MIRACLES AND REVELATION

By the same author

CONFLICT IN CHRISTOLOGY

MIRACLES AND REVELATION

by

JOHN STEWART LAWTON

M.A., B.D., D.Phil., Oxon.; M.A., Cantab.
Sometime Fellow and Chaplain,
Selwyn College, Cambridge
Examining Chaplain to the Bishop of Blackburn

ASSOCIATION PRESS
NEW YORK

Published in the United States by
ASSOCIATION PRESS
291 Broadway
New York 7, New York

Library of Congress Catalogue Card No. 60-6561

*Printed in Great Britain by
The Camelot Press Ltd., London and Southampton*

CONTENTS

PREFACE

To anyone who is interested in the religion of the Bible, the question of miracles can never be merely academic. The religion of the Hebrews became sharply differentiated from the nature religions of the ancient world by the very fact of its awareness of the personal, challenging activity of God in history; and the essence of the New Testament Gospel is that the "Word became flesh" in a particular historic person. To think about the Bible at all, therefore, is to think about the particular ways in which God has intervened in the lives of men. The advent of the scientific study of nature and history has posed many problems for Christian thinkers, not least in connection with miracles. But there is an aspect of the theology of the past two and a half centuries which is far more interesting than the actual controversies over miracles—which have already been written about a great deal. During this period, the concepts of revelation and of faith have undergone a most profound enrichment. Our purpose is to illustrate this metamorphosis by comparing the place of miracles in the theology of the Illumination with their place in the thought of subsequent generations.

The rediscovery of the dimensions of faith is of the utmost relevance to the recent history of the church. We are indeed faced with the phenomenon of multitudes existing with little or no conscious religion. But many thoughtful people would give all they have to be possessed by a dynamic faith. The story of a communist journalist becoming a Christian is a best-seller, whilst the Victorian novels about curates losing their faith interest nobody. For faith there is in modern times, both compelling and creative. Thousands of Christians have been faithful unto death in Nazi and communist persecutions, and countless others have gone on doing their religious duties in the knowledge that the same things could befall themselves. This faith in the 20th century is no nostalgia for a bygone creed, but a compelling personal faith—a proof of the power of the living Christ that would have made the evidence-writers of the 18th century open their eyes with incredulity.

There are other fruits of the creative power of faith in recent times that are equally remarkable: the missionary enterprises and the growth of young churches in diverse cultures; the turning of the tide of separation and the positive efforts towards Christian unity; and the seemingly inexhaustible way in which Christian theology revivifies itself. For those who keep faith, there will be even greater "signs and wonders".

For technical advice I am greatly indebted to three friends: the Very Rev. N. Sykes, the late Rev. Professor C. Jenkins, and the Rev. Professor F. L. Cross. For other indispensable help I am profoundly grateful to my parents and my wife and to a number of other friends.

JOHN STEWART LAWTON

Warton Vicarage,
Nr. Preston, Lancs.

Chapter One

A NEW HEAVEN AND A NEW EARTH

I

FROM the time of the scientific renaissance, the view of western man regarding the character of the universe and his place in it has undergone a profound revolution, both intellectual and emotional. This has not been brought about simply by the vast accumulation of fresh factual knowledge—for what are called scientific data are refined abstractions from the flow of events. The change has come about largely by an interpretation of the new knowledge, in the light of the intellectual technique by which the knowledge was elicited, and by the setting up of this kind of knowledge as the norm over against the more intuitive aspects of human experience. It would be idle to deny that the scientific movement is an epoch of the greatest importance in human development—the validity of its methods, within their proper sphere, can only be challenged at the peril of scepticism regarding reason itself. It would be equally absurd at the present time to deny the departmental character of this revolution: for the present crisis in civilization shows that scientific advancement can proceed without any necessary enrichment of other aspects of the human personality. There is a sense indeed in which the moral and spiritual life of man cannot be thought of in terms of progress: the exercise of such life is conditioned by society, but in essence it consists in the response of each person to God and fellow men. There is, strictly speaking, no such thing as THE philosophy of science, for a great variety of interpretations of the universe have been offered by men who shared a common acceptance of the method and findings of natural science. Moreover, there have been within the last few decades great changes in scientific outlook regarding the most elemental aspects of the universe: matter, motion, space and time. We are in fact dealing with the expression of a highly conditioned mental outlook, rather than with a cut-and-dried philosophical system.

Christian apologetic since the 17th century has not unnaturally been preoccupied with the task of bringing the Christian and the scientific affirmations into an intelligible relationship. The theology of the period of the Illumination, both orthodox and Deist, was unconsciously striving to deal with this question. The 19th century witnessed the struggle to set the Christian dogmas in a working partnership with the scientifically conceived universe; whilst the 19th and the 20th centuries have seen the drama worked out in the field of historical criticism. In the region of open controversy, the points of view adopted by men of religion upon specific questions relating to nature and history have suffered a long succession of defeats at the hands of the men of science. It has therefore been thought plausible to argue that the issue between science and theology could be completely resolved by the evacuation on the part of the latter of all territory rightly belonging to the former—the physical universe being left wholly in the hands of science to describe, whilst religion would deal with the things of the spirit. In many respects this division is obvious and salutary, but as a mode of completely resolving the tension it breaks down.

First, there is one sense in which the two spheres completely overlap: for religion cannot look upon the physical universe as a God-forsaken realm. Like science, theology has things to say about the nature and significance of material things. Secondly, there is overlapping in a more particular sense. Man in his mental as well as in his bodily life is as much part of nature as the ant or the electron. Consequently, man's life as a conscious agent cannot, as was at one time thought, be hedged off as a sphere appropriate to religion and not to science. Thirdly, Christianity, in the New Testament and in its traditional expositions, claims to be a revelation of God in history, not merely a realization by man of spiritual truths. It affirms that a complex of phenomena was specifically caused by God, in which He is revealed and through which He redeems mankind. There has been, as we shall see, considerable variation in the interpretation of what is given in revelation, and in the mode of its supposed authentication. But the point is that within history, within the phenomenal stream which is supposed by many to be the proper sphere of science, there are believed to be events with whose occurrence religion is vitally concerned. To put these points in another way: Christianity asserts that most of what is really significant for human consciousness, though conveyed by the natural world through the senses, consists in those aspects of reality which elude the categories of natural science. In addition, there are certain events which are different in kind from the more usual pattern, brought about by specific Divine initiative for specific ends. These events are recognized by a combination of their inward and outward character, just as the characteristic actions of a human person are recognized. But whereas the unique actions of each human personality tend to appear "natural" by their multiplicity and conformity to the general needs of life, the revealing acts of God, by their very uniqueness, stand in a somewhat irregular relationship to the course of nature.

The question of miracles thus stands in a peculiarly conspicuous position in the modern apologetic endeavour, for it is this aspect of God's revealing action which discriminates the Christian and the scientific worlds of thought most sharply. The miraculous has appeared in the controversies of the past three centuries as the most intractable of the elements of Christian thought which have come within the sphere of criticism from the modern approaches to nature and history. Once the literal inerrancy of Scripture was abandoned, no more difficulty was experienced by churchmen in regard to the Biblical narratives of creation than to the Biblical eschatology. Yet although the idea of miracle seemed somewhat more at home in the older than in the newer cosmogony, the Incarnation could not yield to a levelling-down process without losing its essential character as the personal word of God. Here then was not the defence of the last ditch, where the ruined citadel of a dying world of religious beliefs was being temporarily held; nor was it merely a token struggle on behalf of a religious as opposed to a mechanistic interpretation of the universe. What was at stake was revealed religion itself: the certitude that there is a personal God, who has made Himself known to us in specific personal action, that He has taken a direct initiative for the salvation of man, and thrown light for us upon the meaning of human life and the universe in which it is lived.

Attack and defence, nevertheless, are only the outward side of the story with which we are concerned: the emergence of the scientific approach to nature and history has played a part in much deeper changes for Christian thinking. Before the scientific renaissance began to pull down the medieval cosmogony and cosmology, the Reformation had already dislodged a large part of Europe from its allegiance to the Roman church, in which the continuous and universal witness of the visible church had provided an external authority upon which the individual might lean. Ever since the Reformation, protestant theology has been occupied, consciously or unconsciously, with the problem of the basis of its certitude and the intellectual frame of reference in which this certitude should be expressed. The period with which we are dealing shows this process at work in English theology. There has been a series of remarkable developments in the concept of revelation, the supposed means of its authentication, and the nature of faith. One aspect of this development, which at first sight seems very surprising, is that the function ascribed to the miraculous has shifted from the authentication to the very heart of revelation. To the historian of Christian thought, these developments are of far greater interest than the tiresome arguments about the relation of miracles to the laws of nature, and more attention will be paid to the connection between miracles and revelation than is usually accorded in works on this subject.

II

We must begin by giving some brief account of the outlook upon the world which was in process of dissolution in the 17th century. An entire view of the universe, not only of its nature and functioning, but of its genesis and telos, sacrosanct for over a thousand years, was being replaced. The medieval picture of the universe had been constructed from what was believed to be the teaching of Sacred Scripture, interpreted literally, and taken even from passages of a definitely poetic character. This again was coloured by oriental myths which had percolated into Christian thought via Greek philosophy; and the whole was welded into a rational system by principles derived from Platonic idealism and Aristotelian logic. The fully developed ecclesiastical cosmogony was completed with the writings of the pseudo Dionysius, Peter Lombard and St. Thomas Aquinas, and was finally implanted in the imagination of Christendom by the *Divine Comedy* of Dante.

The all-important focus of the universe was the earth. In the more primitive cosmogony, the earth had been regarded as saucer-shaped, surrounded by four walls which reached up to the solid vault of heaven. With the ripening of scholasticism, however, the earth had come to be regarded as a sphere, immovable in space. Upon the upper side of this globe lived the human race. Around the earth, each in its own perfect sphere, moved the sun, moon and planets. Beyond the outermost sphere, the empyrean, the Blessed Trinity reigned in glory. Below the earth glowed the fires of hell. "Why is the sun red in the evening?" reads a medieval primer. "Because he looketh down unto hell." Through the "windows of heaven" in the solid firmament, the rain was poured down; and from the firmament were hung out the stars, and the comets "for signs and wonders". Many calculations had been made as to the date of the earth on the basis of the Old Testament chronology. The most popular computations in England became those of Ussher and Lightfoot, the latter's date for the creation being October 23, 4004 B.C., at 7 a.m. The whole work of creation was accomplished in six days—including the rock strata, complete with coal-seams and fossils, the first human beings, and every species of flora and fauna. (The fossils were thought by some to have been placed to deceive the unbelieving geologists.) Every inmate of the Biblical menagerie was also there, including dragons, unicorns and basilisks.

Stage by stage, this world picture was replaced: though here it must suffice to illustrate the import of the movement from some of its cardinal episodes. Nicholas Copernicus' *De Revolutionibus Orbium Celestium* was published shortly before its author's death in 1543. In this work was propounded the mathematical hypothesis of the earth's double motion, about its own axis and in a circuit around the sun. For a whole generation the church let sleeping dogs lie, except that this was one of the opinions for which Giordano Bruno was burned by the Inquisition in

1600. But with his telescope, Galileo discovered many facts which fitted in with the Copernican hypothesis, which he now advanced as a statement of fact. He suffered a long and bitter persecution, being twice forced by the Inquisition to retract his opinions, in 1616 and 1630-3. He was made to "abjure, curse, and detest, the error and heresy of the movement of the earth". But the work begun was carried on by Tycho Brahe, Kepler and Newton—the last proving that the planets, of which the earth is one, are all subject to a set of universal laws; the earth's motion being governed by exactly the same laws as the fall of an apple. The controversy, however, muttered on into the 18th century. John Hutchinson published his *Moses Principia* in 1724, as a counterblast to Newton's *Principia*; and it was not until 1835 that an edition of the *Index* appeared which did not contain the works of Copernicus and Galileo.

The change in men's perspective which the new discoveries produced alone makes the theological discussions of the last two and a half centuries intelligible. The whole machinery of ecclesiastical repression and propaganda was not mobilized against Galileo without a supposed weighty reason. Here was something more than an affront to the accepted interpretation of Scripture: if the new conclusions had been acceptable, Scripture might have been treated allegorically in order to accommodate them. The church was faced with an apparent overturning of a universe in which man had stood as the crown of creation. As man was created to serve God, so the universe was created to serve man, wrote the Master of the Sentences. But now it was as though man's home was falling to pieces: he was being left clinging to a tiny planet rotating round one lonely star in an immeasurable ocean of space.

The Galileo controversy is often described as though it was the supreme example of the interference of theology with science. In fact, the pre-Copernican view had on its side the whole weight of the evidence of the human senses previously recorded. There was also scientific opposition to the new theory on the ground that there were facts accounted for by the Ptolemaic astronomy, which were not accounted for by the solar-centric theory as it was at first elaborated. Again, the 17th-century dispute is not primarily a victory for the idea of universal law over caprice. Ever since men had begun to reflect upon what they observed, the movements of the heavenly bodies were associated with the idea of mathematical regularity: for instance, the orientation of Egyptian temples. The concept of astronomical law, then, was nothing new; but so long as man stood upon his immovable earth, his view of reality remained secure. Indeed, to the Hebrews at least, the celestial regularities were yet one more proof of God's character of unchanging faithfulness. The potential influences of the scientific renaissance were not of course all apparent for a long time: the religious outlook of the 18th century was dominated rather by the more theoretical than emotional aspect of the revolution, viz. the exaltation of the more mathematical kind of truth to the position of being looked on as the norm of knowledge.

If the astronomical discoveries shook the traditional beliefs about man's position in space, the researches of the following centuries radically altered the perspective of his position in time, for they set the history of man in the context of a prolonged process of evolution.[1] It is not to be imagined that before the time of Copernicus, men lived necessarily in a much greater awareness of the immediate presence of God: rather, all their thinking about the world around them was done within the context of the Biblical and medieval schema. The fact that scholasticism had a doctrine of secondary causation did not significantly modify the imaginative content of this world-view. The immediacy of God's action upon man—to say nothing of the literal veracity of Genesis—was brought much more into the arena of discussion by the discoveries relating to the antiquity of the earth and of life upon it than by the controversy over astronomy. The inevitable deductions to be drawn from the fossils was for a while sidetracked by such theories as that of John Woodward, who in 1695 advanced the view that they were the remains of creatures which had lived before the Deluge. It has been an unfortunate characteristic of apologetics during the past two and a half centuries to clutch at many dubious pseudo-scientific theories for support. Far more decisive than the fossils, proved to be the discoveries in drift and gravel beds of the pre-historic remains of animals and human activity. As early as 1715, the frame of an elephant

[1] Cf. the remarkable mass of information in A. D. White's *History of the Warfare of Science with Theology.*

with a flint weapon beside it was discovered near Gray's Inn Lane, but it was not until the middle of the following century, through the patient labours and sufferings of men such as Dean Buckland and Lyell, that the true significance of these discoveries became fully apparent. Voyages to distant lands brought to light new species of animals and new races of men who could scarcely have reached their present surroundings since the traditional date of the Deluge.

Finally, there was the impact of the theory of organic evolution. Many tentative approaches had been made towards an evolutionary view of life by such scholars as Benoist de Maillet, Linnaeus, Buffon (who suffered much at ecclesiastical hands), Lamarck (ridiculed by Paley), Treviranus, Geoffrey de Saint-Hilaire and Patrick Matthews. Darwin first gave to the world the fruits of his long researches in a paper to the Linnaean Society on July 1, 1858; the *Origin of Species* appeared in the following year, and the *Descent of Man* in 1871. The publication of Lyell's *Antiquity of Man* in 1863 represents the significant conversion of one who had previously been opposed to Lamarck. The work of Wilberforce, Manning and Wiseman in running the campaign against Darwinism requires no comment, except to point out that, as with the earlier controversies, what was believed to be at stake was not merely the Biblical history but the dignity and destiny of man as a special child of God. Later on, positivist historiography, theories of mental parallelism and Freudian psychology were to blur still further the distinctive differences (as formerly conceived) between human personality and the kingdom of mechanism.

A strenuous effort has been evoked both from philosophers and theologians to analyse the implications of the new knowledge. The presuppositions of science itself have been scrutinized, and the strict limitations of scientific method as applied to the data of human consciousness have been amply exposed. The genuine foundations of man's certitude as to his own spiritual nature have also been elucidated, by the careful interrogation of the facts of conscious experience. Nevertheless, the picture of the universe built up by the various sciences, even to the most confirmed Theist, cannot but have a profound effect upon the manner in which he will tend to think of God's action upon the world and towards himself.

III

We must now examine some of the changes brought about by the scientific renaissance on the level of philosophical method. If we look at English literature, secular no less than theological, at the beginning and end of the 17th century, we see that a great change has taken place in the concept of human reason. Hooker looks back to the medieval scholastic attitude to reason, while Tillotson shares the Deistic concept of it: yet the formal statements of the relation of reason to faith in each are not dissimilar. In the older world-view, the Ptolemaic universe was regarded not merely as a set of mathematical relations, but as a great chain of beings, of ascending planes of existence and of creatures graded according to their utility, excellence and powers. The sun was the noblest planet, the lion was the noblest animal. Characteristic of this aesthetic and intuitional approach to nature was the method of analogical reasoning, by which new truths were arrived at by the extension of observed analogies between objects in the different planes of being. We have the constant interplay of analogy, abundantly illustrated in Elizabethan poetry and theology, between macrocosm and microcosm: God the maker of all things, inferred from man, as maker of things; the spiritual displayed in the natural order; the tragedy of humanity portrayed in the tragedy of an individual. Such judgments were arrived at by the combination of the intellect with the more intuitional faculties of feeling and spiritual discernment.[1] With the second half of the 17th century, however, there came about what Mr. T. S. Eliot has called a "dissociation of sensibility". The intellectual life of England gradually came to be dominated by the kind of attitude towards nature that was evolving in the course of the scientific renaissance; a view which tended to drive apart discursive thought and feeling, and to exalt the judgments of the former in man's understanding of his environment to the exclusion of the latter. In order to explain this change, which has had such momentous results for the history of religious thought, we must turn again to the scientific development of the time.

In the 17th century, on the level of scientific experiment and

[1] *Vide* S. L. Bethell, *The Cultural Revolution of the Seventeenth Century.*

philosophy, the long reign of Aristotle was drawing swiftly to its close, and was being replaced by a very different methodology and cosmology. The older science had sought to arrive at truth by the metaphysical analysis of things, and was preoccupied with teleological considerations and the *a priori* method of reasoning. This method was in a sense the quest for what OUGHT to be rather than for what IS, but it did at least attempt to relate the phenomenal experiences of man with his more intuitional judgments in a comprehensive, meaningful view of life. The method assumed that the actual in nature was controlled by ideal forms; and search was made both for the ideal uniformities underlying the actual, and for teleological explanations of the events in nature. The scholastic outlook persisted in part well into the period of the scientific renaissance. Thus, Kepler is an interesting illustration of the dominance of science by the category of formal causality, though he was also in the van of the new discoveries. He accepted the Copernican hypothesis, partly because, with the sun as centre, he could elaborate an allegory of the Blessed Trinity in the solar system. To Kepler, it is the mathematical form itself which conditions the movements of planets, and therefore to him a scientific definition is a statement of the underlying mathematical harmonies thus at work.

The new discoveries in astronomy were both caused by, and gave the impetus to, the abandonment of this earlier method of reasoning. The renaissance of science, as of the humanities, was a creative and imaginative movement, a revolt against the strait-jacket of the medieval type of reasoning. Men now set out simply to observe, record and correlate things as they are, without reference to metaphysical considerations. The change is strikingly reflected in the types of categories employed before and after the movement. Before it, we have substance, essence, matter, form, quality and quantity: later thought comes to be dominated by the ideas of time, space, mass and energy. The men of the new era believed themselves to be dealing with bed-rock realities, and failed to recognize the selective and abstract character of their categories: they did in fact embrace a very definite cosmology and metaphysic, which was to dominate the thought of the west until the closing years of the 19th century. To use Whitehead's description, the new metaphysic presupposed the ultimate fact of an irreducible brute matter or material, spread throughout space, and existing in absolute time, in a flux of configurations. This matter is purposeless of itself, acting, not by the inner nature of its being, but by reason of its external relations. The new primary abstractions—mass, motion, time and space—were forged to operate this new scientific approach, highly efficient in its own narrow domain, reaching its apotheosis in the 19th-century version of materialism, in which the whole of reality is conceived of in terms of mechanics—the reassorting of the ultimate base ingredients of the universe.[1]

To Galileo, a fact was just what it was, irrespective of human observation or reason. He abandoned the idea of final causes, and he fully accepted the distinction between primary qualities —which he believed to be objective and fixed—and secondary qualities, which he believed to be subjective and unstable. Colourless, beautiless matter is his business: everything non-mechanical is relegated to the imagination and the world of mind is left as a separate world. He had a boundless faith in mathematics, even on its abstract side: the knowledge which it gives us is Divine and absolute. It was on account of this persuasion that he felt himself able to challenge even the accepted interpretation of passages of Scripture.[2]

The new cosmological principles became a consciously rationalized system in Descartes. His universe consists, first, of an undivided physical substance, extended throughout space, of which mathematics gives us real knowledge; secondly, a plurality of human minds; and thirdly, of God. God was a necessary postulate, as the cause of the external relations existing within the physical world, and as the bridge between the self-conscious minds of men and the mechanically-conditioned world. William Temple has suggested (half jokingly, it is true) that Descartes' experience in his stove was the most disastrous moment in the history of Europe.[3] Descartes was certainly one of the fathers of modern anti-supernaturalism: for his separation of mind and matter into exclusive spheres had the effect, on the one hand, of leaving philosophy preoccupied

[1] Whitehead, *Science and the Modern World*, p. 24. E. A. Burtt, *The Metaphysical Foundations of Modern Physical Science*, ch. I.

[2] Burtt, *op. cit.*, pp. 70ff.

[3] *Nature, Man and God*, p. 57.

with the problem of epistemology—how mind can know the physical world which is so dissimilar from itself, whilst on the other hand, natural science, dominated by mechanical abstractions, was left the sole interpreter of the physical universe. The cosmology thus adumbrated was completed by Gassendi and Newton. The former, in reaction to Descartes' theory of vortices, postulated the idea of real Space, infinite in extent, and existing in clock-time. The crowning episode of this line of development was the formulation of the law of gravitation by Newton. In his view of the universe, there were a plurality of minds and a plurality of bodies, in simple space-time: the external relations between the bodies were the expression of the Divine laws imposed upon them. "The whole Cartesian apparatus of Deism, substantial materialism and imposed law, in conjunction with the reduction of physical relations to the notion of correlated motions with mere spatio-temporal character," says Whitehead, "constitutes the simplified notion of nature with which Galileo, Descartes and Newton finally launched modern science on its triumphant career."[1]

This methodology found its way into the study of every aspect of human experience. John Oman points out that, instead of "surveying our environment from the highest standpoint we can reach, with all our experience and all our insight as well as knowledge", the Cartesian method seeks to start as low as possible in our experience and build up from thence.[2] The Illumination was right in its faith that reality if rightly interrogated will not deceive us, but it reduced the conception of truth to what can be proved by abstract reasoning, instead of realizing that each kind of reality has its own witness, which alone can determine the true method of investigation.[3] The teleological view of nature is replaced by the idea of the transformation of what already exists. The illusion was thus created that the new is explained by being represented merely as a reassortment of the old. A long succession of philosophers, of whom Hegel was the most outstanding, had attempted to apply the method even to the ultimate explanation of the universe; whilst a great deal of the historiography of the 19th century was pursued on the assumption that if we got far

[1] *Adventures of Ideas*, p. 145.
[2] *The Natural and the Supernatural*, p. 99.
[3] *op. cit.*, pp. 100-3.

enough back we could begin with simplicity, from which we could see that everything subsequent was merely a little rearrangement of what had existed in the age before. "If this method assume itself to be the only valid method of knowledge," concludes Oman, "it will already have ruled out the possibility that the universe has any supernatural aspect, or at least that this could have any significance for us."[1]

This gives some indication of the breadth of the front on which Christian apologists have had to fight since the coming of the scientific era. The tendency to treat man as a little higher than the brutes instead of as a little lower than the angels is the apex of the endeavour based upon Cartesianism to produce a rationale of the universe. The Christian attitude to the universe, the miracles and dogmas of Scripture and the religious interpretation of many natural events and institutions were all to be challenged. In the 17th and 18th centuries, however, much of this lay in the future. Indeed, many of the most active minds of the time regarded the new science as an ally of religion. In the thought of Descartes and Newton, God was necessary as the nexus between man and his environment and as the imposer of nature's laws. The ripening of the new science did nevertheless coincide with the reaction against the religious controversies of previous generations in favour of a simplified creed, consisting of a belief in the Creator, a rational ethic and a future life. The Newtonian universe and the Deistic creed seemed to fit like hand in glove. Newton was almost a prophet —"God said, Let Newton be, and all was light," sang Pope. The period of the Illumination, which saw the confluence of the new knowledge with the religious reaction, was characterized by the attempt to express the dominant ideas of theology, philosophy and morality in quasi-mathematical terms, that is to say, what were then regarded as the ideal patterns of thought.

IV

Yet although the work of the scientific renaissance was far from being unfavourable to Theism, and in the long run has done a great deal to purify our notions of God's activity,

[1] *ibid.*, p. 108. Cf. Aubrey Moore, *Science and the Faith*, 1889, pp. xvii, xxi.

there was from the outset an element of hostility towards the miraculous. If we examine the effects of the movement upon some of the educated minds of the period of Deism, we find an attitude towards the miraculous with which most modern religious men are to a greater or less degree in sympathy. Most of the sharpest outlines of the modern negative attitude to miracles are already drawn by Spinoza in his striking work, *Tractatus Theologico-Politicus*, of 1670. The modern Christian apologist frequently opens his polemic by denouncing Spinoza's attempt to deal with the question of miracles on *a priori* grounds. To dismiss him on this ground alone seems a folly, for he takes the scientific picture of the universe in deadly earnest and sees in it a presumption of the way in which God in His wisdom will operate. This picture must be taken into consideration too, by orthodox theology, or else human reason is vain. So much is clear even if we dissent from Spinoza's particular brand of rationalism.

The vulgar, says Spinoza, look upon the unusual as the special manifestation of God's activity, and so long as nature proceeds in its accustomed order they think that God is doing nothing.[1] The powers of nature are thought to be suspended when God intervenes; so that two powers are conceived of, that of God and that of nature. The title of miracle, or work of God, is therefore given to every extraordinary natural event: and partly through devotion and partly through opposition to the scientific spirit, men do not care to inquire into the causes of these phenomena. Spinoza attempts a rudimentary anthropological explanation of this attitude, in the Hebrew desire to exalt their God above the gods of heathen nations. He regards the universal laws of nature as the very decrees of God, which necessarily result from the perfection of His nature. Anything which happened in nature repugnant to its universal laws would therefore be necessarily repugnant to the decrees and intelligence of God. Whatever is and happens does so by the eternal will and decree of God. Otherwise it would be implied that God was frequently obliged to intervene to uphold His universe. Miracle can therefore mean no more than that which is inexplicable to the narrator.

From miracles, declares Spinoza, we can neither obtain

[1] *op. cit.*, E.T. 1862, pp. 120f.

knowledge of the existence of God nor of His providence: indeed, these truths are better elicited from the changeless order of nature. The ideas which suggest the existence of God—our observation that all things in nature obey a definite course—ought to be beyond doubt; whereas an irregularity such as a miracle could only cause doubt. From a miracle we could at most infer a cause relatively greater than that of nature; nor is the distinction between "contrary to nature" and "beyond nature" of any value.[1]

The method of Scripture is to represent everything as coming direct from the hand of God; but it is clear that in a great many cases the natural causes are assumed. Some of Spinoza's natural explanations of miracles in Old and New Testaments are rather fanciful, but he confesses himself anxious lest any be scandalized by finding in Scripture things which appear to be repugnant to natural reason.[2] He also shows himself to be alive to one of the chief problems of historical criticism. It is seldom that men relate an event simply as it happened, and mingle nothing of their own fancies or opinions with the narrative. Therefore it is absolutely necessary to be informed of the opinions of those who first witnessed or narrated miracles, and also of those who have left us an account of them in writing, and to make a cardinal distinction between the event in itself and the impression it may have produced upon the minds of those who witnessed it.[3]

In Spinoza, then, lie the seeds of the coming protracted controversies over miracles. He realized both the practical difficulties in dealing with the evidence for miracles and the problems for the philosophy of religion raised by the admission of such events. Spinoza stands at the threshold of the period with which we are to deal: all subsequent apologetic work takes account of him, for he marks the point at which man's recently acquired apprehension of the structure of the physical universe created a tension with the traditional theology. The negative work of refuting the principles of Spinoza and his successors has been surpassed in vigour only by the positive effort to exhibit the organic relationship between the revelation in Christ and its miraculous accompaniments.

[1] *ibid.*, p. 127. [2] *ibid.*, p. 134. [3] *ibid.*, p. 135.

Chapter Two

THE AGE OF ENGLISH DEISM

I

THE question of the occurrence and character of miracles arose in its modern form, as we have seen, when men began to approach the study of history and theology with their minds pre-conditioned by the achievements and technique of the Scientific Renaissance. In England, this crisis took the form of the Deist controversy. Both parties to the dispute are interesting. The Deists represent a well-marked stage in the development of modern rationalism, and the position of their orthodox opponents constitutes an important chapter in the history of post-Reformation theology. The Deist controversialists were an odd assortment of individuals. There were Lords Cherbury, Bolingbroke and Shaftesbury, Tindal the don and Chubb the tallow chandler. They produced a miscellaneous assortment of writings, notable neither for their profundity nor their ingenuousness. Their output has been vastly outstripped by the Rationalist Press Association. Yet the Deists have a claim to historic importance. They were the first to approach many of the problems of natural theology in the characteristically modern way. They set apologetics a quite new task.

Sir Leslie Stephen, our greatest historian of the thought of the period, represents English Deism as the continuation of the work of the Reformation. As the Reformation delivered men from the shackles of the authoritarian church, so Deism emancipated them from subservience to the Bible. No friend of the orthodox Reformation theology will agree with this. If medieval theology represents the synthesis of Biblical and classical thought, and the Reformation and the Renaissance are the splitting apart of the two elements, then Deism marks the victory of the latter over the former—of humanism over Biblical theology. What makes the situation complicated is that Deism had its counterpart in the predominant Christian orthodoxy of the time. The rapid decline of Calvinism in the later years of the 17th century is one of the most remarkable happenings in the history of English religious thought.[1] A new rationalized theology was mapped out in tiers: natural theology, historico-logical proofs of particular revelation and a eudaemonistic ethic buttressed by a belief in a future state of rewards and punishments. The orthodox controversialists were to some extent like dogs barking at their own reflection.

By the time of the Restoration, the nation had become spiritually weary after a century and a half of religious controversy. Not a few minds had been turned to religious scepticism, as we can see from such contemporary writings as Pepys; whilst many others were demanding a theology that was based upon "plain arguments", as opposed to the tortuous controversies over the interpretation of Scripture. If Christianity were to be believed, it must be shown to be "reasonable". The Scientific Renaissance gave natural theology a sudden new lease of life. The truth of God's existence and metaphysical attributes, it seemed, could be inferred from the data which science supplied. The existence of the Deity was therefore known by reason, not by revelation; orthodox Christians of the day agreed with that. Might not God, who had thus revealed His existence, be expected to have implanted in human reason also the moral law by which man was to live? And should it not be expected that the laws of the moral life will be as universal, unchangeable and knowable as the laws which God has imposed upon the physical creation? This was the road along which the Deists travelled.

The Christian orthodoxy of the period of the Illumination shared in the new impetus that had been given to natural theology. Samuel Clark's first series of Boyle Lectures, Richard Bentley's Boyle Lectures and George Berkeley's *Alciphron* show how deeply the traditionalists had drunk of the new spirit. Natural theology was the norm of religious thinking: the need for revelation and the content of revelation had to be related

[1] Cf. G. R. Cragg, *From Puritanism to the Age of Reason.*

to the system which was logically prior to it.[1] But there was another important factor which shaped the orthodoxy of the period. To understand this, we should look at the Anglican divines of the middle of the 17th century, in such works as Jeremy Taylor's *Liberty of Prophesying* and Herbert Thorndike's *Epilogue to the Tragedy of the Church of England*. The Anglicans are engaged in refuting the two dominant theories about the basis of Christian certitude. The Romans appeal to the church; the sectaries, to the inner light, for interpreting the Bible. Yet both are arguments in a circle—it is from the Bible that we learn about the church and the promise of the Spirit. If there is any surety at all, it must be within Scripture itself. It was in these circumstances that the Anglicans turned to the Patristic and Scholastic tenets that revelation is evinced by miracles and the fulfilment of prophecies. The way was thus prepared for a new generation of theologians, headed by such men as Tillotson and Stillingfleet, to harden these insights into syllogisms that could be fitted into a theology that was virtually expressed in the thought-forms of Deism.

II

We can see the problem that was emerging for orthodoxy if we look at Locke's theological writings. In his *Essay concerning Human Understanding* he had attempted to discover the simple matter-of-fact certainties of epistemology. In his *Reasonableness of Christianity as delivered in the Scriptures*, 1695, he makes the same kind of attempt in the realm of theology. The Bible, he contends, is designed by God for the instruction of the illiterate bulk of mankind in the way to salvation, and must be understood, therefore, in the plain and direct meaning of the words and phrases—such as they may be understood to have had in the mouths of those who spoke them.[2] He accepts plenary inspiration, and has a ready-made estimate of the content of the Gospel in terms of the rational morality of his day: and for such thinkers there are no problems in Scripture. Like his Deist contemporaries, he has an implicit faith in the correspondence between the principles of religion and those of

[1] Cf. Tillotson, *Works*, 1752 ed., *Sermons*, vol. II, Nos. 48, 49.
[2] *Works*, 1801 ed., VII, p. 5.

reason; though, unlike the Deists, he does not admit the sufficiency of reason to discover these religious beliefs. "It is no diminishing to revelation," he says, "that reason gives its suffrage to the truths revelation has discovered. But it is our mistake to think, that because reason confirms them to us, we had the first certain knowledge of them from thence."[1] Orthodoxy was faced with a dilemma. If it depressed the rationality of revealed truths, revelation would be shunned as superstition; whereas if it was maintained that every religious truth was demonstrably conformable to the dictates of reason, it might be urged that revelation could be written off as superfluous. We can see how orthodoxy had contrived to wedge itself in this position even in Locke. He takes revelation to mean the truths which are revealed. Now even if these "truths" include far more than simply moral precepts, we still have only "truths", and not the personal revealer. By surrendering the position that Christ Himself is revelation, whom the believer knows, not only "knows about", the apologists of the Illumination made it virtually impossible to defend themselves against Deism. If the idea of revelation is reduced to a set of truths, human reason becomes the hero of the story; and revelation becomes either an instrument for re-kindling man's reason, as in the Illumination theology, or another name for man's evolving religious experience, as in 19th-century immanentism.

In his attempt to reduce the New Testament theology to its simplest terms, Locke seeks what some present-day writers would call a "controlling doctrine". He finds that one single thing was required, viz. that men should believe Jesus to be Messiah. Of the woman of Samaria's faith he writes: "It is plain that believing on the Son is the believing that Jesus is the Messiah; giving credit to the miracles He did, and the profession He made of Himself."[2] Faith thus turns out to be the rational acceptance of a fact about Christ; and with this is linked the proof from miracles.[3] Locke, moreover, offered a definition of miracles which was destined to be the subject of considerable comment. A miracle, he says, is "A sensible operation, which, being above the comprehension of the

[1] *op. cit.*, VII, p. 145.
[2] *ibid.*, VII, p. 17.
[3] *ibid.*, VII, pp. 18, 20, 43-44.

spectator, and in his opinion contrary to the established course of nature, is taken by him to be Divine."[1] Nature's frontiers were thought to be clearly marked, and we must not therefore suppose that Locke doubted the direct Divine causation of the miracles of Scripture. But with the long controversies behind us, it is interesting to see that so long ago a thinker of Locke's calibre realized that the only practicable—as opposed to theoretical—way to define a miracle was by reference to its impact upon the human witnesses.

III

The Deist controversy began to blaze up with the appearance of John Toland's *Christianity not Mysterious*, in 1696. This luckless literary freelance made his attack upon the faith in an oblique manner; for toleration was still only in name, and the book was in fact burned by order of the Irish parliament. He complains that some of our divines would have us always to believe the literal sense of Scripture with little or no regard to reason, whilst others assert that we may use reason as the instrument but not the rule of our belief. "Both of 'em from different principles agree, that several doctrines of the New Testament belong no farther to the enquiries of reason than to prove 'em Divinely revealed, and that they are properly mysteries still." He holds that reason is the only foundation of all certitude, and that nothing revealed is exempted from its "disquisitions".[2] By "reason" he means Locke's "representative ideas", and holds that these give infallible knowledge of things. He identifies these with Spinoza's "clear and distinct ideas"—the quasi-mathematical structures and necessities which were believed to govern reality, not merely the physical universe but the realms of ethics and metaphysics as well.

On this basis Toland rejected all beliefs that appeared to transcend "clear and distinct ideas",[3] and everything that is hypothetical.[4] What is supposed to have been revealed must strictly conform to the quasi-mathematical forms of human reason.[5] Nor are these truths hidden from mankind. As opposed to the doctrine of human depravity, Toland maintains that

[1] *Discourse of Miracles*, Works, IX, p. 256. [2] *op. cit.*, 1702 ed., p. 5.
[3] *ibid.*, p. 25. [4] *ibid.*, p. 15. [5] *ibid.*, p. 46.

reason is whole and entire in everyone whose organs are not accidentally indisposed.[1] In the New Testament, moreover, the word "mystery" is never used of anything inconceivable: faith, therefore, is so far from being an implicit assent to something above reason, that this notion directly contradicts the ends of religion.[2] As a last resort, he says, the advocates of mystery fly to miracles.[3]

But to what purpose were all these miracles if there were no regard to men's understanding—if the doctrines of Christ were incomprehensible, or if we were obliged to believe revealed nonsense?[4] Toland's challenge, then, is that reason is supreme in the realms of faith and morals, and that therefore the orthodox paraphernalia for proving special revelation is otiose. The lengths to which the idea of the inner light could be pressed may be seen in Henry Dodwell's *Christianity not founded on Argument*, 1743.

IV

If we take the most outstanding sets of Robert Boyle Lectures between 1691 and 1732, we have a *Summa Theologica* of the orthodoxy which was elaborated in reply to Deism.

The lecturers dilate upon man's need of a Divine revelation. The wisdom of the ages had made scarcely any appreciable impression upon the bulk of mankind: the degradation of the heathen world bore testimony to the need for a standing authoritative rule of conduct.[5] Why is it, asks Addison who strayed into the realm of apologetics, that the civilization of these islands has outstripped the glories of ancient Greece? It is because we are Christians, professing more excellent and Divine truths than the rest of mankind.[6]

In view of the gravity of the human situation, it is instructive to learn how revelation was thought to achieve its task. Its design, says Samuel Chandler, is "to lead men into just and becoming sentiments of the Divine Being and perfections; to direct and appoint that method of worship which will be

[1] *ibid.*, p. 57. [2] *ibid.*, p. 139. [3] *ibid.*, p. 144. [4] *ibid.*, pp. 48-49.
[5] *Boyle Lectures*, 1739 ed., T. Burnet, III, pp. 462-75. Williams, I, pp. 156, 159.
[6] *Evidences*, 1730, pp. 194, 191.

acceptable to Himself; to recover men from their ignorance, to reform them from their vices, and to lead them into the practice of virtue and true goodness, by proper motives and arguments . . ."[1] It is remarkable that so realistic a view of the condition of unredeemed human nature could have been combined with such a Pelagian view of the manner in which that nature was to be changed.

An authoritative revelation was necessary: therefore it was given—in one certain historical record.[2] It was not designed to convince the most sceptical, said Tillotson, but he knew of nothing that ever carried greater evidence than the doctrine of Christ, preached by Himself and His Apostles to the obstinate Jews, and confirmed by multitudes of unquestionable miracles.[3] The authoritative revelation then, is recognized (1) by its intrinsic excellence; (2) by the miracles wrought in its attestation, and (3) by the prophecies fulfilled by the revealer.[4] One result of treating the teaching, rather than the person, of Christ as the chief content of revelation is that the Resurrection figures mainly in an evidential rather than a theological context. Tillotson had a profound reverence for the mystery of the Incarnation, as anyone may see from his group of sermons on the subject, yet he defines the Resurrection as the outward demonstration of what was done secretly in the Virgin Birth.[5] Particular miracles were supposed to have been wrought to reinforce particular truths: the paralytic is cured to show the power of Christ to forgive sins; and to prove the existence of heaven, Christ miraculously ascended thither.[6]

In order to counter the Deists' objection to the idea of mystery, it was contended that revelation bestowed new truths which fitted into the already existing scheme of natural religion, and that the proofs of revelation were analogous to the proofs of natural theology.[7] The Deists of the time held that the components of nature and hence the laws governing them were constituted according to rational necessities. In order to

[1] *Vindication of the Christian Religion*, 1728 ed., p. 95. Cf. *Boyle Lectures*, Burnet, III, pp. 481f.; J. Clarke, III, p. 245; Bradford, I, p. 449.

[2] Stillingfleet, *Works*, 1709 ed., II, p. 67.

[3] *The Rule of Faith*, 1752 ed., p. 545. Cf. *Sermons*, 1752 ed., II, pp. 394f.

[4] *Boyle Lectures*, Woodward, II, p. 517.

[5] *Sermons*, 1752 ed., II, pp. 420f.

[6] *Boyle Lectures*, Burnet, II, p. 496.

[7] *Boyle Lectures*, Williams, I, p. 158.

accommodate the miraculous, the orthodox had therefore to appeal from Spinoza to Descartes, as it were, to maintain an "imposed", as opposed to an immanental, view of the laws of nature. It is a wrong distinction, they urge, to define a miracle by any absolute difficulty in the accomplishment of it. It is at least as great an act of power to cause the sun or a planet to move at all as to cause it to stand still at any time.[1]

The Scriptures disclose the fact that miracles had been performed by evil spirits, and this made it impossible to define a Divine miracle simply in terms of unusual supernatural causation. Samuel Clarke points out that differing power is given to different creatures; so that unless we knew the limit of communicable power we could hardly affirm with certainty that any effect, however miraculous it might seem to us, was beyond the power of all created beings to have produced. There is no instance of any miracle in Scripture, he says, which, to an ordinary spectator, would necessarily imply the immediate operation of absolute and underived power.[2] These are wise words indeed. The only definition of a miracle which he will admit is "An effect produced contrary to the usual course or order of nature, by the unusual interposition of some intelligent being superior to men."[3] Two questions thus arose in respect of the miracles of Christ: Were they true miracles? and, Could it be shown that they proceeded from God? Such effects as the instantaneous cure of grave diseases and the raising of persons from the dead are beyond the usual powers of nature. These acts were wrought before thousands of enemies, under conditions rendering fraud or delusion impossible, as opposed to the circumstances of medieval miracles.[4] Their Divine origin is proved by the fact that they exhibit marks of outstanding power and beneficence and are accompanied by teachings which commend themselves to human reason. As in the Old Testament we see such signs of superior power as Aaron's rod swallowing up the magicians' rods,[5] so also is the character of

[1] *Boyle Lectures,* S. Clarke, II, p. 161; Leng, III, pp. 119-20; Bentley, I, p. 44; Ibbot, II, p. 860.

[2] *Boyle Lectures,* II, p. 162.

[3] *op. cit.,* II, p. 163.

[4] *Boyle Lectures,* Leng, III, p. 116; S. Clarke, II, pp. 163-64; Gurdon, III, pp. 360-63, 388-89.

[5] *op. cit.,* Leng, III, pp. 117-18, 121.

Christ a pre-eminent argument in favour of the Divine character of His miracles. Christ appeared in His words and works, says Samuel Clarke, neither as an impostor nor an enthusiast: His innocent and spotless life was spent entirely in serving the ends of holiness and charity.[1]

There is clear Scriptural warrant, it is urged, for the belief that miracles are not to be received as a blind, indiscriminate authentication of doctrine (Deut. 13: 1-5). If the doctrine attested by miracles, writes Samuel Clarke, be in itself impious, then without question the miracles are neither worked by God nor by His commission. If, however, the doctrine attested by miracles tends to promote the honour and glory of God and the practice of righteousness, even though it be in itself indemonstrable, the miracles are unquestionably Divine and the doctrine must be acknowledged as an immediate, infallible revelation of God.[2] This thesis has been challenged from that day to this on the ground that it is an argument in a circle. But the 18th-century apologists retort that the miracles are not proved by the doctrine: the good tendency of the latter is simply a necessary condition without which it could not be proved by any miracles.[3] The criticism was thought to be a mere quibble, for in actual fact Christ had wrought incontestable miracles, including victories over the demons, which went hand in hand with the most lofty and beneficent teaching.[4] Why did the Jews reject this incontestable claim, which surpassed the work of Moses on every count? They rejected Christianity, says Bishop Kidder, first on account of a carnal and worldly temper; secondly, malice and pertinacity; and thirdly, pride and "hautiness".[5]

We are thus introduced to the idea that the acceptance of Christianity depends after all not merely upon the rational weighing of the evidences but also upon a moral choice. Thus in another context, Samuel Chandler, arguing for the appropriateness of a historic revelation, says that for God immediately to reveal Himself to every individual person "would be an overbearing the reasonable powers and faculties of men, without giving them any opportunity for the proper

[1] *op. cit.*, II, p. 140. [2] *ibid.*, II, pp. 164-65.
[3] *ibid.*, II, p. 166. Cf. S. Chandler, *Vindication*, p. 96.
[4] *Boyle Lectures*, Williams, I, p. 205; Stanhope, I, p. 646.
[5] *Boyle Lectures*, I, pp. 92-107. Cf. Stanhope, I, p. 68.

exercise and improvement of them".[1] God does not work miracles today for our satisfaction, says Blackall, because "such clear demonstration might be enough to overpower us, so that we could not be infidels if we would; and then there would be no virtue in believing."[2] At this time it was extremely difficult for apologists to find a place for the will in the acceptance of revelation. It was thought that the first essential was to show, as Samuel Clarke put it, that all the Christian doctrines when once revealed are most agreeable to sound, unprejudiced reason.[3] But, though haltingly, the New Testament concept of faith as a personal decision still breaks through the studied logicality of these apologists.

V

Tindal's *Christianity as old as the Creation* is the classic statement of the Deist standpoint. Here the movement on its theoretical side came to a halt; the avenue which continued to invite exploration was the criticism of Christian origins. Tindal reminds one of the sociologist who was said to be shut in his study, working out a new plan for society, "with his mind unclouded by a single fact". His system is doctrinaire in the extreme and was doomed to swift oblivion. The sting of his attack upon the faith was that it tended to make the specifically Christian dogmas appear to be a needless accretion to pure natural theology. The thesis can be stated very briefly. It follows from the perfection and goodness of God that He must always have given men a law by which to live, which itself must be perfect. "It follows, that the Christian Religion has existed from the beginning; and that God both then and ever since, has continued to give all mankind sufficient means to know it . . ."[4] As God gives to all mankind the means to act for their preservation, so He gives to man the means to act for his eternal happiness.

Tindal has no illusions as to the irreconcilability of this standpoint with traditional Christian orthodoxy—unlike some less clear thinkers nearer to our own day. He rejects the traditional view of revelation on two counts. First, it is incompatible

[1] *Vindication*, pp. 4, 78.
[2] *Boyle Lectures*, I, p. 608.
[3] *Boyle Lectures*, II, p. 71.
[4] *op. cit.*, 3rd ed., p. 4.

with the wisdom and goodness of God that He should make a special revelation of Himself to some men and not to others. Secondly, when we turn to the records of the supposed particular revelation, the Bible, we find the purest to the most unworthy motives attributed to the Deity. When all the dross is taken away, we are left with those universal principles of morality which are as old as the creation. For several years before 1730 when Tindal's book was published, a violent controversy had been raging over the authenticity of the New Testament miracles (cf. next chapter). Tindal does not engage in this controversy, for he believed he had sufficiently refuted the traditional idea of revelation on *a priori* grounds. He merely reiterates a few of the more superficial objections to the proof from miracles, and concludes that "If the doctrines themselves, from their internal excellency, do not give us a certain proof of the will of God, no traditional miracle can do it; because one probability added to another will not amount to certainty."[1] This complete confidence in the certainty of the accepted ethical principles was one aspect of that unbounded trust in the rationality of the universe which characterized the Illumination.

VI

Christian apologetics should concern itself primarily with setting out the whole economy of God's saving acts in a manner intelligible to the thought of each generation. But many of the replies to Tindal create the impression that they belong to a system that was wholly on the defensive. Silence would have avoided the implication that Tindal had set up a system which was a serious rival to the faith. For example, Waterland's attempt to reply to Tindal's strictures on the Old Testament drew the attention of thoughtful men to one of the weakest strands in the orthodox case. Some of Israel's worthies are said to have performed acts at the behest of God which it is difficult to reconcile with Christian ethics.[2] Apologists were on surer ground when they attacked Tindal for his picture of the whole human race enjoying equal opportunities of knowing and

[1] *op. cit.*, p. 338; cf. pp. 169, 337.
[2] D. Waterland, *Scripture Vindicated*, 1730.

serving God.[1] If he had explored the underworld of one of the cities of his own time, he would have discovered men and women who, through heredity and environment, had little opportunities for observing the moral law as he understood it. Whatever difficulties there may be thought to be in the idea of special revelation, they equally apply to Tindal's doctrine of natural illumination. Even the Stoics, with whom the idea of *lumen naturale* originated, thought that it expressed itself in relative forms in different ages and cultures. Tindal's opponents attempt to avoid the doctrinaire character of his system by arguing that revelation is "expedient" and "desirable" rather than that it is necessary as a correlate of the Divine character.[2]

At this time, "internal evidence" of the truth of doctrines means their excellence and good tendency, whilst "external evidence" comprises the miracles wrought and the prophecies fulfilled by him who teaches the doctrines. Tindal had argued that, on Clarke's premises, the precepts of Christianity should be self-authenticating. In reply, Conybeare, Leland and Law tend to tilt the balance away from the self-evident character of Christian beliefs. Strictly speaking, says Conybeare, there can be no internal evidence of a revelation.[3] Leland, to whom we owe the first history of English Deism, contends that Tindal has confused the truth of doctrines with their good tendency. We may discover that a doctrine would have a good tendency if it were true—such as the existence of hell; but where the doctrine relates to a matter of fact, the tendency itself would not render the belief one jot more probable.[4] In rejecting the purely moralistic view of religious truth, and any merely pragmatic view of its apprehension, these writers are on the Christian side of the chasm that divides the faith from Deism, despite their difference of approach from our own.

Conybeare does make one attempt to create a closer relationship between miracles and the truths they authenticate. Miracles are like seals on a document, or like the

[1] Leland, *An Answer to a late book entitled "Christianity . . ."*, I, ch. V. J. Jackson, *Remarks on a book entitled "Christianity . . ."*, p. 7.

[2] J. Conybeare, *A Defence of Revealed Religion*, 1732, p. 427. Other replies are: J. Foster, *Usefulness, Truth and Excellency of the Christian Revelation*; H. Stebbing, *A Defence of Dr. Clarke's "Evidences"*; Berkeley, *Alciphron or the Minute Philosopher*.

[3] *op. cit.*, p. 431.

[4] *op. cit.*, pp. 82f.

sounds we utter in relation to the meaning of our speech. It is the application of miracles which gives them their significance.[1] It was all too easy, as subsequent discussion proved, for miracles to be treated as a question *in vacuo*, unrelated to the actual life and work of Christ. It is, however, to Law and Butler that we must turn for a more positive retort to Deism.

VII

To those who know William Law as a devotional writer, it will come as a surprise to meet him in the guise of a controversialist. It was not a rôle for which he was ideally suited, for it obliged him to deal in the categories of the day which were inadequate to express his more comprehensive understanding of the faith. Like other apologists, Law begins by challenging the Deists' assumption that nothing can come from God save through nature. There is nothing in man to oblige him to think this: and if humility is the foundation of our attitude towards God, and pride the source of evil, confidence in our own reason in the face of God is highly questionable. "Shew me," he says, "according to what fitness, founded in the nature of things, God's infinite wisdom was determined to form you in such a manner, bring you into such a world, and suffer and preserve such a state of things as human life is, and then you may have some pretence to believe no revealed doctrines, but such as your own reason can deduce from the nature of things and the fitness of actions."[2] Suppose some supernatural means is necessary to destroy the guilt and power of sin; and supposing that the mediation, sufferings and intercessions of the Incarnate Son of God is that supernatural means; it necessarily follows that a revelation of such supernatural means cannot be made obvious to our reason and senses as the things of human life, but must be revealed in such a way as to be a just occasion of our faith, humility, adoration and pious resignation to the Divine wisdom and goodness.[3] Unfortunately Law is dealing in merchandise unsaleable to his contemporaries.

[1] *op. cit.*, p. 460.
[2] *The Case of Reason or Natural Religion fairly and fully stated*, 3rd ed., p. 10.
[3] *op. cit.*, p. 36.

The Deists had become so infatuated with the idea of the rationality of nature's forms and laws that they were practically saying that nature MUST be as it is—has a quasi-necessary existence; the "best possible of all worlds" outlook. Law strikes at the root of this attitude with the Christian assertions that nature's forms and working are nothing but the fiat of God Himself.[1] His position required an even stronger emphasis than that of many of his contemporaries upon the external evidences, as his doctrines were of so far-reaching a character. Internal excellence, he urges, far from proving revelation, might be a presumption against it; for God would scarcely make a special revelation of matters sufficiently known without it. In fact, "if God has no ways of acting so peculiar to Himself, as to be a sufficient proof to human reason of His action, then no revelation can be sufficiently proved to be a Divine external revelation from God."[2]

Law concentrates rather upon arguments illustrating the unity of Christian truth, and the inconsistency of the Deists' position. There is nothing, he argues, half so mysterious in revelation as there is in providence—which all Theists and Deists admit.[3] Moreover, "as we can only know what is worthy of God in creation, by knowing what He has created; so we can no other way possibly know what is worthy of God to be revealed, but by a revelation."[4] It follows also that if we can appeal to the creation as proof of God's existence, we can as surely appeal to miracles for proof of revelation.[5] It must be adjudged that Law's first parallel, between creation and the things revealed, is more convincing than the second, between creation and miracles. If miracles had been conceived of as germane to the substance of revelation, then both the parallels would have been apt indeed: for the comparison is really between God's two acts of creation and redemption as they are brought about by the Logos. There has been a persistent notion in modern times that it is easier to believe in God than in Christ. This idea has not unnaturally been engendered by the fact of men living in a nominally Christian society; and of course there were Theists in Israel and Greece before the coming of Christ. But Theism does not appeal to any

[1] *op. cit.*, p. 48. [2] *ibid.*, p. 90. [3] *ibid.*, p. 86.
[4] *ibid.*, p. 80. [5] *ibid.*, p. 92.

different elements within the human personality than does revelation. Law is concerned to show that the same scepticism which Tindal applies to revelation might equally be turned against his own doctrinaire Theism: and this actually came to pass a few years later in the sceptical philosophy of Hume.

VIII

To those who continually demand from their theologians some fresh insight into the faith, Butler's *Analogy of Religion*, 1736, must appear unsatisfying. He epitomizes the best theology of his time and employs only such arguments as had been already tried in the fire of controversy. He possessed that virtue, so hard for an apologist to acquire, absolute honesty; for like a master engineer, working out the stress and strain upon every girder, he never exaggerates the force of any single argument. In his conception of the cumulative argument, taking a broad view of the Old and New Testaments, the person and work of Christ and the existence and work of the church, Butler was far ahead of most of the men of his century. He saw that there was no "Short and Easy Method" to demonstrate in the logical sense the Divine character of the Christian dispensation. Hence his skilful use of the concept of analogical reasoning for natural and revealed religion.

The Christian religion consists of two parts, natural and revealed. Butler rejects outright the Deist contention that mankind has sufficient knowledge of natural religion without revelation.[1] The miracles and prophecies of Scripture were intended to prove a particular dispensation of providence, the redemption of the world by the Messiah; but this does not prevent them from proving God's general providence. He admits the apparent theoretical difficulty of miracles proving moral precepts, but points out that the historic connection between them is undeniable. The doctrine of the future state of rewards and punishments, so necessary to natural religion, could certainly not have been apprehended by mankind without revelation.[2] In addition to reinforcing natural religion, certain

[1] *op. cit.*, 1900 ed., p. 137. [2] *ibid.*, p. 141.

specific truths otherwise unattainable by human reason are conveyed by revelation. These are of no mere speculative interest, but vitally affect our conduct and worship: they are the functions of the Son and Spirit as Redeemer and Sanctifier.[1] Butler does not therefore have to balance on a tightrope with regard to the capabilities of human reason.

Butler does not conceive revelation to be an abrupt interference in a world which otherwise functions by its own momentum and laws. It is God's continuous supervision which alone preserves to everything its proper nature and functioning. The Incarnation is strictly speaking a miracle. It is not, however, self-evidencing; and we could possess no analogy to it, except some possible Incarnation upon another planet. It must therefore carry with it ancillary proofs of a miraculous character.[2] It is analogies from God's working through nature which make it possible for us to apprehend the significance of these supernatural evidences.

Some of Butler's most frequently quoted observations on miracles appear in his three arguments for their intrinsic credibility. We shall allude in the following chapter to his summary of the positive evidences for revelation. First, "There is," he says, "a very strong presumption against common speculative truths, and against the most ordinary facts, before the proof of them; which yet is overcome by almost any proof. There is a presumption of millions to one against the story of Caesar, or of any other man."[3] In the case of a miraculous event, is there any peculiar or significant presupposition against its occurrence? Let us admit, he says, that there is an additional presupposition against a miraculous fact: such a peculiar presupposition, added to the immense presupposition against ordinary events before they have actually occurred, cannot be estimated, and is as nothing.[4] J. S. Mill complains that Butler has confused the question of probability before the report of an event with probability after it. In the case of a reported miracle, says Mill, the probability against it remains enormous even after its reported occurrence.[5] Even if Mill's views about the grounds of induction be rejected, it remains that in the

[1] *ibid.*, p. 145. [2] *ibid.*, pp. 157, 159. [3] *ibid.*, p. 159.
[4] *ibid.*, pp. 159-60. [5] *System of Logic*, II, p. 169.

reports of miracles we have to reckon with the factor of human fallibility. Butler does realize that a great deal more testimony is required in the case of reported miracles; but he is arguing that men are led to accept many otherwise incredible statements simply on human testimony, just as new scientific truths have often won their way in the face of great prejudice. He concludes that there is no presumption against miracles as to render them incredible, but "that, on the contrary, our being able to discern reasons for them, gives a positive credibility to the history of them, in cases where those reasons hold; and it is by no means certain that there is any peculiar presumption at all from analogy, even in the lowest degree, against miracles as distinguished from other extraordinary phenomena. . . ."

Secondly, Butler goes on to explain that apart from religion "we are in such total darkness upon what causes, occasions, reasons, or circumstances, the present course of nature depends; that there does not appear any improbability for or against supposing that five or six thousand years may have given scope for causes . . . from whence miraculous interpositions may have arisen."[1] Having some conception of general laws, he says elsewhere, we conclude that the whole of nature is capable of being reduced to them; and if so, it is also legitimate to argue that "God's miraculous interpositions may have been all along, in like manner, by general laws of wisdom."[2] There may even be beings to whom the whole Christian dispensation appears "natural", i.e. "analogous or conformable to God's dealings with other parts of His creation."[3] The theologians of the 18th century were well acquainted with St. Augustine's dictum that miracles might be "*non contra naturam, sed contra quam est nota natura.*"[4] A number of rationalizations on this basis were attempted in the following century. Butler is concerned simply to make the point that we may not unreasonably expect nature to have been created on a long-term policy, many aspects of which will lie beyond the limited powers of man to foresee or correlate with the ordinary course of things.

Thirdly, when we take religion into consideration, and the

[1] *Analogy*, p. 160. [2] *op. cit.*, p. 181.
[3] *ibid.*, p. 28. [4] *De Civ. Dei*, XXI, 8.

moral system of the world, "we see distinct particular reasons for miracles: to afford mankind instruction additional to that of nature, and to attest the truth of it. And this gives a real credibility to the supposition, that it might be part of the original plan of things, that there should be miraculous interpositions."[1]

IX

At this stage of the investigation we shall concentrate upon one question regarding the 18th-century apologetic: What kind of a revelation was it that miracles were supposed to have proved?

It will be apparent that there are two common factors in the systems of the Deists and their orthodox opponents. First, the mode of apprehending Divine truth in both cases is in essence the same—the acceptance by the discursive intellect of facts and principles. Secondly, the content of revelation is thought of in not altogether dissimilar terms by both parties. Leland lists the objects of the Christian revelation thus: Disclosures of the main principles of the law of nature; disclosure of the method by which God wills to reconcile sinners to Himself; and disclosure of the terms He requires from men, together with knowledge of the final rewards and punishments.[2] Butler indeed speaks of the functions of the Son and the Spirit as essential to revelation, and there was no lack of interest at the time in dogmatics as such: witness the searching Trinitarian controversy. Orthodoxy is a correlate of revealed religion; but in an "age of reason" there is the subtle temptation to assume that religion is concerned predominantly with knowledge about God rather than with knowledge of God. Long before Buber wrote his famous book it was realized that there is a fundamental distinction between knowing about a person, and knowing a person in that peculiar way in which one spiritual being can know and be known by another. We can only know a person as such in the full sense, points out C. C. J. Webb, when he discloses himself to us in a personal relationship.[3] This is what God has done for us in revelation. Yet the 18th-century

[1] *Analogy*, p. 160. [2] *Answer to a late book* . . ., I, p. 11.
[3] *Problems in the Relations of God and Man*, p. 39.

dogmatics and apologetics concentrated nearly all its attention upon God as an object to be known about. This theology was impressive in its thoroughness and self-consistency: no woolliness blurred its doctrines, nor sentimentality its ethics. But a religion which does not centre upon the living personal relationship between the church and its Lord, and the supernatural dimension of the believer's life, is not the whole Gospel of God.

The matter becomes still clearer when it is realized that the ethics which were held to form so central a place in the content of revelation comprised a system of thought and behaviour which falls short of the categories of New Testament experience and reflection. Scarcely is it suggested that the Christian ethic may differ radically, if at all, from the principles of humanism. Deist and traditionalist alike believed in an objective norm of morality, whose fulfilment leads to happiness; and morality was taken much more seriously at this time than many people have supposed.[1] But to neither party does it appear that the New Testament offers an outright challenge to their eudaemonistic scheme. The rational humanism of the 18th century was nominally set in the context of eternal life; but the other-worldliness was simply concerned with the rewards and punishments meted out in respect of an ethic whose demands were largely contained within the requirements of civil society and personal uprightness: "A theology which regarded Christianity as an admirable auxiliary to the police-force."[2] But the Christian character is supernatural in its cause and its results, because it is the work of Christ and the Spirit. Such a power in human life, whose efficient cause is grace and whose final cause is God's glory, is at home in an atmosphere where the miraculous activity of God is taken for granted, be it in the Incarnation, the sacraments or interior prayer.

It is not surprising that in the 18th-century scheme of doctrine the connection between miracles and the revealed doctrines came to appear so artificial. When revelation and faith are both rationalized and externalized, miracles become the bridge between a rational creed and its rational acceptance.

[1] Stromberg, *Religious Liberalism in Eighteenth-Century England*, 1954.
[2] Lecky, *Rationalism*, I, p. 165.

The supernatural character of miracles came to be thought of almost entirely in terms of their non-conformity to nature: hence their appeal was directed exclusively to the discursive part of man's mind rather than to his moral and spiritual judgment.

Chapter Three

THE DAWN OF HISTORICAL CRITICISM

I

THE Deists did not content themselves merely with stating their theoretical objections to the idea of a particular revelation; they set themselves to discredit the Christian revelation on historical grounds. This aspect of Deistic polemics is of even closer interest at the present day than their theoretical work: for whereas the duel between reason and revelation has assumed new forms, the historical attack raised questions of which the apologist to this day must take cognizance. One may heartily agree with the censures passed upon the spirit of the Deist writers by such 19th-century historians of the controversy as Van Mildert and A. S. Farrar, but it can scarcely be regretted that the church was so abruptly awakened to the examination of the historic origins of its faith in this formative period of modern thinking. The historico-critical controversy of the 18th century was a very different affair from the struggle in the following century for the acceptance of higher criticism. A century was still to elapse before the storm over *Essays and Reviews*, 1860, and Bishop Colenso's *Introduction to the Pentateuch and Book of Joshua*, 1862. At this later period, the scandal was clearly that the new views were being propagated by men who were official representatives of the church, whilst in the 18th century the criticisms were advanced by men who were already enemies.

In every instance, a seemingly complete refutation was forthcoming from the orthodox side; it was made to appear that Deism was as dead as Donatism. But once the literal infallibility of the Scriptures had been questioned on rational grounds, nothing could put Humpty-Dumpty together again but the deepest researches into Christian origins—and the church did not yet possess the necessary critical armour, but was obliged to go on restating its historical affirmations backed by such "evidences" as could then be marshalled. (This explains a fact which seems to have puzzled Mark Pattison: that long after the controversy, the "clergy continued to manufacture evidence".[1]) The Deists were at liberty to attack at whatever point they chose, whilst the orthodox, with their belief in plenary inspiration, were obliged to defend their whole perimeter with equal tenacity. Again, the Deists' weapons were crude, as compared with which the hypodermic needle of a modern sceptical historian may be far more deadly. It was here that traditionalists had a certain advantage. It is intellectually conceivable that Christians may be mistaken in their beliefs; but it is morally impossible for men of good will to be blind to the majesty, uniqueness and beauty of the life and personality of Christ. It is equally morally impossible to believe that the first promulgators of Christianity were scoundrels. Yet it was on charges which ignored these insights that the Deists sought to discredit the faith. It is in the writings relating to historical matters that we feel the full throb of the Deist controversy; the age when theological questions were argued at dinner parties and in coffee houses, and the time when the views of one's opponents were attributed to their moral decrepitude.

There were numerous indications of the coming storm. In 1680, Charles Blount, an early Deist, published a translation of the first two books of Philostratus' life of Apollonius of Tyana—the insinuation of which was that the miraculous element in history is like a fungus which grows around the memory of all religious leaders. In 1683, a tract appeared under the title *Miracles no violation of the laws of nature*, ascribed to Blount, which was actually a paraphase translation of sections of Spinoza's *Tractatus*.[2]

[1] *Essays and Reviews*, 5th ed., p. 261.

[2] Dr. A. Richardson says that the Deistic objection to miracles did not arise from any historical examination of the evidence. *Christian Apologetics*, p. 157. For a more adequate judgment cf. V. F. Storr, *Development of English Theology*, pp. 46f.

II

The two names chiefly associated with the first onslaught upon the citadel of tradition are Anthony Collins and Thomas Woolston. In 1713, Collins, a gentleman of leisure, published a tract entitled *A Discourse of Free Thinking*, outlining a rationalistic approach to religious dogma, which brought down upon its author the wrath of Bentley. In 1724, Collins followed up his pamphlet with *A Discourse of the Grounds and Reasons of the Christian Religion*, and continued his theme in *The Scheme of Literal Prophecy*, 1727. The *Grounds* was like a thunderbolt: no less than thirty-five written replies to it were counted.[1]

Collins narrows down his task by asserting that Christ and His Apostles based His claim to Messiahship exclusively upon the fulfilment of Old Testament prophecies; the proof from miracles rests upon the prior proof from prophecy.[2] He uses as a cat's-paw a book by William Whiston, *Essays towards restoring the true text*, 1722, in which the hypothesis was advanced that Jewish scribes had rearranged much of the Old Testament material so as to obscure a great part of the original prophecies of the Messiah. For instance, the Messianic prophecy, "A virgin shall conceive . . .", had been deliberately conflated with words relating to a child of the prophet. Collins has no difficulty in ridiculing this hypothesis, and concludes that the prophetic writings have their primary reference to events in the lifetime of the prophets. The only method of discovering prophecies of Christ is by allegorical interpretation. He then solemnly parades ten rabbinical methods of clipping and reshuffling the text, and declares that here if anywhere is the true foundation for Christ's claims.

The *Grounds* was easily recognized as a thinly disguised attack upon the Christian faith. The apologists of the time made a strenuous attempt not only to reinstate the validity of the proof from literal prophecy but also to press the importance of the proof from miracles.

Collins had promised to write a work on miracles himself, but the gauntlet was thrown down by a rougher hand, for from 1727 to 1729 there appeared the six discourses on miracles

[1] *Essays and Reviews*, 5th ed., p. 259. [2] *Grounds*, pp. 27, 31.

by Thomas Woolston, a Cambridge don whose unstable mental condition was a good enough target for his orthodox opponents. He was subsequently indicted for blasphemy and died in prison. His ribald attacks upon the character of Christ and the Apostles evoked, amongst many replies, Bishop Thomas Sherlock's *Tryal of the Witnesses of the Resurrection*, one of the most popular apologies of the time. This latter work is cast in the form of an imaginary trial of the Apostles on a charge of fraud, and belongs to the class of writings which Dr. Johnson aptly called "Old Bailey theology". The tone of the book is somewhat secular; there is no hint of the crucial importance of the event at stake or of the splendour of Christ's person; and the book ends with a touch of comedy in bad taste. As the arguments in Woolston's sixth discourse are repeated by the imaginary counsel for his defence in the *Tryal*, we may consider the two books together.

The Resurrection, contends Woolston, was the most notorious and monstrous fraud ever put on mankind, engineered by the disciples who stole the body of Christ from the sepulchre.[1] The persistence of the belief in the Resurrection is no argument, since contemporary Jewish documents exposing the fraud are lost. The chief priests, both because of Christ's predictions and the "Lazarus fraud", sealed the sepulchre—a precaution impotent against violence yet proof positive against fraud. Similarly, the guards were not numerous enough to prevent an assault, but were undeniable witnesses to any fraud. The seal implies that the priests had agreed with the disciples to open the sepulchre on the third day in their presence—the disciples forestalled the exposure by stealing the body a day earlier, i.e. on the Sunday morning. The crowning proof of the fraud is that Jesus never once appeared to His enemies, to the leaders of His nation or to impartial witnesses; and the Gospels show amazing discrepancies in their accounts of the appearances. The concomitant evidences are useless: the testimony of the women is but one apparition to support another apparition; and every false doctrine can show martyrs in its cause.

Sherlock replies that all other supposed resuscitations show wide differences from the accounts of Christ's Resurrection; whilst such legends as Mahomet's ascension into heaven have

[1] VIth *Discourse*, p. 5.

nothing but the subject's word for them. It was easy for him to show the hollowness of some of Woolston's more superficial objections—for instance, by pointing out that the Jews numbered their days inclusively, so that Sunday was in fact the third day. But he is at his best when he shows how Woolston's reconstruction is riddled with contradictions. Woolston's picture makes nonsense of the person of Christ. It had been suggested that Jesus Himself was party to the plot: but what would this have served Him seeing He Himself was to die! Nor is the suggestion any better that He only prophesied resurrection when He saw that His death was inevitable: in that case why not have saved Himself?[1] Genuine knowledge of Jesus' miracles could alone have made the Jewish authorities take notice of His predictions.[2] The character of the disciples is even less comprehensible on Woolston's view. They are first represented as harmless dreamers looking for the Messiah, and then as bold bad men: and if they had been looking for a temporal kingdom, what could it have served them to steal a body? That they had a compact with the priests is preposterous, especially in the light of the fact that they had fled.[3] The chief priests do not charge the Apostles with fraud in the examinations recorded in the Acts, nor does Tertullus mention it in his speech.

Sherlock also enlarges upon the sufficiency of evidence received on the testimony of others: a subject which from now on was to loom large in apologetic writings. If testimony that conflicts with normal experience is unacceptable, he says, then men who live in the tropics should never believe that water freezes.[4] A man from the dead can provide as much evidence of his being alive as any living man.[5] Moreover, evidence of a miracle given to chosen witnesses is the only kind of evidence that is practically acceptable.[6]

The apparently artificial character of this controversy derives in part from the peculiar nature of the evidence at our disposal. Woolston's talk about lost Jewish writings is an attempt to escape from the narrow confines of the evidence. Many of the arguments on both sides are based upon the assumption that the New Testament provides a complete description of the

[1] *Tryal*, 1729, 4th ed., p. 27. [2] *op. cit.*, p. 38. [3] *ibid.*, pp. 40f.
[4] *ibid.*, p. 60. [5] *ibid.*, pp. 61–62. [6] *ibid.*, pp. 74f.

matters with which it deals. Woolston works out his case by denying the truth of specific statements in the New Testament, and then builds upon the assumption that the rest of the material is the last word in historical veracity. For instance, he assumes the story of the seal and the guards to be the truest section of the post-crucifixion narrative, yet he rejects the account of the interview of the guards with the chief priests. The futility of discussing the subject on the terms adopted in this controversy brings out very sharply the fact that historical certitude is something very different from logical or experimental certitude, and it is part of the scandal of particular revelation to share in the nature of historical knowledge. In the early 18th century it was not yet sufficiently grasped that questions of historical probability must largely turn upon judgments of human personality: the whole of man, all his cognitive and intuitive powers, are needed to determine, let alone to evaluate, the deeds of men in the past. In the case of Christ's life, historical enquiry which does not take into account the whole impact of His life-giving personality is sterile. Sherlock attempts to meet rationalism on its own ground, not without success; but he seems unaware that the strongest arguments in his book are those in which he shows the fraud theory to be morally impossible. The long story of the rationalistic attacks upon the Resurrection from Woolston to Kirsopp Lake must be countered not merely by detailed refutations of the theories but by the widest consideration of the facts of Christ in the historical setting.

[Until 1748, the historical controversy continued to be waged with the same pieces on the board. On the Deist side there were Chubb and Annet, and on the orthodox side, the two Chandlers and Gilbert West—see Bibliography.]

III

We come now to critical work of more permanent significance, to writers whose work was ultimately to cause the reshaping of the structure of apologetics. The year 1748 saw the publication of two books which were to provide the miracle controversy with its characteristic points of reference for the next hundred years. They advanced no arguments which were really new; rather, they acted as lenses which focused the light and heat to burning points, concentrating the critical work of a whole generation.

Hume's *Treatise of Human Nature* had been "still-born" in the press, as its author put it, and he was therefore obliged to publish his philosophical opinions in a more popular form. This he did in the *Enquiry concerning the Human Understanding*, of 1748, into which he introduced some material of a startling, if not altogether relevant, character—namely two sections dealing with miracles and providence.

In the tenth section, on miracles, he refers to Tillotson's *a priori* argument against transubstantiation, and makes the following boast: "I flatter myself that I have discovered an argument of a like nature, which, if just, will, with the wise and learned, be an everlasting check to all kinds of superstitious delusion, and consequently will be useful as long as the world endures. . . ."[1] The most widely differing verdicts as to the success of this boast have been offered: from contemporary apologists, who urged that the argument contained a most blatant fallacy, to Leslie Stephen who declares the argument to be "unanswerable".[2] Be this as it may, Hume's essay helped theologians to ask themselves whether in fact the truth of Christianity could be based upon the argument from miracles—events which require sympathy with the Christian position for their credence.

Hume begins his essay with a general attack upon the reliability of human testimony, and proceeds to the assertion that certain events are found to be conjoined constantly in experience. Here, as A. E. Taylor points out, he takes the first step outside the magic circle of his metaphysics; for it is a postulate of Hume's philosophy that all events are for all we know quite separate.[3] Hume goes on to argue that a wise man will always proportion his belief to the evidence in any statement about a succession of events: which presumably means basing one's judgment upon the number of times that such and such have been previously conjoined—since according to him,

[1] Philosophical Works of D. Hume, 1854, vol. IV, p. 125.
[2] *English Thought in the XVIIIth century*, I, p. 339.
[3] *David Hume and the Miraculous*, 1927, a lecture.

all our knowledge is founded solely on our experience of the "constant and regular connection of events". Thus, the Siamese prince, in the hackneyed story, was justified in refusing to believe in ice, since the testimony to its existence contradicted the whole of his experience. But there is one case where the weighing of testimony is unnecessary, since evidence in support of the statement would not, by its very nature, outweigh the evidence against it. He writes:

> In order to increase the probability against the testimony of witnesses, let us suppose that the fact which they affirm, instead of being only marvellous, is really miraculous; and suppose also, that the testimony, considered apart and in itself, amounts to an entire proof, in that case there is proof against proof, of which the strongest must prevail, but still with a diminishing of its force, in proportion to that of its antagonist. A miracle is a violation of the laws of nature; and as a firm and unalterable experience has established these laws, the proof against a miracle, from the very nature of the fact, is as entire as any argument from experience can possibly be imagined.[1]

Philosophers and apologists have not been slow to point out that the seeming success of this argument depends upon assumptions which Hume has already discounted in his philosophy. Elsewhere he had urged that we know nothing directly of the laws and causes which prescribe certain patterns in nature, except the bundle of sense data. Now he assumes that e know of such laws and causes, enabling us to declare with certainty the course of nature outside our own experience of it; and—what is even more surprising to a modern thinker—that we can distinguish between what is natural but unusual, and what is beyond nature's powers to produce.[2] Since Hume's argument is directed against anything which contradicts experience, it has often been pointed out that it equally militates against the acceptance of new scientific discoveries.[3] A. E. Taylor concludes that on Hume's own principles the only

[1] *op. cit.*, p. 130.

[2] Cf. Hume's distinction between a resuscitation and a darkness over the earth, *op. cit.*, p. 147; cf. also T. H. Green's incisive criticisms of the argument on technical grounds, *Works*, vol. I, pp. 269f.

[3] Cf. Tennant's discussion of the argument, *Miracle and its Philosophical Presuppositions*, 1924, pp. 81-82.

legitimate definition of a miracle could be that it is something unusual, and that it is natural to be incredulous. Again, Hume had argued that our only knowledge of nature was derived from sense-experience. This must either mean "my own personal experience", in which case there is an end of all correction of personal errors; or "the whole human experience", in which case it is a *petitio principii* to say that there is a universal experience against any event to which any man claims to be able to testify.[1] Now this is fair criticism of Hume as he stands; but to those who regard nature as a rational system created by God, and not a bundle of possibly disjointed fragments, there must be very special reasons for believing that that order has ever been radically transgressed. Indeed, the various attempts in the 19th and 20th centuries to conceive the Biblical miracles as being in some sense "natural" bears witness to the difficulty to the Christian mind.

In the second part of the argument, Hume would appear to retrace his steps. For after having declared that in the case of the miraculous the question of the weight of testimony is irrelevant, he returns again to consider the question from a fresh angle. This latter section has generally been regarded as the most deadly portion of the argument, and for the very good reason that it forsakes the merely *a priori* and deals with the actual fallibility of human evidence. "No testimony," he says, "is sufficient to establish a miracle, unless the testimony be of such a kind that its falsehood would be more miraculous than the fact which it endeavours to establish: and even in that case there is a mutual destruction of arguments, and the superior only gives us an assurance suitable to that degree of force which remains after deducting the inferior."[2] A. E. Taylor points out that, to arrive at such a solution of a given case, one would have to have considered all the available testimony to calculate what it amounts to. As a suggestive *modus operandi*, however, the argument has had far-reaching consequences. As already suggested, Hume's attempt to distinguish the miraculous from the merely extraordinary is scarcely justified on his own principles. Suppose, he says, all authors agree that from January 1, 1600 there was a total darkness over the whole earth for eight days, our present philosophers ought to receive it as certain and ought

[1] A. E. Taylor, *op. cit.*, p. 10. [2] *op. cit.*, p. 131.

to search for its causes: whereas a report of the resuscitation of Queen Elizabeth would be believed by no one.[1] Hume, in spite of himself, has here stumbled on a fact of importance, namely, that the human mind tends naturally to accept some things almost without question whilst it rejects others with almost equal ease. But, like Mill, he does not give an adequate explanation of it: for beyond empirical experience there are deeper questions of congruity at work.

Hume makes three admissions, which would seem to take the sting out of the essay. First, he says that testimony may justify belief in something which "seems" miraculous, though it cannot prove such an event to have been worked by God.[2] Similarly, a miracle can never be proved so as to be the foundation of a system of religion.[3] And finally at the end of the essay he says that his argument will not convince anyone who already accepts the Christian faith. But though the essay has not destroyed and will not destroy the belief in miracles, it did in fact help to undermine the 18th-century theological view of miracles as an independent external authorization of religious truth.

IV

There was no lack of immediate theoretical rejoinders to Hume's arguments. William Adams urges that Hume has confused the credibility of facts with that of witnesses: if a thing has happened it is presumably possible to have adequate testimony to it. Miracle, far from militating against natural uniformity, actually implies it as its background; and in fact the uniformity of nature is no more disturbed by a miracle than by an iron ship that floats. In moral agents we look for moral causes, for reasons or motives to induce them to act, as well as the natural powers of acting. The laws of the moral world are as certain as those of the physical order. With adequate evidence and understandable moral causes at work, therefore, it is reasonable to accept the testimony to miracles.[4] Bishop Douglas argues that nothing can be justly asserted to be incredible in its own nature the possibility of which must be

[1] *op. cit.*, p. 147. [2] *ibid.*, p. 131. [3] *ibid.*, p. 146.
[4] *An Essay in answer to Mr. Hume's Essay on Miracles*, 1752.

allowed, and the possibility of miracles follows from the existence of a Being who superintends the universe.[1] Hume's argument proved too much, and therefore nothing at all. Its speciousness was shown by the fact that its author was prepared to believe a story such as the hypothetical darkness in 1600: the distinction was purely arbitrary, and showed that he would believe anything where religion was out of the question.[2]

George Campbell's *Dissertation on Miracles*, 1762, is especially interesting as it was acknowledged by Hume to be a fair treatment of his essay. The crucial point of the *Dissertation* is its discussion of the relative values of experience and testimony. Hume had posited, first, that all our knowledge comes to us through experience, and secondly, that human testimony is fallible. Campbell takes it that Hume was contrasting experience and testimony as distinct sources of knowledge, the former being greatly superior to the latter. But, says Campbell, children give unlimited assent to testimony long before they have experience to act for themselves: how then can the acceptance of testimony be grounded in experience? Even the commonest peasant derives vastly more of his knowledge from testimony than from personal experience: if our acceptance of testimony were to be based only on personal experience, our belief in matters of fact would have very narrow bounds.[3] Hume himself replied that he had not in fact been seeking to distinguish experience and testimony as separate sources of knowledge. But Campbell's general criticisms of the pretensions of empiricism are just in themselves—the part played by our instinctive trustfulness that the future will resemble the past was not taken proper account of by these philosophers. On the other hand, the modern apologist must show that the events surrounding the Christian revelation are consonant with man's highest reasonings; for the modern rejection of the miraculous is in one sense due to a refining and intellectualizing of man's intuitive expectation of the orderliness of nature.

As time went on, apologists concentrated upon the argument that Hume had merely considered the question of testimony *in vacuo*, without any reference to the character of the witnesses or the moral significance of the event alleged.[4] Miracles, says

[1] *The Criterion*, pp. 11-12. [2] *op. cit.*, p. 29. [3] *op. cit.*, pp. 38-40.
[4] e.g. Richard Price, *Four Discourses*, 1768.

Paley, are not nearly so incredible as the future state which they attest, and which natural theology finds none the less not difficult to accept. A narrative, he continues, would be contrary to experience only if the person were at the time and place of the event and therefore knew it to be false; the only other meaning of the word is "contrary to general experience", which assumes the subject of the controversy. If miracles were necessary for the first promulgation of Christianity, would it be so obvious that they would be so much repeated as to become objects of general experience? Finally, when a mathematician is presented with a proposition, the first thing he does is to put it to a simple test. Suppose, then, twelve trusted men recount a miracle and die in attestation of it. According to Hume, they should be disbelieved: yet there is scarcely a sceptic in the world who would not believe them.[1]

By setting side by side the uniformity of nature and the fallibility of human testimony, Hume undoubtedly showed that the difficulty of crediting a rare occurrence increases by leaps and bounds in proportion to its strangeness from customary experience. In an oblique way this was no disservice to Christianity, for it obliged theologians to undertake a radical criticism of the way in which the historical credenda may be apprehended. But the thing which really out-dates Hume, is that he—and Leslie Stephen[2] too for that matter—envisaged a picture of natural uniformity which was relative to the scientific reflection of their times. Against that background the miracles of the Bible appeared totally strange, and therefore totally unacceptable. Modern psychical research, however, has provided undeniable testimony to many strange phenomena bearing a remarkable resemblance to occurrences attributed over and over again to the saints and mystics.[3] The important question now is not so much the truth of these reports as their significance for religion. Hume's pronouncements are quite useless at this level. Furthermore, looked at from a standpoint which takes all the known psycho-physical phenomena into account, many of the "miracles" of the Bible do not now appear strange to the nth degree as they did to Hume.

[1] Preface to the *Evidences*. [2] *English Thought*, I, p. 339.

[3] Cf. Fr. H. Thurston's extensive researches: *The Physical Phenomena of Mysticism*, 1952.

V

An illustration of the standards of criticism laid down by Hume is provided by Middleton's *Free Inquiry into the miraculous powers, which are supposed to have subsisted in the Christian Church, from the Earliest Ages through several successive centuries.* The work also focuses attention upon a peculiar problem which was henceforward to embarrass evidentialist writers. Heretofore apologists had found it sufficient to deal simply with the authentication of the Scripture miracles; heathen and popish miracles might be dismissed with contempt. This was but one instance of the freedom from the canons of secular history which the Biblical narratives enjoyed. It followed from the evidential view of miracles that miracles in the Roman church had to be denied in order to rebut the claims of that church to continuous inspiration. Some Anglican divines were prepared to allow the reality of certain miracles in the church down to the time of Constantine and the Council of Nicaea. The New Testament miracles form indeed a unique corpus of narratives, organically united as they are to the saving acts and teaching of Christ. But the evidentialist distinction was purely arbitrary: it denied the belief that God would ever act in response to prayer in a supernatural manner; and sooner or later also it was bound to be realized that superficially the New Testament miracles do not stand by themselves. Nor is there any break in the church's record of miracles: in the very year that Woolston began to sneer at the Gospel miracles, 1727, there died François de Paris, at whose tomb the Jansenists claimed a great number of miraculous cures.

It was Middleton who struck the characteristic blow against the traditional protestant distinction between the miracles of the New Testament and those of the church. He was a man whose scholarship was admired by Bishop Warburton, and who had taken great pains to study the Roman claims for purposes of refutation (cf. his *Letters from Rome*). The gist of the *Free Inquiry* lies in its preface: for the body of the large book, though it contains much shrewd critical work, laid itself open to serious attack by such scholars as John Wesley on account of its orgy of special pleading. The original object of Middleton's studies—and still the ostensible object of the *Free Inquiry*—was to set the New Testament miracles on a firmer foundation, by disentangling them from the mass of miracles purporting to have been wrought in the church. But he employs canons of criticism which might well be turned upon the Apostolic miracles, and this was recognized by his opponents as the true goal of his work.

Middleton first plays upon the inconsistency of orthodox apologists regarding the date when the church's miraculous powers are supposed to have ceased. Leslie, Dodwell, Marshall, Whiston and Waterland all had their own favourite dates.[1] Some writers had said that history provided no conclusive evidence as to the date of cessation, and in any case that it did not matter. Yet if miracles were for authentication, this was surely a most extraordinary evasion.[2] Many writers had argued that the gift of tongues was indispensable during the first era of missionary activity: but Xavier would equally have benefited from such a gift.[3] Lastly, apologists urged that miracles occurred in the period when the church's doctrine and practice was most pure; yet it was precisely within the first three centuries that we saw the firm establishment of those features of the catholic religion which these apologists so much abhorred.[4] The fact was that the whole of ecclesiastical history stood or fell together: if the church historians of one century were to be believed, so must those of another.[5]

The truth of the ecclesiastical miracles, Middleton tells us, depends upon the joint credibility of the facts and of the witnesses who attest them. If either be infirm, their credit must sink in proportion; and if the facts especially be incredible, their credit must disappear. The credibility of facts lies open to the trial of our reason and senses, but the credibility of witnesses depends upon a variety of principles, wholly concealed from us.[6] As witnesses to the miraculous, the Fathers can be ruled out practically en bloc, on account of their prejudices, superstitious temperament and interest in proving the events to be true.[7] We find them roundly affirming things evidently fictitious, in order to strengthen as they fancied the evidences of the Gospel.[8] Nor do they ever show how the testimony which

[1] *op. cit.*, pp. xiv, xlix. [2] *ibid.*, p. xviii. [3] *ibid.*, p. xx. [4] *ibid.*, p. lii.
[5] *ibid.*, p. xvi. [6] *ibid.*, p. ix. [7] *ibid.*, p. xxxi. [8] *ibid.*, p. xxxii.

they give had been verified at the time. The body of the *Free Inquiry* is occupied with the attempt to substantiate this indictment. One point which characterizes all Middleton's work is what may be called the canon of intrinsic absurdity—what the Deist God might be relied upon never to have done for His creatures. It is impossible to exaggerate the implicit no less than the explicit influence of this idea since the 18th century.[1]

VI

Amongst the many retorts to the *Free Inquiry*, two are outstanding: Newman's second essay on miracles of 1843 (see *infra* ch. 4) and Wesley's letter to Middleton. The latter, written in twenty days, is a little masterpiece of scholarly polemic. Wesley has no illusions as to the drift of Middleton's argument, which he summarizes thus: "1. That there were no miracles wrought in the primitive church; 2. that all the primitive Fathers were fools or knaves, and most of them both one and the other. . . . 3. that no miracles were wrought by Christ or His Apostles; and 4. that these too were fools or knaves, or both."[2] The principles from which these conclusions were drawn, however, could lead to nothing but complete historical scepticism. For if the credibility of all witnesses is certainly known in no case, then "farewell the credit of all history, not only sacred but profane."[3]

Wesley deals acutely with Middleton's picture of the early church. He protests himself to be interested solely with the first three centuries—"because after the empire became Christian (they are your own words) 'A general corruption both of faith and morals infected the Christian church'."[4] St. Chrysostom, in fact, complains of the lack of miracles in his time owing to the want of faith, virtue and piety. Middleton had not quoted one Father in support of his contention that the

[1] An interesting commentary on the question of ecclesiastical miracles is afforded by the career of Gibbon. Sensing the connection between the Biblical and ecclesiastical miracles, he temporarily seceded to Rome; but becoming sceptical of miracles in general, he lost his hold on the Christian faith altogether. Cf. Gibbon's remarks on the place of miracles in the early church, *Decline and Fall*, Bury's ed., 3rd ed. II, pp. 28ff.

[2] *Letters of the Rev. J. Wesley*, Standard ed., J. Telford (1931), II, p. 312.

[3] *op. cit.*, II, p. 314. [4] *ibid.*, II, p. 313.

characteristics of catholicism—monkery, image worship, invocation of saints, etc.—were established within the first three centuries. Prayers for the dead and anointing with oil there had been, but were these corruptions?[1] There was ample evidence both of the miraculous powers in the Apostolic and sub-Apostolic periods, and of the expectation that such powers would continue to reside in the church.[2] If the Fathers had claimed miraculous powers, Middleton would have called them frauds: as they do not, he tries to use the fact as evidence that such powers did not exist. In actual fact the Fathers give ample evidence of miraculous powers. Middleton's assertion that in Patristic times miracles were merely worked by boys, women and private or obscure laymen, whereas in New Testament times they were performed by Apostles, will not bear examination. There is testimony to miracles performed by such outstanding Fathers as Cyprian, Justin, and Dionysius of Alexandria. But if the assertion had been true, it would simply have signified a more literal fulfilment of Joel's prophecy.[3] Finally, we may note a significant argument advanced in reply to a cavil of Middleton that certain miracles of raising from the dead were not done publicly. Such miracles, says Wesley, were not performed for the conversion of the heathen but for the good of the church; to support and confirm the Christians, who were daily tortured and slain, but sustained by the hope of obtaining a better resurrection.[4] This is one of the earliest divergences from the strictly evidential view of miracles in the 18th century: it was a sign of better things to come.

Such were the Deistic attacks upon the faith on historico-critical grounds, and such were the immediate orthodox rejoinders to them. We must now turn to the long-term policy of defence that was built up.

[1] *op. cit.*, II, p. 319. [2] *ibid.*, II, p. 327.
[3] *ibid.*, II, p. 337. [4] *ibid.*, II, p. 349.

Chapter Four

CHRISTIAN EVIDENCES

THE writing of "Christian evidences" forms an important chapter in the history of English theology. It predominated over other theological interests roughly from the close of the Deist controversy to the third decade of the 19th century. The Deists had offered a direct challenge to the historical credentials of Christianity and the evidence writers therefore set out to substantiate the claim that a Divine revelation had been given in Christ, witnessed to by miracles. In seeking to establish the continuity of the primitive Christian tradition, these apologists were not primarily concerned with the continuity of revealed truth in the church nor with the church's unbroken life of sacramental grace, as were the historians in the Tractarian movement. Their concern was the testimony to the life of Christ, and especially to the miraculous seals of His doctrine. This is very clearly to be seen in their treatment of the Scriptures. First of all they claim the authenticity of the Scriptures in virtue of the early church's witness. They then use the Scriptures as the central evidences for the miracles of Christ and His Apostles; and only after this do they appeal to them as the vehicles of the content of revelation.

The interest of theology today has shifted away from the evidentialists' immediate objective, but the work which they did is of permanent value. It is characteristic of the state of historical criticism at that time that they were able to present their case in the form of an either—or: the Christian tradition must be accepted or rejected *in toto*—more subtle alternatives were as yet unknown. Deistic criticism had been for the most part crude, but on the other hand, scholarly ingenuity working on the assumption of plenary inspiration produced a harmony which is far from reassuring to the modern reader. The evidence writers appear sincerely to have believed in their work, and within the very narrow corridor in which they argued out their case they may be deemed to have carried their point.

I

Despite the acute historical questions raised by the Deists, some evidence writers believed that the authenticity of revelation could be clinched by an appeal to some principle of historical criticism. Further, since faith was a moral act, and wilful doubt sinful, the ends of religion might best be served by the suppression of anything which might detract from the comprehensiveness of the writer's argument. Indeed, the method of cutting a highway through the jungle of historical problems provides an excellent insight into the thought of the 18th century.

Charles Leslie's *Short and Easy Method with the Deists*, 1701, is the earliest celebrated attempt to counter the Deists on the ground of historical criticism. He sets out a fourfold canon by which we are to judge the account of the miraculous institution of a religion. The following conditions must be present: "1. That the matter of fact be such as that men's outward senses, their eyes and ears, may be judges of it. 2. That it be done publicly in the face of the world. 3. That not only public monuments be kept up in memory of it, but some outward actions to be performed. 4. That such monuments and such actions or observances be instituted, and do commence from the time that the matter of fact was done."[1] From this starting-point he finds little difficulty in setting up the claims of Christianity. But so far has the study of history travelled since Leslie's day, that the canons as they stand present serious difficulties. Nothing need be said here about the first two: the observation of miracles. The latter pair, regarding the continuity of historical monuments and institutions, naturally are of great weight, but Leslie's own application of them is far from satisfactory. No man, he says, could conceivably persuade the people of London that he had once divided the river Thames: no more could Moses have deluded the people of Israel that he had

[1] *op. cit.*, p. 5.

brought them from Egypt had it not been so. Suppose a man wrote a book alleging that Stonehenge had been set up by Hercules, who would believe him? How then did the story of the stones at Gilgal ever gain credence had it not been true?[1] The science of comparative history has eaten the heart out of this argument as it stands; for the admission of the principle would involve the acceptance of a multitude of folklore explanations of customs, place-names and unusual natural objects.

Almost a century later, Joseph Priestley shows a similarly optimistic approach to the task. Like Leslie, he yokes together the fortunes of the Gospel history and those of the Pentateuch. How did the deliverance from Egypt take place?—"Moses, whose account was written at the time, and with all the minuteness, and other marks of authenticity, of any modern journal, informs us, that it was in consequence of a series of miraculous interpositions . . ."[2] Moses could not have effected the deliverance by mere statesmanship, because, says Priestley, he was really a very credulous person; he really thought that the Egyptian magicians produced frogs.[3] So after all, Moses was not the ideal witness to the miraculous by modern standards! The fact that the Hebrews lapsed into idolatry shows that they were not naturally monolatrous, but held their faith in Jehovah only on the evidence of revelation.[4] A favourite theme, this, with the evidentialists—to assume that the Hebrews, like 18th-century divines, based their creed on miracles.

Despite his adoptionist Christology, Priestley was a staunch upholder of supernatural revelation. He strides through the evidential questions regarding the Gospels. Jesus' miracles were of a vast number, performed under the very eyes of His enemies; one failure would have meant His ruin.[5] The same affirmative approach is found in Priestley's opponent in the Socinian controversy, Bishop Horsley, a celebrated pre-Tractarian high-churchman. Such an event as the Resurrection, he tells us, must have been accompanied by irresistible evidence, and this indeed we find to be so. If any human testimony

[1] *op. cit.*, p. 17.

[2] *Discourses on the Evidence of Revealed Religion*, 1794, p. 58. See also his polemical writings against Hume and Gibbon.

[3] *Discourses*, p. 64. [4] *ibid.*, p. 168. [5] *ibid.*, pp. 253-54.

ever attained the certainty of demonstration it is in this instance.[1]

II

The attempts to find "A Short and Easy Method" for settling the historical problems of Christian origins is but one example of the general lack of historical imagination in the 18th century. Another aspect of this state of mind had a profound influence upon the shape of apologetic writings. Whereas a modern apologist may dilate upon the perfect timing of the Incarnation, and speaks of the *Pax Romana*, the Greek language, the religious yearnings of the time and the advantageous dispersion of the Jews, some of the evidentialists took great pains to play down the natural conditions favouring the spread of Christianity.

Francis Atterbury, later Bishop of Rochester and subsequently banished on a charge of treason, preaching before the Queen in 1694, contended that the swift progress of the Gospel through the Roman world was certainly miraculous. For the natural causes were wholly inadequate to the effect produced—viz. twelve very ignorant men, preaching a doctrine repugnant to all men's natural desires and inclinations.[2] Four things may conduce to the spread of a new doctrine, of which Christianity had none: If its principles are suited to the lusts and interests of men, like the teaching of Mahomet and Hobbes; if it is supported by persons in power and authority; if it be first brought into the world in dark and barbarous ages; or if it is not proposed to men directly, but insinuated secretly and gradually. God did not suffer human learning or the civil power to come to the support of the Gospel for one hundred and three hundred years respectively in order to show the supernatural power of the Gospel.

Richard Watson, the Cambridge scholar and Bishop of Llandaff, wrote two apologies, one for Christianity, against Gibbon in 1776, and another for the Bible, against Paine in 1796. The former is especially interesting in the present connection, for he takes one by one the natural causes which Gibbon had assigned for the spread of Christianity and whittles

[1] *Nine Sermons*, 1815, pp. 127-41.
[2] *Sermons*, 1708 ed., Nos. III and IV.

them down to the barest minimum. On Gibbon's point regarding the inflexible zeal of the Christians, Watson argues that it could not have proceeded from any alluring prospect of worldly interest or ambition, or from any motive other than a love of truth.[1] Again, the Christian hope of a future life was no allurement, since it was neither agreeable to the expectations nor corresponding with the wishes, nor conformable to the reason, of the Gentiles. Nothing but the Divine power could have induced them to conform their loose morals to the rigid standards of Gospel purity "upon the mere authority of a few contemptible fishermen of Judaea."[2]

III

The limitations in method and insight, however, are seen most clearly in the writings which were directly provoked by Tindal. Butler, even, repeats some of the evidentialist commonplaces of the day. Like a modern apologist, he begins his examination of the evidences with the Epistles of St. Paul, and he points to the credibility of the Biblical history in itself, apart from the miracles.[3] But he repeats the common assumption that the Gospel was received by the Gentile world on the evidence of Christ's miracles.[4] It never seems to have occurred to these writers that a world in which portents of every kind were matters of common belief would scarcely have been convinced of the truth of Christ's unique claims by such manifestations alone. All the evidence writers, moreover, before Paley, laboured under the disadvantage of not possessing an adequate critique of the materials at their disposal. Many valuable testimonies to the veracity of the New Testament were collected from Jewish, pagan and early Christian sources, but these were mingled with a mass of uncriticized material, some of it purely legendary. Joseph Addison enumerates Tacitus' mention of the Crucifixion, Julian the Apostate's and Celsus' acknowledgment of Christ's miracles, Phlegon's refer-

[1] *Apology for Christianity*, 1806 ed., p. 11. Cf. Gibbon, *Decline and Fall*, ch. XV.

[2] *Apology*, p. 30. Another excellent example of the playing down of the natural causes is Tillotson's sermon for Ascension Day, 1688, *Works*, 1752 ed., II, No. 20.

[3] *Analogy*, 1900 ed., pp. 224, 246. [4] *ibid.*, pp. 225-27, 247-48.

ence to the Good Friday darkness and earthquake, the miracle of the Thundering Legion, the tale that Tiberius would have deified Christ but for the opposition of the senate, and the legend of the letter of Abgarus of Edessa to Christ and of the Lord's reply to him.[1] To gather together anything quoted by anybody within four hundred years of the time of Christ and to set it out as evidence of Divine revelation was a method calculated to bring little permanent credit to the Faith.

Bishop Berkeley's *Alciphron*, 1732, which is also a reply to Tindal, contains some evidential material. He is chiefly concerned with elucidating specific problems. For example, it had been urged that the collateral evidences were two-edged: if people in Apostolic times were able fully to investigate the facts, why were not more of them converted? Berkeley contends that our evidence is adequate, since we do know of the conversion of many great men both Jews and Gentiles, whilst we know nothing of the motives of those who rejected Christianity.[2] The real father of English evidence writing, however, was Nathaniel Lardner. It is remarkable into what oblivion he has fallen: Leslie Stephen scarcely deigns to mention him. Lardner's two main works are *The Credibility of the Gospel History*, 1727-57, which, along with its supplement, comprises sixteen large volumes, and *A Large Collection of Ancient Jewish and Heathen Testimonies to the Truth of the Christian Revelation*, 1764-67, in four volumes. Although his work was begun at the height of the Deist controversy, it is not topical in the same sense as that of Addison and Berkeley. His aim rather was to meet the situation as a whole, by setting up a vast positive structure of evidences. In the first work he is concerned with establishing the credit of the Gospels and the primitive tradition of the church through their mutual corroboration, and in the second he deals with the collateral proofs. Lardner is thorough and painstaking, and if he falls short of the scholarly standards of our own day in his sense of the relative value of historical data, that must be ascribed to the influence of his time. He has little to add to the theoretical and doctrinal questions about revelation, and we may therefore return him to his long repose.

[1] *Evidences of the Christian Religion*, 1730. [2] *op. cit.*, II, p. 105.

[Three prominent evidence writers of the latter half of the 18th century continue the conventionalized pattern: Gregory Sharpe, *An Argument in Defence of Christianity*, 1755, James Macknight, *The Truth of the Gospel History*, 1763, and John Hey, *Lectures on Divinity*, 1796-98. The last two works are systematic rather than controversial, and Hey's lectures are an early attempt to treat the progress of Christian doctrine historically.]

IV

A special problem became acute with the propagation of Middleton's implicit thesis that the miracles of Scripture and those of the church rested on much the same kind of insecure evidence. Apologists had therefore to show that the miracles of the New Testament stood upon evidence altogether more cogent than those purporting to have been worked in the church in subsequent ages. True miracles in later ages might also buttress the claims of the Roman church. The evidentialists were seriously embarrassed by this side-issue: they who had staked all upon the truth of a certain cycle of miracles were now obliged to discredit all other miracles, even many seemingly well attested ones held to have been wrought in answer to Christian prayer. To these writers, the belief that God had intervened miraculously in revelation gave a strong presumption that He would never do so in other circumstances. To Christians of many other times, however, this inference has not seemed to follow; far from it.

On the level of evidence, the evidentialists' task was a hard one. The New Testament miracles do not stand out in history as unique, considered as individual wonders. They belong to types which recur in the history of most ages and peoples. There was this further complication, that the same Fathers who provided collateral testimony to the primitive Christian tradition had to be disbelieved when they recounted miracles of their own time. To cover up this by acknowledging real miracles in the church down to the time of Constantine was but a makeshift.

It fell to Bishop John Douglas to write the first full-scale retort to Hume and Middleton. He has much to say that is interesting about the credibility of the Gospels on their internal evidence, and about the early Christian preaching with the Resurrection as its centre, but the special importance of his book lies in the principles by which he seeks to discriminate the miracles of Scripture from those of the church. The evidence for "real" miracles must be free from every suspicion of fraud; whereas, in ecclesiastical history, the reports of miracles are always to be suspected without the strongest evidence to confirm them.[1] Since suspicion alone is enough to disqualify a miracle, it is a simple matter for Douglas to write off every ecclesiastical miracle as exhibiting one of the following defects: A miracle is suspect (1) if it is not published until long after the supposed event, or (2) where it is published only at a distance from the supposed place of performance, or (3) if, under the circumstances, it might be transmitted unchallenged because it coincided with the superstitions and prejudices of the propagators, or because the accounts were originated or encouraged by those who alone had the power to detect the fraud.[2]

The rest of the *Criterion* is a detailed if diffuse application of this triple canon, first to the ecclesiastical, and then to the Gospel, miracles. When Douglas comes to a set of miracles to which his canon will not give the lie, he introduces us to a pair of new arguments. The cures at the tomb of the Jansenist, François de Paris, were too recent and well-attested to be dismissed as fictions. But, says Douglas, we must look for natural causes for these cures. In any case, the fact that there were some failures is proof of the non-miraculous character of the cures as a whole.[3] He strenuously denies that these canons might disqualify the Gospel miracles. Jesus was never applied to in vain for healing: there were no failures in His ministry.[4] Finally, he goes back to the theological *a priori*: miracles are vouchsafed only as credentials of teachers; so we can reject all miracles of those who do not claim to be teachers sent by God.[5]

To read Douglas is to realize how much our attitude to these questions has changed. We are not now afraid of saying that many of Our Lord's works were brought about through natural

[1] *The Criterion*, 1754, p. 50. Cf. Middleton, *Free Inquiry*, p. 217.
[2] *The Criterion*, pp. 51-53. [3] *ibid.*, pp. 182f.
[4] *ibid.*, p. 257. [5] *ibid.*, pp. 352f.

means: indeed we feel it to be congruous with the perfection of His human personality that this should be so. The attempt to set up an absolute distinction between the New Testament and the ecclesiastical miracles in terms merely of evidence was doomed from the start. For it has become apparent that the miracles of Our Lord only have significance, let alone credibility, if they are seen as an integral part of the new spiritual life that He brought to mankind. It is not by accident that the men who denied miracles in the church were also those who had little grasp of the church's life of supernatural grace.

V

We come now to the man whose name is most commonly associated with the writing of Christian evidences. The first impression which Paley's works produce in the modern reader is one of impatience. In the *Natural Theology*, not only does he seem insensible to the intrinsic objections to his system, but the appearance of the theories of organic evolution seems to necessitate an almost complete restatement of the teleological argument. Again, adequate though the *Evidences* may have been against the contentions of the earlier rationalistic schools, a whole world of new questions has been raised since the time of Strauss. There is, however, a valuable parallel between the method of the two works—which, if Paley was aware of, he does not comment upon. His teleology of nature and of revelation are analogous, as Romanes astutely observed.[1] First, Paley directs our attention to a large number of natural objects: a leaf, an eye, a certain ligament in a cow's back. Severally and cumulatively, these objects exhibit creative design. Secondly, if we consider the evidences of the Christian revelation—the separate remarkable concurrences in the different strands of testimony, and the cumulative strength of all these strands together—it must be found that we have a very strong indication of the supernatural intervention of God at the outset of the church's history.

He sweeps away all the theoretical questions in his introduction to the *Evidences*. Mankind stood in need of a revelation from God, and the probability that such a revelation would be

[1] *Thoughts on Religion*, 5th ed., p. 179.

given carries with it the same degree of probability that miracles would accompany it. (Cf. his arguments against Hume, ch. 3 *supra.*) He deals in the body of the work, first, with the direct historical evidences, and then with the auxiliary evidences; the latter including the internal evidences, such as the character of Christ. The ninth chapter of the first part deserves special mention: it is a well-stated argument for the primitive character of the four Gospels. Paley appeals to our possession of genuine ancient manuscripts, to arguments derived from the style and language of the New Testament, to the acceptance of these writings by the whole church from the beginning, to their being regarded from the first as sacred and authoritative, and to their embodiment in the church's liturgy. He appeals also to the acceptance by the primitive Fathers of all four Gospels, to the ancient commentaries, harmonies and collations, to the reception of the Gospels even by heretics, and to ancient lists of the New Testament canon.

Here, as in Lardner and others, the canon of the New Testament is established largely upon evidences external to it. Later, however, the centre of theological interest was to move back to those vital years between the death of St. Paul and the emergence in the second century of a more continuous tradition. In this twilight period, contemporary Patristic support is insufficient to bear the weight of authenticating the Scriptures; hence the rise of New Testament criticism as we know it, with its attempt to reconstruct the life and thought of the primitive church from evidence extracted from the Scriptures themselves. Paley's *Horae Paulinae*, with its study of the coincidences between the Acts and the Epistles, makes a promising start towards such criticism. Moreover, it is interesting to note that a contemporary of Paley, Herbert Marsh, was actually engaged upon an enquiry into the formation of the Gospels, the results of which he published along with a translation of Michaelis' *Introduction to the New Testament* in 1801. Marsh examines possible explanations for the combination of agreement and divergence to be observed between the Synoptic Gospels, and he posits a common Hebrew source existing in several recensions; each of our Greek Gospels being a translation from a different recension. It is remarkable that so keen-sighted a scholar should not have even considered the Marcan hypothesis as a possible solution. The essay is none the less a landmark, not only for Biblical criticism, but ultimately also for apologetics.

Paley's critique for disposing of the ecclesiastical miracles is similar to that of Douglas, though more systematized. First come disqualifications of narratives from the character of the evidence, and secondly there are disqualifications from the nature of the reported facts.

His first two disqualifications of evidence are Douglas' canons about distance in time and place from the supposed event. The miracles of St. Ignatius Loyola, not published until sixty years after his death, and those attributed to St. Francis Xavier by persons writing at vast distances from the scenes of his work, are the familiar illustrations cited here. Thirdly, there are cases where we have merely transient rumour unsupported by the permanence of the belief or its subsequent collateral confirmation. Fourthly, there are cases where we have merely a naked or fragmentary report, with no evidence that it was well attested or that the truth of the supposed miracle produced any effects. Paley explains this canon by contrast with the miracles of Scripture which come down to us along with the institutions which they helped to create. Fifthly, we may reject stories which require merely an otiose assent; they concern simply the love of the marvellous. Finally, we may reject miracles which come in attestation of beliefs already held: Popish miracles happen in Popish countries, whereas Jesus had not one follower when He began His ministry.[1]

Of disqualifications from the nature of the reports, Paley tells us first that it is not necessary to admit as miraculous what can be resolved into a false perception. Such were the visions of St. Anthony. These experiences are generally confined to one of the senses, and are not confirmed by the coincident experience of other people. It may be pointed out in passing that whilst such experiences cannot be accepted as useful material by evidentialism, their spiritual significance may be very great when looked at in the light of the subject's whole religious experience. Secondly, Paley tells us that we may

[1] *Evidences*, Works, 1825 ed., vol. II, pp. 184-94.

reject "tentative" miracles, where out of a great number of trials, some succeed—like the supposed cures of the King's Touch.[1] Thirdly, we may dismiss all accounts in which, allowing the fact to be true, it still remains doubtful whether a miracle were wrought.[2] He instances the miracle of the Thundering Legion, the liquefaction of the blood of St. Januarius and the cures of hypochondriacal and nervous complaints. Fourthly, narratives may be excluded in which the variation of some small circumstance may have transformed an extraordinary appearance, or a critical coincidence of events, into a miracle.

Such incisive criticism immediately raises the query whether the miracles of Scripture do not themselves fall within the categories of disqualification. Paley admits that there are miracles in the New Testament which fall within some of the exceptions here listed, yet they are united with others to which none of these exceptions apply, and their credibility stands upon this union. Thus, St. Paul's visions were attested by his own outward miracles.[3] Now the historic Christian revelation is closely bound up with the miraculous, and the apologist must be very discriminating, therefore, in his treatment of all accounts of miracles. In the 18th-century theological scheme, all that was thought to be necessary was the discrimination of the true miracles on their physical side. But a further step turned out to be required. The miracles of Our Lord had still to be distinguished in respect of their revealing character, their intimate relation to His person and work. This could only be worked out by a later generation of theologians, who had gone far beyond the evidentialists in their conception of the nature of revelation. Hence Paley's canons reflect, not the lack of historical acumen, but the theological needs of his time.

VI

The plight of Newman is an interesting epilogue to the discussion of miracles from the evidentialist point of view, for undoubtedly the ecclesiastical miracles were an Achilles' heel to the 18th-century system. The question of miracles arose for Newman in connection with his secession to Rome, and raised

[1] *op. cit.*, p. 198. [2] *ibid.*, p. 200. [3] *ibid.*, p. 202.

a problem to the solution of which he brought all his dialectical skill. He published two essays on miracles, the first in 1825, in which he adopts an attitude differing little from that of Douglas and Paley, and the second in 1842, in which he drastically modifies his position. (The two are printed together in an 1870 edition, with a preface that naïvely attempts to gloss over the divergence between them.)

The first essay opens with a statement of the evidentialist position, that miracles are necessary to authenticate Divine revelation, for which task reason is inadequate. But Newman is less sanguine than his predecessors about the possibility of drawing in every case a clear line between the miraculous and non-miraculous. The nature miracles of Christ were clearly beyond human powers, but a few of the Gospel miracles would be improbable if taken by themselves—such as the Gadara story. Miracles, too, are only a part of apologetics, appealing to certain types of mind, and would be no evidence to an atheist. But the evidence as such for the Christian miracles is stronger than that for the occurrence of many of the other historical facts commonly accepted.[1] Newman contends that a miracle is an instance of the priority of the moral order over the physical—an argument that was to assume great importance in the 19th century. But on the other hand he describes the ecclesiastical miracles as "unmeaning, extravagant and useless."[2] He applies all the rigorous disqualifications of these miracles from Douglas and Paley; his incisive criticisms even outshine Middleton. One canon is quite explicit: "Answers to prayer, however providential, are not miraculous; for in granting them, God acts by means of, not out of, His usual system."[3] One wonders what Scriptural support he could have invoked for such a dogma!

The essay of 1842 opens on a very different note. Sacred history is distinguished from profane by the nature of the facts which enter into it: "Miracles are its characteristic, whether it be viewed as Biblical or ecclesiastical." Newman's thesis now is that there may be other final causes for miracles than the authentication of doctrines. The ecclesiastical miracles have sometimes no discoverable object. Often they partake of what may be called a romantic character. For the most part, they

[1] *op. cit.*, 1870 ed., pp. 4-12. [2] *ibid.*, p. 48. [3] *ibid.*, p. 67.

are contained in no authoritative document.[1] But they are not thereby to be rejected: there was no age of miracles after which they ceased. Newman's exposition of nine typical miracles, which he presumably regarded as among the best authenticated, certainly bears out his warnings.[2] But Newman contends that revelation has stood the brunt of the antecedent objections to miracles, and by establishing the certainty of miracles in fact has disproved their impossibility in the abstract.[3] Nor are the ecclesiastical miracles without their proper significance. Gregory of Neo-Caesarea, "Thaumaturgus", found only seventeen Christians in his diocese, but through his miracles he converted the whole district.[4]

It is shallow to reject miracles because they are not what we should have expected: he compares the inadequacy of such a judgment with a person's surprise on first visiting a menagerie—not perhaps a very happy analogy![5] The miracles of Scripture were a far greater innovation upon the economy of nature than were the ecclesiastical miracles upon the economy of Scripture: and there are actually ample precedents in Scripture for the type of miracles found in the church, such as those wrought in connection with Elisha's bones, St. Peter's shadow and St. Paul's handkerchiefs.[6] If only we realize what Christianity is, Newman concludes, and what stupendous facts are involved in the doctrine of a Divine Incarnation, we shall feel that no miracle can be great after it.[7]

At the time, it was possible for this essay to be written off as the product of a mind seeking at all costs to justify the Roman position. Today we have not indeed come to share Newman's credulity regarding the miracles of Gregory Thaumaturgus, but for other reasons we have come to realize that a hard and fast line cannot be drawn between the acts of God in New Testament times and in the life of the church down the ages.

[A number of works of the evidentialist school appeared during the first half of the 19th century. Their general standard of historical

[1] *ibid.*, pp. 116-17.
[2] Cf. E. A. Abbott's withering attack on this essay, entitled *Philomythus.*
[3] *op. cit.*, p. 103. [4] *ibid.*, p. 118. [5] *ibid.*, p. 148.
[6] *ibid.*, pp. 148, 162-63. [7] *ibid.*, p. 185.

scholarship does not compare unfavourably with that of Paley, but their basic theological concepts show little advance. Bishop Van Mildert's Boyle Lectures of 1802 and 1805, *An Historical View of the Rise and Progress of Infidelity*, is an excellent book of its time. The following may also be noted: Thomas Chalmers, *Works*, 1836-42, vol. III. Milman, *The Character and Conduct of the Apostles considered as an Evidence of Christianity*, Bampton Lectures for 1827. Wardlaw, *Systematic Theology*, 1856.]

VII

There are two matters for debate arising out of the foregoing survey: the appraisement of the historical endeavour itself, and the elucidation of the theological presuppositions of the movement.

If we ask how far these writers were successful in achieving what they set out to do—to establish the supernatural origin of Christianity—it may be suggested that they did succeed, but not precisely in the way that they understood the matter. It has come to be realized that certain types of historical judgment are not arrived at merely by mechanically sorting out data, but involve a personal assent to the meaning and value of the data. The activity that we call faith has furthermore regained much of its deeper Biblical meaning. From such a standpoint it becomes fair to say that, in so far as the historico-critical demands of their day went, the evidentialists did present a prima facie case for the supernatural origin of Christianity; an adequate spring-board, so to speak, for the act of faith. In regard to this historical technique itself, it is possible to trace a considerable growth in critical acumen during the period covered. There is better discrimination of the relative value of materials. It is gradually realized also that the general arguments regarding the way in which Christianity spread require to be modified by a closer study of the New Testament and the situation in the Graeco-Roman world. Thus it comes to be better understood that the crux of the argument lies in the Apostolic age itself, and hence in the internal historical evidence provided by the New Testament. The movement unquestionably provided an invaluable training-ground for the later schools of English constructive criticism that flowered in

Lightfoot, Westcott and Hort. The failure to allow for a residuum of genuinely abnormal happenings in the later history of the church is simply the temporary effect of a particular theory of miracles upon an immature critical judgment.

In an age in which the discursive reason was exalted above intuition as the acme of the human powers of apprehension, it was natural for the attempt to be made to construct a rationale of Christian certitude in terms of a series of deductions from occurrences in the phenomenal world. In a previous "Age of Reason", St. Thomas Aquinas rejected the intuitional arguments for the existence of God, preferring rather to stake his whole case upon such rational deductions as could be drawn from the world of outward experience. Correspondingly we find the traditionalist theologians of the Illumination attempting to find an anchorage for revelation in the world of sense and rational deduction. Thus, Christ's Resurrection, says W. Sherlock, "gives us the same sort of evidence for the Divine authority of Our Saviour, and the Truth of all His Promises, which we have for the being of God by mere Natural Reason; that is, the Argument from visible Effects to an Invisible cause."[1] The fact that Christianity was an historical religion led easily to the supposition that its supernatural origin was intended to be demonstrated pre-eminently by a rational technique; and we shall see what element of truth there was in this supposition. In the criticism of this theology and in the misunderstandings of the critics one of another lies the whole subsequent history of the discussion of the Christian miracles.

As a working scheme of Christian persuasion, evidentialism has three principal defects. First, the scheme presupposes a highly developed system of natural theology. Occasionally a writer is to be found who suggests that the evidences for revelation also provide positive evidence for the existence of God, but the more usual view is that "the very supposition of God's interposing by miracles supposes also the certainty of His Being, perfections and providence."[2] There must indeed be a certain capacity in the human mind for recognizing Divine revelation,

[1] *Discourse concerning the Happiness of good men* . . . , 1704, p. 360.

[2] S. Chandler, *Discourse of the Nature and Use of Miracles*, 1725, pp. 44-45.

a religious sense which feels after God and a mind which can formulate such aspirations into religious evaluations of the universe. This needs to be stressed today, in reply to the Dialectical Theology with its virtual denial of natural religion. But it remains that we cannot draw the same hard and fast line, as was done in the age of Deism, between natural and revealed religion. We cannot think of natural religion as a self-contained and self-sufficient system of belief as the evidentialists did. Today we find it more natural to think of revelation as the key which unlocks the enigmas of life, itself validating the hitherto tentative arguments of natural theology.

Secondly, the upshot of the long debate regarding the possibilities of historical criticism appears to be that, the more a reported event differs from the accustomed pattern of nature, the more difficult it becomes to adduce convincing evidence of its occurrence—except to those who see in it a meaning and value relative to the significance of the whole of life. Evidentialists tell us that one of the marks of Divine miracles is their beneficent character, but they assume without question that the occurrence of miracles can be established by evidence which is independent of our religious intuitions, and this makes the task they set themselves look so formidable.

Thirdly, even supposing we had enough evidence to prove the occurrence of the recorded miracles, and assuming that miracles in the traditional sense could establish a Divine revelation, there remains the fact of our ignorance of the bounds of nature's powers. Apologists nearer to our own day have contended that to admit Our Lord's miracles to have been wrought by a power not different in kind from that possessed by man does not detract from His uniqueness as a spiritual agent. But this view would be fatal to the neat structure of evidentialism.

But even if these difficulties were surmounted it still remains questionable whether the scheme is appropriate to the Christian revelation. It will have been observed that in the characteristic theology of the 18th century there is a certain congruity between the substance of revelation and its proof: the sovereign Lord of the universe reveals His commandments and the future destiny of man by mediators whose bona fides are mighty signs and wonders. Even before the above-mentioned difficulties became apparent to English churchmen, the evidentialist theology began to crumble from within, as men came to realize the inadequacy of its view of revelation. We need not repeat what was said of this at the end of the second chapter. Thus, in the 18th-century scheme, the person of Christ is envisaged predominantly as the instrument of the revealing of Divine truths. The New Testament language regarding His atoning work is expounded without being really integrated into the theological system. But when Christ's very person came to be thought of as revelation, and the life of the believer as a personal relationship to Him as Lord and Saviour, it gradually came to seem strange that Christ's Divine mission had to be proved by a set of logical inferences from prophecy and miracles. It has come to be realized that the only compelling evidence for the Divine mission of Christ is His personal appeal to the whole human personality.

In some quarters the reaction against the Illumination has gone much further. The assertion that faith in Christ is essentially a personal act has led many Ritschlians and Barthians not only to reject the inferential proofs from prophecy and miracle as alien to the true nature of faith, but also to regard the work of establishing the historic foundations of Christianity as not in itself a religious activity. They do not, as the catholic modernists, regard the historical element as irrelevant to Christian belief. What they appear to contend is that belief in the events of Christ's life is a purely intellectual, almost secular, activity: upon this intellectual sub-structure man builds his saving faith in Christ.[1] But this reaction runs the grave risk of by-passing the most characteristic element of Christianity—that God has been incarnated as man, and that this, the central fact of history, can be known about as a most assured tradition enshrined in the memory of the supernatural yet human society which Christ created. To attempt to dissect one's faith in Christ from one's knowledge about Him is an utterly meaningless and misleading abstraction. The theologians of the 18th century did indeed over-emphasize the rational aspects of

[1] Cf. Brunner, *Revelation and Reason*, pp. 6, 167-68, 206-7.

Christian belief, but, in opposing a religious philosophy whose emphasis was laid primarily upon an illumination of the individual soul, they vindicated for their own day and for ours the essentially historic character of the Christian revelation.

Chapter Five

THE SCIENTIFIC INTERPRETATION OF NATURE

We now come to consider the way in which new forces tended to break up the structure of 18th-century theology. The most significant changes, as we shall see, were generated from within religious thought itself; but we shall first give some account of the forces working from without—the scientific interpretation of nature and the scientific interpretation of history.

With the 19th century there came what may be called the self-consciousness of scientific thought—the belief that the new knowledge and methods were not simply a miscellaneous accumulation of useful information, but that they opened up a new way of viewing the constitution of the universe. It is even now difficult to enter into the feelings of those who lived in the springtime of the 19th-century optimism regarding the possibilities of science, which was hailed by some of the greatest minds of the period as the solvent for most of the world's ethical, philosophical and theological problems. In its philosophical optimism the new spirit was the successor of 18th-century Deism. This may be seen in the writings of Robert Fellowes, who combined a rational Theism of an earlier type with a crass optimism regarding the possibilities of scientific thought. In a religion based on scientific thought, he says, priest and schoolmaster would henceforth be one person. Science alone can make man adequately contemplate the Divine perfection, and a religion based upon science has the possibilities of endless progression and growing certitude—as opposed to a particular revelation in a past age supported by miracles, whose narratives have passed through the dark and distorting medium of hundreds of years. Every village should be equipped with a telescope for the inhabitants to contemplate God's universe.[1]

It is easy to point out the weaknesses in Fellowes' thought, but he is an interesting witness to the spirit of his time. Even more striking than the work of the theorists, however, have been the widespread effects upon mankind's beliefs in the supernatural of the mental conditioning brought about by scientific method. W. E. H. Lecky, himself an enthusiastic disciple of the 19th-century secular attitude towards science and the supernatural, pointed out that men had come to be prepared to admit almost any conceivable concurrence of natural improbabilities rather than resort to a supernatural hypothesis. He says, "If you connect a nation which has long been insulated and superstitious with the general movement of European civilization by means of railways, or a free press, or the removal of protecting laws, you will most infallibly inoculate it with this spirit."[2]

The tide of human opinion was running fast against the belief in miracles. The most telling influence on the intellectual level was the scientific study of history; but the influence of scientific thought in general has also vitally affected the belief. Its influence has been felt in two successive stages. In the first place there was the attempt to rule out the admission of the miraculous on the basis of the philosophy of induction; and in the second place there came the admission of the provisional character of scientific laws, which has rendered it well-nigh impossible to say of any given event that it lies outside the domain of nature.

The vast increase in man's knowledge of the world of nature led to the enthronement of the method of induction, whereby this knowledge had been acquired, as the sole legitimate method of enquiry. In the thought of the Positivists and those who came under their influence, the knowledge gained by observation and induction was regarded as the only kind of information that was worthy of human attention. This assumption was destined to have a far-reaching effect upon the capacities of men to receive Christian truth, since it discounted all judgments of value except on the hedonistic level. It was also claimed for induction that it provided not only the means of correlating existing information but also a chart by which to

[1] *The Religion of the Universe*, 1836, pp. 12f. [2] *Rationalism*, I, pp. 156-58.

fill out our knowledge of the unobserved past and to predict the future course of events. On such an assumption, the anomalous could only be admitted in so far as it provided a basis for further experiment, with a view to relating it to the pattern of nature.

In J. S. Mill, 19th-century science found its schoolman, who attempted to give to scientific method a philosophical and rational basis. He is a grim warning of what can be achieved by skilful education with religion excluded from the curriculum; for he grew up an intellectual giant, yet with one side of his personality atrophied. Before Mill's time, it seems to have been assumed that induction which was short of complete enumeration was not a fully logical process. Yet the whole of scientific research is based upon this very practice of inferring general statements from particular experiments. Mill came to the conclusion that the method of inference from crucial instances, and the uniformity of natural causation which it presupposes, must represent a fundamental truth about nature. He formulated four principles of induction, which are devices for isolating a particular pair of cause and effect from a complex process in nature.

Clearly, it is not the method, but the assumption of uniformity of causation, which is Mill's real dogma. He strenuously denies that belief in the universality of natural causation is merely an "instinct", for it is not right to make the truth of anything in the external world dependent upon the disposition of the mind to believe it.[1] Nevertheless, Mill's critics have pointed out that, if we have no other knowledge of a thing than the number of times it has occurred, no logical reason can be advanced why the thing should occur again. F. R. Tennant calls this a pseudo-scientific attempt to inflate empirical science into the equivalent of the older *a priori* systems. Hume had not scrupled to assume the uniformity of nature, but, unlike Mill, had been too shrewd to try to prove its universality. Mill had thought that the principle of uniformity could be proved cumulatively by particular inductions: but he constantly begged the question by appropriating universal terms, like "invariable" for "hitherto unvarying".[2] Lord Balfour, on the same topic,

[1] *System of Logic*, 6th ed. (1865) II, p. 95. Cf. I, p. 344.
[2] Tennant, *Miracle and its Philosophical Presuppositions*, pp. 14f.

points out that a chick a few hours old rejects food once found nasty. The empirical philosophers lag behind the chick, which expects and gives no reason: the empiricist expects, and gives a bad one.[1] Mill's philosophy was doomed under the shattering attacks of more incisive critics of scientific thought, and his treatment of miracles, as we shall see, was relatively harmless. But the position into which he had helped to elevate the method of induction became ever more influential as new areas of knowledge bore witness to its efficacy. There were many who were led to the position that belief in miracles must be denied in practice as a matter of principle. Carlyle believed that the newer scientific method had succeeded where the *a priori* method had failed, and that it was as sure as mathematics that a miracle had never happened.

Mill himself held that there was a theoretical case where there is not simply a matter of not believing, but the need for actual disbelief. The proof against an improbable assertion is never complete, but is based upon the comparison of approximate generalizations. If, however, the alleged fact be in contradiction, not to any number of approximate generalizations, but to a completed generalization grounded on a rigorous induction, it is said to be impossible and is to be disbelieved totally.[2] To those who contend that Hume's argument against miracles is a *petitio principii*, Mill replies that we have the right to declare such a proof, without complete enumeration, "whenever the scientific canons of induction give it to us; that is, whenever the induction can be complete. We have it, for example, in a case of causation in which there has been an experimentum crucis."[3] As Tennant points out,[4] it is difficult to see when we could have such a thing as a complete induction; and Mill himself seems to have had no illusions as to the limitations of his own argument. Mill argues that we cannot admit a proposition as a law of nature and yet believe a fact in real contradiction to it. But the question is different when viewed from the standpoint of causation. In order that any alleged fact should be contradictory to a law of causation, he continues, the allegation must be, not simply that the cause existed without being followed by the effect, but that this happened in the

[1] *Theism and Humanism*, pp. 194-95. [2] *System of Logic*, II, pp. 160-61.
[3] *op. cit.*, II, p. 162. [4] *Miracle . . .*, p. 84.

absence of any adequate counteracting cause. Now in the case of an alleged miracle, the assertion is the exact opposite of this: i.e. that the effect was defeated not in the absence of, but in consequence of, a counteracting cause—God. Hume, thinks Mill, has simply made this out: that in the imperfect state of our knowledge of natural agencies, no evidence can prove a miracle to anyone who did not previously believe in God.[1]

Mill's treatment of causation, whilst adding little to Hume's, tended to discount still further the notion that the hand of God may be seen in irregular phenomena. It also illustrates the attitude of 19th-century naturalism to that intractable spiritual factor in life: human volition. On the argument that only in volition have we any experience of causation, and thence infer that all causation is from mind, Mill says that this assumes that everything in nature is efficient causation and that human volition is really an originating cause.[2] But our experience of volition is quite different from the kind of causation we see in nature, and the power of will is not known as an originating force as something separate from the acts we exert: will does not originate force, but only directs it.[3] The facts of human consciousness, indeed—volition and the power of reason—were the realities which stood in the way of the construction of the perfect picture of the mechanistic universe. All such attempts have foundered on this rock: that to construct a mechanistic explanation of human reasoning and action is to make sheer nonsense of all intellectual effort.

The effect of the positivist attitude towards knowledge upon the apprehension of religious truth is nowhere better illustrated than in Mill's own three essays on *Nature*, *the Utility of Religion*, and *Theism*. Religion, he says, should be tested scientifically to see what it can offer that science can recognize.[4] Monotheism is the only form of Theism which can claim any footing on scientific grounds, as it assumes one rather than a multiplicity of causes. Nothing in science prohibits belief that the laws of nature originate from a Divine will; but the *a priori* arguments for God's existence are unscientific, whilst the *a posteriori* arguments are inconclusive. Mind and force may be coeternal;

[1] *System of Logic*, II, pp. 163-64.
[2] *op. cit.*, II, p. 389.
[3] Cf. *Three Essays*, 2nd ed., p. 147.
[4] *op. cit.*, pp. 128f.

mind is not explained by a prior mind; whilst analogies in nature show that the lower can produce the higher. The whole treatment is destitute of many of the most vital religious considerations: no recognition is given to the human personality with its possibilities and its plight; arguments drawn from the human situation are dismissed outright; whilst the discussion of revelation is confined to a criticism of evidentialism in which the assumption is made that revelation could only be proved by external evidences.

In Professor Baden Powell's contribution to *Essays and Reviews*, the principles of inductive philosophy are carried to a complete denial of the admissibility of the miraculous. Some of the wider implications of the essay will be discussed in later chapters. First, Baden Powell points to the extreme difficulty in eliciting the truth when dealing with the report of the abnormal, which arises not so much from conscious dishonesty as from the uncertainty attaching to the transmission of testimony. Even when we ourselves are the witnesses, there is the enormous influence upon our judgment of our prepossessions; and when we have no prepossessions the situation is equally uncertain, since the more startling the event, the less prepared we are to view it accurately.[1] But he does not regard the question of testimony as the chief issue: we must turn rather, he says, to those antecedent considerations which must govern our entire view of the subject.

Testimony, this writer argues, cannot reach to the supernatural, but can only prove an extraordinary occurrence. The phenomena of speaking with tongues had been common and well attested among the Irvingites: yet even if the physical cause were obscure, no one outside the sect, of ordinary cultivated mind, doubted that they were in some way to be ascribed to natural causes.[2]

> On such questions [says Baden Powell] we can only hope to form just and legitimate conclusions from an extended and unprejudiced study of the laws and phenomena of the natural world. The entire range of the inductive philosophy is at once based upon, and in every instance tends to confirm, the immense accumulation of evidence, the grand truth of the universal order and consistency of natural causes, as a primary law of belief; so

[1] *Essays and Reviews*, 5th ed., p. 106. [2] *op. cit.*, p. 108.

strongly entertained and fixed in the mind of every truly inductive inquirer, that he cannot even conceive the possibility of its failure.[1]

If it be thought that this statement (which amounts to saying that mechanism is the last word that can be said of any circumstance in the physical world) is a surprising statement for a Theist to make, it should be compared with another passage, which attributes an almost metaphysical self-sufficiency to the physical universe:

> The simple but grand truth of the law of conservation, and the stability of the heavenly motions, now well understood by all cosmic philosophers, is but the type of the universal self-sustaining and self-evolving powers which pervade all nature. Yet the difficulty of conceiving this truth in its simplest exemplification was formerly the chief hindrance in the acceptance of the solar system—from the prepossession of the peripatetic dogma that there must be a constantly acting moving force to keep it going. This very exploded chimera, however, by a singular infatuation, is now actually revived as the ground of argument for miraculous interposition by redoubtable champions who, . . . inform us that "The whole of nature is like a mill, which cannot go on without the continual application of a moving power."[2]

There is a curious parallel between Baden Powell and Hume. First, like Hume, he declares the question of testimony to be irrelevant, since we have higher grounds for believing that miracles do not happen; the Irvingite phenomena were genuine but not miraculous. Then, again like Hume, he keeps returning to the question of testimony with fresh arguments. For instance, testimony, he says, can never be believed against reason. If a whole ship's company attested that they had seen a mermaid, they could not be believed.[3] So there are classes of phenomena which cannot even be believed—let alone be considered in the matter of causality. An alleged miracle, Baden Powell concludes, can only be treated in one of two ways: as a physical event, to be investigated by reason and referred to physical causes—when it ceases to be supernatural; or asserted on the authority of inspiration, when it ceases to be capable of investigation by reason.[4]

[1] *ibid.*, p. 109. [2] *ibid.*, p. 134.
[3] *ibid.*, p. 140. [4] *ibid.*, p. 142.

Many Christian thinkers have come to believe that there is an important sense in which Baden Powell is right, in his contention that testimony cannot itself reach to the supernatural. Testimony can only acquaint us with an abnormal event: it is the believer who sees its religious significance. Baden Powell's own conclusion, that no miracle can ever justly be believed in, does not follow from his premise. We are not concerned here to enquire how this writer reconciled his view of nature with his Theism, but simply to call him as an important witness to the effects upon many minds of the inductive philosophy.

Of more immediate concern to the Christian apologist than the scientist or the philosopher as such, has been the popularizer of scientific ideas. The most eminent of such persons in the 19th century was T. H. Huxley. He was well equipped for his task, for not only was he a gifted expositor and a shrewd controversialist, he also stood in the front rank of the scientific thinkers of his day. In controversy, indeed, he often showed himself the gentler party; in the controversy with Dean Wace, his tone contrasts sharply with the latter's tone of reprehension; whilst the terms of the controversy with Bishop Wilberforce are well known. As regards the question of miracles, Huxley points out what is probably the cardinal difficulty for the scientific mind: not the *a priori* postulate of uniformity, but the actual insufficiency of evidence. In his biography of Hume he sets aside some of the *a priori* questions as meaningless. The vast accumulation of evidence relating to the unbrokenness of nature made it reasonable to ask for evidence for a miracle, not only equal, but superior to that required for a natural event. But to define a miracle, as Hume did, as a "violation of the laws of nature" was an employment of language which could not be justified.[1] Hume had argued that such an event as a dead man's coming to life could not happen, since it would be a violation of the laws of nature; in other words, that which never has happened never can happen. If a dead man, says Huxley, did come to life, the fact would be evidence, not that any law of nature had been violated, but that those laws are necessarily based on incomplete knowledge, and are to be held only as grounds of more or less justifiable expectation.[2]

Nevertheless, though Huxley envisages no definition of a

[1] *David Hume*, pp. 129-31. [2] *op. cit.*, p. 133.

miracle further than that it is a very extraordinary event, he is persuaded that as regards the grounds for believing any particular miracle, "The more a statement of fact conflicts with previous experience, the more complete must be the evidence which is to justify us in believing it." He would believe the report of one who alleged he saw a piebald horse in Piccadilly without hesitation. If the same person said he saw a zebra there, he would hesitate about accepting his testimony, unless he were well satisfied, not only as to his previous acquaintance with zebras, but as to his powers and opportunities of observation on this occasion. If, however, his informant assured him that he had seen a centaur there, he would emphatically decline to credit his statement.[1]

Huxley's argument has been held by some apologists to retain an element of the illegitimate *a priori*, since on empiricist grounds the past gives no rational presumption as to what the future will be like. To others, the argument appears as one way of stating the anthropological difficulty, i.e. the factors of human fallibility.[2] The argument in its various forms has, nevertheless, proved a powerful dissuasion to belief in miracles. Nor can the apologist afford to treat the argument from induction merely as a Godless prejudice. For he himself is pledged to an expectation of order in the universe, and he therefore not only has to exhibit the cogency of the evidence for the Biblical miracles but has to show that their character is the very converse of such hypothetical abnormalities as mermaids and centaurs. There inhered in the inductive method, however, the seeds of a more formidable difficulty in the way of accepting the miraculous in the traditional sense: for there arose the problem of how to declare any event to be beyond the powers of nature to have produced. Mill, Baden Powell and Huxley all show themselves aware of the possibility that large classes of alleged miracles might conceivably be explained by unusual natural processes, but they were so confident that the traditional Biblical miracles would not stand up to the test of evidence that they could afford to neglect this further explanation. Mill explains that scientific thought conceives of two kinds of law: ultimate or absolute, and empirical or derivative. The latter are statements of the behaviour of nature as we observe

[1] *ibid.*, p. 134. [2] Cf. A. E. Taylor, *Faith of a Moralist*, II, pp. 151-54.

it, and are deducible from or resolvable into the more general laws. We are not sure that any of the uniformities we now know are ultimate laws, though we are sure such laws must exist.[1] It might have been thought a general law of nature that all swans were white, before any black ones were observed. Thus, when exceptions to a law appear, it means that the law was not complete enough or that the really ultimate cause had not been properly understood.[2]

Some of the Deists had urged that the miracles of Scripture might have been the work of nature's powers; but the state of scientific knowledge at the time made it easy for apologists to ridicule the suggestion. However, subsequent criticism of the idea of natural law, together with the growing understanding of the possibilities of psychological and psycho-physical phenomena, brought the old suggestion back with a new incisiveness. The recognition of the provisional character of scientific schematization has had a profound effect upon the attitude of apologists towards miracles: it is not too much to say that it has finally sealed the fate of the older evidentialist attitude to miracles as a self-evincing proof of Divine intervention. Frederick Temple's Bampton Lectures of 1884, on "The Relations between Religion and Science", are a notable landmark in the recognition by theology of this new situation. The state of the question of miracles in relation to the laws of nature is summed up in F. R. Tennant's little book, *Miracle and its Philosophical Presuppositions*, 1924.

In the idea of miracle in its pre-scientific origin, writes Tennant, there inhered a twofold reference—the source of later ambiguity: first, a relation to other objects, and secondly, a relation to human subjects. Wonderfulness thus resolved itself, on the one hand, into unprecedentedness, novelty or rarity (which are objective traits); but also into impressiveness, which is a subjective quality. The objective sense implies reference to an ordinary background; though in the Old Testament the reference is almost wholly subjective, little distinction being drawn between miracle and the other works of God in nature. Before the scientific age, indeed, there was no

[1] *System of Logic*, II, pp. 5f.

[2] Cf. K. Pearson's important discussion of "law" in *The Grammar of Science*, 2nd ed., pp. 77-112, and the relevant chapter in H. W. B. Joseph's *Introduction to Logic*.

difficulty in giving credence to miracles, nor was any hard line drawn between the natural and the supernatural; but "The marvellous, in order to possess evidential value as to Divine interposition, needed, in a scientific age, to be conceived as the unaccountable, as evincing inexplicability in terms of natural law."[1] It was thus that difficulties arose, as theology sought to render definite and intellectually serviceable the vague notion of miracles that it had inherited from pre-scientific beliefs.

Tennant shows how the late 19th-century logicians had demonstrated the principle of uniformity to be no more than a postulate, whilst the psychologists had arrived to show that the expectation of uniformity was no more than a survival of man's primordial credulity. One of the older assumptions had been that nature was built up out of a few natural kinds or substances, all the instances being exactly alike and completely permanent. This view had gradually been transformed, and with it had also gone the idea of a "reign of law", in the sense of "immutable connection characterizing all change in a closed system."[2] Laws, now said physicists of repute, were no more than empirically devised descriptions; as to their verbal form, they underwent remodelling as knowledge increased. If an exception to a law turns up, whether it be the behaviour of radium or the resuscitation of the dead to life, we must, if we can, widen the law to include the abnormal case.[3]

Theology had at first rejoiced that science had lost its weapon for declaring miracles impossible; but in fact the new position involved the loss of a criterion by which any given marvel might be recognized as a miracle, in such a sense as to warrant for it evidential value for proving supernatural intervention.[4] The recognition that nature might produce such phenomena as faith-healing and the stigmata does not remove the possibility that bygone miracles were produced supernaturally, but it does remove all certainty that they were so produced.[5] When we turn from the idea of law to that of causation, the situation is the same, Tennant tells us. Science proper does not and cannot assert the non-existence of the supernatural: it may be "atheous", by the rules of its game, but is not atheistic. Its world is not proved, or even asserted, to be a "closed system",

[1] *op. cit.*, p. 4. [2] *ibid.*, p. 21. [3] *ibid.*, p. 22.
[4] *ibid.*, p. 23. [5] *ibid.*, pp. 30-31.

or a dead mechanism and no more. But, so long as the constitution of nature is not exhaustively known, it is no more possible to assert that a given marvel is beyond the unaided powers of nature than to affirm that an event indescribable in terms of natural law, as systematized up to date, is for ever or intrinsically incapable of being subsumed under natural law.[1]

If the scientific expectation of uniformity and scientific standards of evidence forced theology to make a radical re-examination of the New Testament witness to Christ, the further development described by Tennant drove the process of reinterpretation still further. Scholastic theology, accentuated in this particular in the 18th century, had fastened upon one aspect of the Biblical miracles for its scheme: their physical non-conformity. Such a use of these significant acts of God was tenable only so long as men believed they knew the determinate nature of many things in the universe. The more developed understanding of scientific thought has removed the keystone from the evidentialist structure. Nevertheless, as we shall see, this grave disturbance has not meant the end of belief in the Biblical miracles nor prevented their continuing to play a rôle of considerable importance in the Christian apprehension of revelation.

[1] *op. cit.*, pp. 41-54.

Chapter Six

THE SCIENTIFIC INTERPRETATION OF HISTORY

GREAT as were the changes brought about in the modern intellectual outlook by the philosophy of science, the problems raised for the Christian apologist by the creation of a scientific method and philosophy of history were even more profound. It is claimed by some historians today that the science of history grew up to some extent independently of the natural sciences, and there still remains much questioning as to the extent to which scientific categories may be appropriately applied to the interrelation of human actions. But for our purpose it will suffice to show how the science of history became the means by which the 19th-century picture of the world of man and nature was projected back through history. No longer was the past a heterogeneous patchwork of men and miracles, with the former almost as unconditioned as the latter, but a seamless weave of causes and effects.

Until comparatively recent times the study of history was treated predominantly as an art: to Cicero it was "*Magister vitae*"; to Dionysius "Philosophy by examples". Indeed, to the writers of ancient Greece and Rome, history was a storehouse of warnings to statesmen or of moral maxims. To the ecclesiastical historian, the chief interests were the lives of the saints, the acts of the martyrs, and the chronicles of the church's deeds and triumphs. (The attempts of some modern writers to restore the approach to history as an art—Windelband to Croce—need not detain us here.) The beginnings of the new spirit were evident in the 18th century, in such labours as those by which Bentley had exposed the spurious character of the Epistles of Phalaris.[1] Rationalistic criticism at this time, however, got

[1] G. P. Gooch, *History and Historians in the XIXth century*, p. 6.

little further than denying this or that to be true; and even the monumental works of Adam Smith and Gibbon were doctrinaire in character. The modern science of historiography is generally dated from the appearance of Wolf's *Prolegomena to Homer*, 1795, B. G. Niebuhr's *History of Rome*, 1838, and Ranke's *History of the Popes*, 1834. These writers brought to their study a systematic and minute method of examining, criticizing and comparing historical sources, which has become the hall-mark of modern scholarship.

With this new apparatus, which was motivated by an interest in facts, simply as facts, there came an elevation of the standards of historical truthfulness; a scrupulous conformity to historic reality. No doubt the historians of every age believed themselves to be conveying a faithful representation of the truth, but whilst history was pre-eminently a sermon, the same store was not set upon that kind of accuracy which came to be required when historiography was raised to the pantheon of the sciences. Thus, a modern historian, perusing an ancient narrative, may well believe that the suppression of a vital detail here, or the heightening of a circumstance there, may have transformed the natural into the miraculous.

The criticism of ancient documents, however, does not constitute the whole of the science of history. The breath which animates the frame is the conception of history as a genetic causal process. Three passages from J. B. Bury will illustrate this. The right idea of history, he says, could not be formed until men had grasped the idea of human development. "This is the great transforming conception, which enables history to define her scope."[1] The conception, he thinks, has brought history into line with the other sciences, and marks a definite stage in man's growing self-consciousness. Thus, "The 'historical' conception of nature, which has produced the history of the solar system, the story of the earth, the genealogies of telluric organisms, and has revolutionized natural science, belongs to the same order of thought as the conception of human history as a continuous, genetic, causal process."[2] History could only become a science when it "is conceived as lying entirely within the sphere in which the law of

[1] *Selected Essays*, ed. H. W. V. Temperley, p. 9. [2] *op. cit.*, p. 23.

cause and effect has unreserved and unrestricted dominion."[1]

But the science of history did not content itself with the claim that history is a causal process. Further theories of an aprioristic character were introduced into the very texture of the subject, and were often identified with the actual logic of historical criticism. Superimposed upon the genetic idea was the teleological doctrine of progress, which Collingwood has described as a piece of sheer metaphysics foisted upon history by the temper of the age.[2] This subjection of the process to a judgment of value runs somewhat parallel in time to the growth of historical science itself. Condorcet, though not the first in the field, clearly enunciated the idea of progress in 1795, the same year as Wolf's *Prolegomena*, and the idea is illustrated in De Tocqueville's apotheosis of democracy—man's progress towards equality. It is also seen in Spencer, where society is thought to be progressing from a militaristic to an industrial state. Another powerful influence in the formative period was Hegel, who saw history as the successive periods corresponding to the ascending phases in the self-evolution of the absolute being. Although this view—that ideas create history—was the exact opposite of the view which was later to predominate, it proved a powerful stimulus in the mid-19th century to the causal, evolutionary view of history, especially as regards the evolution of religious ideas.

Perhaps more decisive than the influence of Hegelian idealism was the philosophy of positivism. Condorcet had emphasized the part which the mass of mankind play in the movements of history, and Comte, in the fourth volume of his *Course de Philosophie Positive*, 1839, made the study of mass behaviour the pivot of his historical study; he created social psychology, it has been said. The study of statistics, with the astounding uniformities they appear to exhibit, added weight to this movement; so that extremists such as Buckle sought for historical laws in the same way as a scientist looks for physical laws. Indeed, it is precisely when the individual historical "fact" is artificially isolated, like an object in a laboratory experiment, and when masses of these artificial units are studied en bloc, that it becomes possible to apply scientific categories to history. Positivism might, in fact, be described as the

[1] *ibid.*, p. 26. [2] *The Idea of History*, p. 144.

methodology of natural science elevating itself to the very essence of knowledge, declaring itself to be the only kind of knowledge that can exist.[1] The most penetrating and progressive historians of our own century have come to realize that history can be treated in the positivist manner only by excluding the most significant elements in each human situation: though we still have with us the disciples of Marx, whose system combines considerable insight into the effects upon society of economic environments mixed up with a tangle of Hegelian metaphysical dogmatism.

The stage was thus set in the 19th century for the wedding of the science of history with the conception of evolution drawn from biology. History having been described as a causal process, whose terms were of the same order as those of scientific classification, it could take its place as one more chapter in the story of life upon the planet. Few in the 19th century questioned whether, being constituted of an aggregate of conscious, free personalities, history could yield all its secrets to such treatment.

In order to understand the general effects of the new science of history upon the study of sacred history, we may begin by turning again to Bury. The historian, he claims, need not and should not call upon transcendental causes to explain historical facts: in the actual pursuit of his science he must dismiss their possibility. The historian himself may be a Theist, but as far as his work goes his belief is otiose. Ideas, says Bury, have no existence except in the minds of those who think them.[2] Thus, if we dismiss the Theistic-providential and the Hegelian thought-manifesting views of history, we are left with a natural development which is made up of two factors. First, there are general laws. These do not, however, account for the particular in human history any more than they do in biology. Secondly, therefore, what makes the individual what it is may be called the factor of chance; not in the popular sense of the word, but as a point where two different lines of causes meet and bear consequences. History thus becomes the study of contingencies such as the consequences of the shape of Cleopatra's nose.[3]

It must be granted that the scientific treatment of history as a

[1] Collingwood, *op. cit.*, p. 134. [2] Bury, *op. cit.*, p. 33. [3] *ibid.*, p. 60.

natural continuum has produced a rich harvest of knowledge regarding the past. The difficulty for apologists in the 19th century was that, whilst history was drawing ever closer into the family circle of the natural sciences, its principles could not be criticized without the counter-charge of obscurantism. As we shall see, they held grimly on to the fundamental facts of spiritual experience in man, free will and the moral imperative, as the sure witnesses against a movement which would seemingly reduce human affairs to a web of laws and chance. Their tenacity has been rewarded, for within the present century a reaction against the positivist approach has set in amongst secular historians.

The science of history was born at a time when physics and biology were still dominated by developed forms of the Cartesian and Newtonian pictures of the universe, when the idea of matter shaping and reshaping itself according to mechanical laws gave rise to a view of history in which life and action were thought to be likewise woven simply of law and contingency from already existing entities. The more recent biology and scientific philosophy, which appears to envisage leaps forward in creative evolution, has been paralleled in historical study by a renewed emphasis on the uniqueness of the realm in which consciousness manifests itself. The ethos of the historical, in Tennant's words, is now seen to be "the actual and changing, the concrete and particular, the qualitative and may be the unique, as contrasted with the universal, the abstract, the timeless or the quantitative."[1] In the 19th century, however, the positivist conception of history insinuated its influence into every philosophical and theological question. As Oman writes:

> all problems became historical. Scientific explanations were an account of how things came to be; philosophy was largely a theory of history; religion seemed to be at the mercy of critical historical questions, and there was an active school which taught that all its problems could be determined wholly on grounds of historical evolution. But a historical scheme constantly turns out to be merely what we might call an illustrated edition of the Cartesian method.

[1] *The Philosophy of the Sciences*, p. 86.

That is, the idea that if one gets far enough back one will come to the simple elements from which everything subsequent is a mere reshuffle.[1] Furthermore, it has been abundantly shown that the historiography of the 19th century was by no means the impartial study that it claimed to be. The notion, says Whitehead, "of historians, of history devoid of aesthetic prejudice, of history devoid of any reliance on metaphysical principles and cosmological generalizations, is a figment of the imagination."[2]

The science of history was born with a strong bias against the supernatural. Voltaire, for example, had immense confidence in the power of enlightened reason: he thought that history could be neatly divided up into fable and fact—a principle he learned from Bayle. Even for matters which he might accept as facts he demanded a high degree of testimony; whilst for the rest—"*Ce qui n'est pas dans la nature n'est jamais vrai.*"[3] Historiography continued to be handled with a naturalistic bias; the spirit of Bayle and Voltaire lived on, for the new science never quite forgot its origin in Deism.[4] The persistent work of the evidentialists also sharpened the weapons of their adversaries: as Canon Storr points out, "Investigation of the external evidences of a religion based upon the life and doings of a historical person must, in course of time, lead to enquiry into the method and canons of historical criticism."[5] Furthermore, there was a practical incentive towards scepticism regarding the supernatural owing to the fact that the first task to which the new science set its hand was the elucidation of the histories of Greece and Rome, which could only be carried out by a thorough process of separating the genuine history from its fabulous superstratum. This was no mere scissors-and-paste procedure; it involved such questions as inferring a natural explanation for an event from the surrounding evidence as opposed to the supernatural explanation offered by the ancient author. It was in fact in connection with the histories of ancient Greece and Rome that the principles of historical criticism in something like a systematic form came into England, in the writings of Thirlwall, Grote and Thomas Arnold. (Thirlwall's history of

[1] *Natural and Supernatural*, p. 116. Cf. Berdyaev, *Destiny of Man*, p. 11.
[2] *Adventures of Ideas*, p. 4.
[3] J. B. Black, *The Art of History*, pp. 33, 51, 52.
[4] Gooch, *op. cit.*, pp. 6f.
[5] *Development of English Theology*, p. 33.

Greece appeared in 1835, and Grote's in 1846-56.) In a letter to Bunsen in 1835, Arnold wrote that what had been done for the histories of ancient Greece and Rome by Wolf and Niebuhr ought to be done for the histories of the Old Testament.[1] This work was indeed already being done; but the story of the foundation of Biblical criticism through Simon, Astruc, Herder, Eichhorn and the rest is well known. In the very year that Arnold's letter was written, Lachmann propounded the ultimate solution of the synoptic problem and D. F. Strauss published his first life of Jesus—regarded by many as the high-water mark of sceptical Gospel criticism.

Until late in the 19th century, the number of English churchmen to embrace the new critical views on Scripture was quite small. Milman's *History of the Jews*, 1829, in which he pleaded that the Biblical history should be treated scientifically, was regarded as but one example of the contemporary Godlessness, which had a few years previously led Bishop Van Mildert in his Boyle Lectures to ask whether the end of the world might not be close at hand. Dean Stanley built his *History of the Jewish Church* upon Ewald's *History of the People of Israel*, which began to appear in 1843. He treated the pre-Mosaic narratives as mythical, and the crossing of the Red Sea as historical but non-miraculous. These writers, however, were regarded as the extreme liberals of their day; and the receptions accorded to *Essays and Reviews*, Colenso's work on the Pentateuch, and Robertson Smith's essay on the Bible in the 9th edition of the *Encyclopaedia Britannica*, 1887, give some idea of the long struggle for the recognition of this field of enquiry.

The technique of historiography impinged upon the traditional belief in miracles in two chief ways: first, in regard to the want of adequate evidence, and secondly, in regard to the conditions under which the belief in miracles naturally arises. First, then, as we have seen, the question of testimony was the characteristic issue in the earlier part of the miracle controversy. The question was raised by Hume, Middleton and the Deists, and it continued to hold pride of place in the controversial work of Mill and Huxley.[2] T. H. Huxley epitomized the scepticism produced by the merely mechanical comparison of the New Testament with other historical sources in an essay

[1] Gooch, *op. cit.*, p. 522. [2] Cf. Mill, *Three Essays*, pp. 237-42.

of 1889, entitled *The Value of Witness of the Miraculous.* He describes an intriguing story from Eginhard, the court chronicler of Charlemagne, relating to the adventures involved in the stealing and transporting of certain relics from Rome—a story of cheating and counter-cheating, mixed up with the pious account of a number of miracles connected with the relics. No one, says Huxley, has any difficulty in rejecting these stories of the miraculous: yet no one doubts either the good faith of the writer or that he was a contemporary enquirer who had access to the witnesses of the facts. These stories are rejected, yet the Gospel miracles—far worse attested—are accepted![1] Against the contention that to discredit the miraculous is to throw a cloud of scepticism over all history, it is often pointed out that it is possible, for example, to recognize in the Venerable Bede the work of an excellent historian, whilst rejecting the miracle stories with which his work is strewn.[2]

The sceptical attitude towards miracle stories was also partly fostered by apologists themselves, in their work of distinguishing the New Testament miracles from pagan and ecclesiastical miracles. In the eyes of many 19th-century thinkers—even of many Theists—such a dichotomy was impossible. James Martineau points out that the protestant, as opposed to the Roman, is obliged to reject the evidence of present miracles whilst demanding credence for others in ancient times. In dealing with the authenticity of the New Testament books Martineau gives two modern instances of the ease with which misplaced authorship can pass unnoticed. A paper on Christian paradoxes by Herbert Palmer was erroneously attributed to Bacon, and commented on as such by scores of writers, whilst the paper itself was actually in print under the name of its true author. Again, Toland, in his life of Milton, had referred to the supposed autobiography of Charles I, which by Toland's time was known to be spurious. Toland, corroborating Milton's critical judgment of the work, had added the reflection that if forty years of modern daylight, when criticism was awake and keen, sufficed for the establishment of such a fictitious claim, it could not surprise us that in the early Christian times many spurious productions found their way

[1] *Collected Essays*, vol. V, "Science and Christian Tradition", 1892.
[2] Glazebrook, *Faith of a Modern Churchman*, p. 68.

into circulation under the names of Christ and His Apostles.[1]

It has come to be perceived, however, by many thinkers, secular no less than religious, that miracle stories as a class cannot be dismissed on the supposed want of evidence. Many miracles even of ancient times are far better attested, on the level of sheer historical evidence, than some other facts of history accepted by most reputable historians. Further, if the question devolves upon the nature of the alleged events, then our increasing knowledge of the physical world renders many an alleged miracle credible—such as the stigmata of St. Francis.[2] The critics already discussed were moved by a further consideration, which came to the fore as the 19th century advanced. This newer and more deadly attack is best described by Edwyn Bevan:

> The real attack upon miraculous stories today . . . is made by psychology and anthropology. For these sciences claim to show how naturally the stories would arise under certain individual and social conditions of mind, even if the events they allege never took place. They do not attempt to prove that the events could not have taken place; all they purport to do is to take the value out of the testimony that they did take place.[3]

Canon Storr sees this process already at work in Middleton, who, he thinks, realized that an explanation of the belief in miracles might be found if an investigation were made into the general intellectual conditions of the age in which miracles were recorded as having happened.[4] But whereas the Deists attributed the belief in the miraculous to knavery and priestcraft, more mature study has led to a minimizing of the part believed to be played by fraud and conscious fiction.[5] The relation of the spiritual to the natural order presupposed in the belief came to be commonly regarded as a product of the animistic stage of human culture. At this stage of reflection, forces of will are believed to pervade nature: and from this it is inferred that there is a continual interference on the part of spiritual beings with human life, and that in exceptional circumstances men, like the spirits, have power over other men's

[1] Martineau, *Seat of Authority in Religion*, p. 179.
[2] A. E. Taylor, *Faith of a Moralist*, II, pp. 161-64.
[3] *Hellenism and Christianity*, p. 233.
[4] *Development of English Theology*, p. 34.
[5] Thompson, *Miracles in the New Testament*, p. 42.

bodies and over nature.[1] We have long been put on our guard against the process of reasoning by which an idea is explained away by exhibiting its lowly historic origins. The Christian belief that the living God is in direct rapport with men through the plastic medium of the outward world may have as little to do with the animism of the jungle as self-sacrificing love has to do with lust. Nevertheless, when we come to deal with the actual forms of miracle stories, we not only discover a similarity of types within one culture but types which have their direct analogies in many different cultures. Thus, miracles follow the saint, by what Gardner calls "an inevitable law of human nature".[2] So akin are the myth-making processes in different cultures that it is possible to explain isolated phenomena in our knowledge of the beliefs of one people by reference to similar beliefs and processes studied in other parts of the world.[3]

The study of the Old Testament Scriptures as historical documents led inevitably to the examination of the character and evidence of their miracle stories, and to the comparison of them with general Semitic beliefs. Several miracle stories were at once deemed to be poetic and literary: the story of the sun standing still at Beth-horon belonged to the same form of thought as the stars fighting against Sisera; whilst the Book of Jonah was a satire on Israel's failure to respond to its vocation. A large number of stories were recognized as illustrations of folk-explanations of natural phenomena, topographical features or ritual. In the miracles recounted of Elijah and Elisha, there were features reminiscent of primitive magic, whilst the cycle of miracles surrounding the Exodus might be assumed to be abnormal natural occurrences. Above all, the reconstruction of the development of Hebrew religion offered by 19th-century Biblical criticism had a profound effect upon the question of miracles. The emergence of ethical monotheism through the work of the prophets, and the transformation through their influence of the ceremonial and moral ordinances, threw a fresh light upon the manner in which the activity of God towards men should be envisaged. This was but an indirect

[1] P. Gardner, *Historic View of the New Testament*, p. 141.
[2] *op. cit.*, p. 147. Cf. J. E. Carpenter, *First Three Gospels*, p. 178.
[3] Gardner, *ibid.*, pp. 11-12.

inference from historical conclusions, but its practical influence upon historical study has been enormous. The same processes of comparison came to be applied to the miracle stories of the New Testament; and a serious problem was raised when it was realized, not only that these stories are instances of well-known types in the histories of many peoples, but that in heathen and rabbinic circles contemporary with the New Testament the process of creating miracle stories was actually at work.[1]

The application of scientific methods to history seemed to be overwhelmingly justified by the results. A technique had apparently been perfected by which to eliminate the last semblances of discontinuity in the world process. The theoretical thinking of the 18th century had assumed that human nature was a given entity, the same at all times. The following century came to be characterized by its sense of history: even the rediscovery of the importance of the intuitive aspects of human thought, which gave rise to the great religious revivals, opened up understanding of the evolution of human ideas and beliefs. The historical approach becomes typical of all sorts and conditions of thinkers: it marks Newman's Essay on Development no less than the work of an agnostic anthropologist. The rationalism with which the apologist came to have to deal was clothed in the guise of historical analysis; at every point, an air of empirical justification was given to philosophical and theological criticism.

The philosopher of history, with his exposition of the way in which the miraculous had once been serviceable to religion but could be so no longer, was probably as serious an opponent as the apologist was likely to encounter. The Oxford idealist, Edward Caird, argues that in the Homeric stage of religious thought, owing to the lack of abstract language and generalized thought about nature, the poet is obliged to represent the powers of nature and the principles of action within us as a host of particular Divine beings who are constantly interfering with the fate and action of men.[2] As the consciousness of the order and connection of nature becomes more distinct, and the idea of God gains greater purity and elevation, it becomes more

[1] J. E. Carpenter, *First Three Gospels*, p. 185.
[2] *The Evolution of Religion*, Gifford Lectures 1894, I, p. 289.

difficult to combine the natural and the supernatural, or simply to intercalate the supernatural in the natural.[1] Caird contends that when the spiritual is treated as another realm working parallel to the world of sense, and its effects as just one more set of objects alongside the other sensuously perceived objects, then the whole of religion is in jeopardy: for just as sophism succeeded the age of poetic religious thought, so the Illumination ended in positivism—we begin by conceiving Divine action like the other separate objects of sense, and we end by believing in nothing but the objects of sense. Only a spiritual interpretation of the whole of nature is at all adequate.[2]

Matthew Arnold was also interested in what he believed to be the unfortunate transformation of poetry into metaphysic. Religion he defines as morality touched by emotion, and claims that in the Old Testament this is embodied in the key word "righteousness"; in the Hebrew conception of God there is not a particle of metaphysics.[3] Around the simple universal notion of the law of righteousness there clings the *Aberglaube*, the fairytale element, which should not be confused with science, for unlike morality it is incapable of proof. The work of Christ was to bring a fuller description of righteousness: He extricated His disciples from the *Aberglaube*, but in time it returned in the form of the expectation of the parousia and the proof of His mission from miracles and prophecy.[4] On the phenomenal level, Matthew Arnold sees no more in miracles than a mere party trick, turning a pen into a pen-wiper.[5] Miracles like witches and fairies are doomed. The men of the Apostolic age being what and when and whence they were, the miracles were certain to grow up for them in the wake of Jesus. The Resurrection, for example, is a beautiful legend, whose very growth can be discerned in the New Testament documents.[6] The belief in literal miracles and the theology based upon them is one glaring example of the mistaken interpretation of literature.

The spirit and principles adumbrated in this chapter came at a later date to be appropriated by certain sections of religious opinion, and hence became not merely the objects of rejoinder

[1] *op. cit.*, I, p. 309. [2] *ibid.*, I, pp. 302-9.
[3] *Literature and Dogma*, 1873, pp. 11ff. [4] *op. cit.*, pp. 77ff.
[5] *ibid.*, pp. 116f. [6] *ibid.*, p. 250.

for apologists but matters of debate between Christians themselves. We may therefore postpone our further discussion of these topics, and turn at once to the revolution in religious thinking which preceded the crisis precipitated by scientific and historical reflection.

Chapter Seven

THE TURN OF THE TIDE

THEOLOGY and the day-to-day preaching of the Christian faith often appear to be far removed from one another, and since the implications of the Gospel have to be thought out at every intellectual level, it is inevitable that wide divergences of thought-forms should arise. But ideally, at least, there can be no fundamental distinction between dogmatic and apologetic theology: a fact which Anglican thought has largely recognized. Rather, we must think of the whole Christian intellectual activity as the attempt at different levels of reflection to precipitate into language something of the overwhelming fact of Christ. On the purely intellectual side, there has been in protestant Christendom an ever growing sensitivity to the surrounding currents of secular thought—indeed, the number of times that German theology has changed its intellectual clothes is almost bewildering. Here, however, we are to consider something far more striking than the adjustment of theological expression to current philosophy: for in the latter half of the 18th century in England, a revolt began to take shape against the prevailing theology, not through any pressure from without, but from the Christian experience itself.

The thing that came about was the reawakened understanding of the place in religion of the emotional and intuitive aspects of human nature. The thinkers of the Illumination had contrived to envisage a dualism in the mind of man analogous to their distinction of primary and secondary qualities in objects. There was the discursive reason, and there were the misty refracting areas of emotion around it. But it came to be seen that man's response to life, and his response to God and His revelation in Christ, must be an act of the whole personality and not merely the operation of the intellect, artificially set apart. It was inevitable that this revolution in the attitude towards the human personality in religion should come to be reflected in the idea of revelation itself and the manner of its reception. The revival of fully personal religious thinking, through the various schools of thought which it inspired, proved not only to be an advance of permanent significance in the understanding of the basis of Christian certitude but a mighty antidote to the external forces which were gathering against Christian truth.

The seeds of the new movement were sown during the period of the Illumination: human nature was bound to take its revenge upon those who had deliberately suppressed one aspect of it. As the 18th century proceeded, confidence in the possibilities of reason declined in religious circles, and theologians settled down to cataloguing the evidences. Theologians, says Canon Storr, had to learn the lesson that reason means more than the logical understanding, and that by the roads of logical demonstration or abstract generalization little progress could be made towards solving the concrete problems of life and history.[1]

I

We must begin with John Wesley, for his contribution to our subject was by no means confined to his rejoinder to Middleton; he holds a unique position in the history of English apologetics. On account of his general dogmatic orthodoxy, Wesley does not figure conspicuously in works dealing with the history of doctrine and the impact of free thought upon theology. Yet it is precisely such giants as he who lift apologetics out of the pedestrian levels of passing controversy into the firmament of the church's enduring faith. The neglect of Wesley in our present connection is particularly unfortunate. Whole works have been written on the miracle controversy with scarcely a mention of his name. Yet his place here is crucial. For just as Hume and Middleton canalized the forces which were to render the evidentialist apologetic impotent, it was Wesley who initiated a movement which was to provide the new direction in apologetics that was to replace evidentialism.

[1] *Development of English Theology*, pp. 26-27, 32.

Wesley had a robust faith in the reality of the miracles of Christ and His Apostles and of the church in the first three centuries.[1] We may expect miracles in answer to prayer, for the idea of a general providence, as opposed to that of a particular providence, is simply nonsense.[2] As we saw in Wesley's attitude to the miracles of the primitive church, he had no difficulty in ascribing other final causes to miracles than the authentication of doctrine. Miracles are to him the manifest signs of God's working; and indirectly they are evident proofs of Christ's Divine mission, though their immediate *raison d'être* was far different. This appears again in his reply to those who demanded miracles in attestation of his own doctrines. Such a demand he rejects as wholly unreasonable: we prove our doctrines by Scripture, and by reason, and by the conversions of men and women, he retorts.[3]

Wesley frankly averred the supernatural character of many of the cures performed amongst his followers, but he was far from being credulous. His letters show a keenly critical spirit; he was always willing in doubtful cases to attribute many seemingly supernatural phenomena to natural causes.[4] To Bishop Warburton's sneers that the Methodists were mad, he urges with great force and dignity that miracles do happen, and that genuine cases attest themselves by the whole tenor of the patients' lives.[5] Yet undeniably, he confesses, the most signal miracles which the Holy Spirit now performs are of a different kind from those which characterized the Apostolic age. Christ had promised to His brethren that they should do greater works than He: what could these greater works be? Surely, the conversion of sinners, the complete transformation of lives: that must be the answer.[6] Inspiration is now different in kind from that of the Apostles, but those who have experienced the power of the Holy Spirit "believe the change wrought by it in the heart to be equivalent to all outward miracles; as implying the selfsame power which gave eyes to the blind, feet to the lame, and life to the dead."[7]

Further—and here we come to the most significant deviation of Wesley's thought from the 18th-century pattern—the new

[1] *supra*, ch. 3. [2] *Sermons*, 1825 ed., II, p. 193.
[3] *Letters*, ed. Telford, II, p. 105; V, p. 247. [4] e.g. *op. cit.*, II, pp. 251-64.
[5] *ibid.*, IV, p. 362. [6] *ibid.*, II, p. 136. [7] *ibid.*, I, p. 234.

manifestations of the Spirit carry with them convincing evidence of the truth of the Gospel, just as much, nay more so, than the testimony of the Gospel miracles. The Christian character and the gift of faith are the chief evidence to the Gospel's truth; and this evidence, the experience of reconciliation, is actually within the soul. The Christian character and hope are to be obtained by faith; and faith is not a set of opinions or an assent to creeds, but a power wrought by the Almighty in our immortal spirit, enabling it to see through the veil into the world of spirits, into things invisible and eternal. Faith "is a Divine evidence or conviction wrought in the heart that God is reconciled to me through His Son . . ."[1] Faith gives a more extensive knowledge of things invisible than the intellect, and shows such things "in the clearest light, with the fullest certainty and evidence."[2] Wesley does not wish to undervalue the traditional evidences, but cannot set them on a level with the interior proof. "It is generally supposed," he says, "that traditional evidence is weakened by length of time, as it must necessarily pass through so many hands in a continued succession of ages. But no length of time can possibly affect the strength of this internal evidence. It is equally strong, equally new, through the course of seventeen hundred years. It passes now, even as it has done from the beginning, directly from God into the believing soul."[3]

Here, then, a generation before the evidentialist theology ripened in the work of Paley, we find the approach to Christian truth which was destined to supersede it. We must therefore pause to note some of the lines of subsequent development that are here in embryo. To begin with, the whole concept of the Christian religion, whilst retaining its historic lines, is painted in fresh colours. The ethos of the evangelical movement is well known, and a little reflection serves to clarify the differences between it and Paley's theology. Wesley realized that the revelation of the love of God, the personal salvation through Christ, applied to the believer through the regeneration of the Holy Spirit, must require an epistemology which goes far beyond the logical inferences from miracles and prophecy. Far more was involved in the Christian's act of faith than the acceptance of the historical evidences of the life of Christ, even

[1] *ibid.*, II, pp. 381-82. [2] *ibid.*, II, p. 383. [3] *ibid.*, II, p. 384.

though salvation had been wrought in history. Whilst accepting in the fullest sense the historic redemption of Christ, and hence the necessity of the historical evidences, Wesley was prepared to tilt the balance towards ascribing a pre-eminence to the inward conviction produced by the Spirit. He did not, however, like some modern protestants, drive a wedge between the historical evidence and the interior conviction, as though the latter alone was of the essence of faith as opposed to belief on authority. To him, personal faith is in the Christ who lived and died and rose again: the reception of the knowledge of Christ through the tradition of the church is no scandal to him.

The expression "internal evidence" undergoes a decisive change in Wesley's writing. It ceases to refer to the beneficent character of the Christian precepts, as in the theology of the Illumination, and comes to mean the inward persuasion of the Spirit, and the experience of reconciliation and new life in Christ. In 19th-century religious thought the connotation of the expression was to be extended still further. On the objective side, appeal came to be made to the perfection of the Gospel dispensation, the quality of the personality and influence of Christ, and the spiritual forces which He brought into the world. On the subjective side, attention came to be focused upon man's faculties for recognizing revelation,—his reason and intuitions informed by grace.

If we look carefully at this striking development, it is clear that Christian certitude has come to be based upon a value-judgment, made by the whole human personality, of the Gospel history and the Christian experience: something very different from the old business of weighing the external proofs. It has sometimes been contended that the appeal to religious experience is a subterfuge by which the semblance of the traditional argument from miracles is retained, by the appeal to things which are not really miraculous. Now it is obvious that in the case of Wesley there was no desire to belittle the importance of the historic Christian tradition; but his work did in fact open the way for a redefining of the supernatural. The experience of conversion scarcely qualifies as a miracle in the sense required by evidentialist theology. In what sense, then, can it be recognized as supernatural? For a human character, bound by the triple chain of heredity, environment and habit to exhibit an altogether new moral energy can only be achieved by the introduction of some adequate force from without. If we start with some at least of the Christian presuppositions, we may well be convinced that a miracle has taken place in such a case; a Divine intervention in the course of nature no less than the raising of the dead. But if the discursive intellect is competent to judge the occurrence of outward miracles, as the evidentialists claimed, it is certainly not competent by itself to judge the quality and causation of a spiritual rebirth. Spiritual things must be spiritually discerned, as St. Paul pointed out: only fully personal perception can judge of the quality and significance of personal experience. Wesley reorientated apologetics by calling special attention to the supernatural activity of God in the soul. Ultimately this led to the abandonment of the attempt to distinguish miracles simply in terms of their physical non-conformity, which had been an altogether inadequate starting-point for apprehending the supernatural.

II

For the time being, the movements of religious revival which followed Wesleyanism were preoccupied with the aspects of Christian faith and life which they had rediscovered, and except in rare cases they did not question the validity of the older structure of apologetics. The whole traditional Christology, with the assumptions that Christ's Divinity was primarily manifested in His supernatural knowledge and power, continued to be assumed until it was questioned by churchmen themselves in the latter years of the 19th century. The evangelicals, in contrast to Newman's view of them, had a very definite scheme of doctrine to teach;[1] which, however different from evidentialism, none the less presupposed the certitude of the Biblical history.

William Wilberforce's *Practical View*, 1797, is a striking evidence of the revolution in Christian thinking that was being carried out. As opposed to the contemporary morality of enlightened self-interest and tacit rejection of the supernatural doctrines of Christianity, he set out the key positions of the

[1] Storr, *op. cit.*, p. 66.

faith. He offers a trenchant discussion of human depravity, and proceeds to an exposition of the atoning work of Christ and the sanctifying work of the Spirit—fresh indeed after the theology of the Illumination. But we get a more vivid insight into his task in the dissertation on the question whether religion should be merely an affair of the reason, or whether the passions and feelings should have a part in it.[1] He argues that the affections are not in themselves unreasonable, but part of the mechanism of the human mind with their proper part to play in human life. There was an abuse of language, whereby that species of religion which was opposite to the warm and affectionate kind had been suffered almost without disturbance to usurp to itself the epithet "rational". It was wrong to exclude from religion so grand a part of the composition of man—all the most active principles of our nature. Scripture inculcated love as of supreme importance: the life of heaven itself was not represented as a cold intellectual investigation but as a worship of gratitude and love. Christ was the proper object of our affections, of personal faith and love, as opposed to mere historic recognition of His merits. Wilberforce's chapter on the "Real excellencies of Christianity" is also characteristic of another growing tendency of the time. He deals with such matters as the wonderful harmony between the theological doctrines and the moral precepts. He was impressed by the great variety of evidences that had been adduced in support of the Christian claims: he mentions prophecy and miracles amongst many other arguments, without singling them out for particular comment.[2]

The Oxford movement and all that flowed from it was likewise a product of the rediscovery of the part played by the intuitional elements in human personality, together with the fresh understanding of the relevance of the central doctrines of the faith—especially the understanding of the nature of the church. On the subject of miracles, the contribution of the Tractarians and their successors lay chiefly in appreciating the doctrinal significance of the Gospel miracles.[3] One important aspect of revelation the Evangelicals and Tractarians had in common was the literal inspiration of the Bible. This belief separates the pre-critical period distinctly from all that has

[1] *op. cit.*, 1834 ed., pp. 62f. [2] *ibid.*, p. 270. [3] *infra*, ch. 10.

followed, be it Barthianism or Anglo-catholicism.[1] There was an obvious congruity between the belief in literal inspiration and the scheme of rational proofs from prophecy and miracles; and likewise there is congruity between the enriched view of revelation, which we are considering, and the view of Biblical inspiration that looks to the events and the experiences of the men of the Bible rather than to the letter of the text. It was most providential that, before the upheaval caused by the advent of higher criticism, theologians had already largely abandoned the 18th-century scheme of apologetics in favour of a deeper understanding of revelation and of faith into which the new knowledge about the Bible could be assimilated.

[An excellent example of the way in which plenary inspiration of Scripture was linked to the older apologetic is afforded by the writing of the pre-Tractarian Thomas Rennell, *Proofs of Inspiration*, 1822. He seeks to show from Scripture itself that the inspiration of the Apostles reached not merely to their oral teaching and their miracles but to their written testimonies also. Bishop Thirlwall's Diocesan Charges show the problems and anxieties that were raised for a deeply learned and liberal-minded man by the onset of Biblical criticism.][2]

III

It is all too easy to speak of movements of thought as though they were like waves of the sea, ebbing and flowing, crossing and recrossing, and to forget the part played by the individual thinkers who created them. Nowhere could this neglect be so dangerous as in the case of the revival of religious feeling in England. Much has been written about Rousseau and the romantic revival, but Wesley was an individual creative personality, and another was Coleridge. He not only interpreted such German thinkers as Schleiermacher and Hegel, but must himself be considered a powerful influence upon religious thought in England. There are those to whom Coleridge's seeming eclecticism is an offence. He is charged with exhibiting confusion regarding the basis of Christian faith and

[1] Creed, *Divinity of Jesus Christ*, pp. 12-17.
[2] *Remains*, ed. J. J. S. Perowne, 3 vols.

the relation of natural to revealed theology. Yet this very catholicity is an object lesson for our own day: for he maintained an outright loyalty to the incarnational approach to Christology together with a luminous insight into the strength of the faith in its personal appeal. Thus, he combines a traditional statement of the efficacy of miracles as evidences with a penetrating criticism of the method of evidentialism.

The traditional standpoint is represented in the following oft-quoted passage. "Most readily do I admit, and most fervently do I contend that the miracles worked by Christ, both as miracles and as fulfilments of prophecy, both as signs and as wonders, made plain discovery, and gave unquestionable proof, of his divine character and authority . . ."[1] Coleridge was not a writer of apologetics in the then accepted sense, but by his discursive examination of the meaning of the faith, he put new life and vigour into Christian thought, and made the Christian profession more of a living issue for an educated man. By revitalizing even the most recondite articles of faith such as the Trinity and the Incarnation and by employing ideas from the leading philosophers of his day, he placed himself at the head of that long line of apologists who have deliberately sought to create a living Christian philosophy combining elements both old and new. But he was not interested in religious ideas merely for their own sake: he took his stand on "the belief that a Means of Salvation has been effected and provided for the human race by the incarnation of the Son of God in the person of Jesus Christ; and that his life on earth, his sufferings, death and resurrection are not only proofs and manifestations, but likewise essential and effective parts of the great redemptive Act."[2] This position was to assume tremendous importance in later 19th-century theology, for the supernatural activity of Christ and the miracles associated with His person become the substance, and not merely the authentication, of revelation and redemption.

In the *Confessions of an Enquiring Spirit*, the question of the miraculous arises in connection with Coleridge's protest against

[1] *Aids to Reflection*, Preface to Aphorism XXIII on Spiritual Religion, 1884 ed., p. 231.
[2] *op. cit.*, 1884 ed., p. 130.

the tyranny of the belief in the literal inspiration of the Bible: a view which, he thought, would regard the words of Scripture as an instrument to compel belief of itself, irrespective of any corresponding operation of grace within the soul of the believer. The only convincing argument for the inspiration of Scripture could be that it found an echo in the believer's soul for its every need—that it finds me at a far greater depth than all other books put together. The miraculous dictation of the Scriptures turns the writers into mere ventriloquists, and makes nonsense, for example, of a work such as the book of Job. Inspiration, as opposed to literal infallibility, must appear vague to those to whom belief is wholly external, and, like the objects of sense, common to all alike. The superstitious view of inspiration is parallel, he claims, to the idea of miracles as things which must compel belief. "Whatever is spiritual is, *eo nomine*, supernatural; but must it be always and of necessity miraculous? Miracles could open the eyes of the body; and he that was born blind beheld his redeemer. But miracles, even those of the Redeemer Himself, could not open the eyes of the self-blinded . . ."[1] The distinction between the Divine will working with the agency of natural causes, and the same will supplying their place by a special fiat, had none so weighty a use as in liberating men from the idea of verbal inspiration.[2] Today it is difficult to realize that such ideas were pathfinders. We assume without question that the business of the apologist is not to present the faith as a series of logical inferences but as a message to the heart and mind.

Coleridge's view of revelation is that it consists of two complementary elements, objective and subjective. It is thus analogous to all other human experience. On this view, the essential rôle of the objective event does not infringe the peculiar activity of the soul in its God-inspired faith. He writes:

> Revealed religion (and I know of no religion not revealed) is in its highest contemplation the unity, that is the identity or co-inherence, of subjective and objective. It is in itself, and irrelatively, at once inward life and truth, and outward fact and luminary. But as all power manifests itself in the harmony of

[1] *Confessions*, 1849 ed., p. 78. [2] *op. cit.*, pp. 78-79.

correspondent opposites, each supposing and supporting the other—so has religion its objective, or historic and ecclesiastical pole, and its subjective, or spiritual and individual pole. In the miracles, and miraculous parts of religion . . . we have the union of the two, that is, the subjective and supernatural displayed objectively—outwardly and phenomenally—as subjective and supernatural.[1]

It will become apparent that Coleridge is here enunciating what has become the characteristic position of modern conservative theology with regard to the historical element in religion. Some writers at the beginning of the 19th century were content simply to adduce the internal appeals of revelation, either setting them side by side with the older arguments or allowing the latter to slide into obscurity. Coleridge, however, recognizes the essential part played by the historical and miraculous element in religion, but is aware that, if religion is to be fully personal, the reception of the historical element cannot be merely a matter of external authority or demonstration. The appeal of Coleridge's own writings shows what a great liberating influence this conclusion proved to be, in freeing apologetic to pursue its proper functions.

In another work, Coleridge offers some penetrating criticisms of the miracle apologetic: not in respect of any weaknesses in the evidence as such, but on the ground that the miracles *per se* were inappropriate instruments for the task they had been assigned. Have we not, he says, the authority of Scripture itself for putting the question whether miracles can of themselves work a true conviction in the mind? There are certain spiritual truths which must derive their evidence from within, which whoever rejects will not be persuaded though one rose from the dead to confirm them. Is not the creating of a new heart, which collects the energies of a man's whole being in the focus of the conscience, the one essential miracle, the same to the ignorant and learned, which no superior skill can counterfeit? "Is it not that implication of doctrine in the miracle and of miracle in the doctrine, which is the bridge of communication between the senses and the soul;—that predisposing warmth which renders the understanding susceptible of the specific impression

[1] *Confessions*, p. 98.

from the historic, and from all other outward, seals of testimony?"[1] To Coleridge, the gravest defect of evidentialism was the sub-Christian morality with which the apologetic was linked. Paley's degrading of the spirit of honour into a mere club law could, he thought, be easily exposed by comparing it with 1 Corinthians 13.[2] What can we think of a theological theory which, adopting a scheme of prudential legality, makes its whole religion consist in the belief of miracles?! "As well might the poor African prepare for himself a fetisch by plucking out the eyes from the eagle or the lynx, and enshrining the same, worship in them the power of vision."[3] He argues that "The feelings will set up their standard against the understanding, whenever the understanding has renounced its allegiance to the reason: and what is faith but the personal realization of the reason by its union with the will?"[4]

The use of terms here is characteristic of Coleridge's psychology. The "understanding" means the discursive intelligence, whilst "reason" is reserved for man's highest powers of intuitive and rational perception. Faith, then, is the act of the whole personality: the reason expressed through the will. There is here an advance on the early Evangelicals in the analysis of man's spiritual constitution. The Evangelicals had drawn attention to the experience in the soul of the work of Christ as an intuitive certainty, and they had stressed the importance of the feelings in the religious approach to life. It remained for Coleridge to relate the part played by the higher intuitions and the will to man's discursive intellect, and to show how the conceptual aspect of religious thinking is necessary to the personal act of believing.

How firmly Coleridge helped to fix these ideas in the minds of religious thinkers may be seen if we consider the work of one who in many respects was poles away from him: J. H. Newman. In the *Grammar of Assent* he considers the question, "Can I attain to any more vivid assent to the Being of God, than that which is given merely to notions of the intellect? Can I enter with a personal knowledge into the circle of truths which make up that great thought?"[5] On reflection, it is found that such an assent is within human reach. It is phenomena that provide

[1] *The Friend*, 1863 ed., sec. II, Essay II, p. 144f. [2] *op. cit.*, p. 139.
[3] *ibid.*, p. 145-46. [4] *ibid.*, p. 146. [5] *op. cit.*, 1870, p. 99.

us with our evidence of the existence of creatures, together with the instinctive certitude that such phenomena do provide real evidence. The thought of God is not gained by an instinctive association of His presence with any sensible phenomena; "but the office which the senses directly fulfil as regards the external world, that devolves indirectly on certain of our mental phenomena as regards its Maker."[1] God, in fact, is inferred from our sense of moral obligation: a sense which should be carefully distinguished from our judgment as to what is right and wrong. Newman is not here engaged upon stating the grounds of belief, but he leaves us in no doubt as to the place where he looks for his certitude. His unqualified acceptance of the moral argument is a noteworthy fact in the history of 19th-century thought, which should make us ready to hear what he has to say of the place of conceptual thought in religion.

To the anti-intellectuals of his day, Newman replies in a striking passage. He has already pointed out that, as in matters of this world, sensation, instinct and intuition supply us with facts which the intellect uses, so in regard to our relations with God we receive our facts from the witness of nature and revelation, and these issue in our doctrines through the exercise of abstraction and inference.[2] Theology deals with notional apprehension, whilst religion deals with imaginative apprehension of these data.

> Here [he says] we have the solution of the common mistake of supposing that there is a contrariety and antagonism between a dogmatic creed and vital religion. People urge that salvation consists, not in believing the propositions that there is a God, that there is a Saviour, . . . but in believing in God, in a Saviour, in a Sanctifier; and they object that such propositions are but a formal and human medium destroying all true reception of the Gospel, and making religion a matter of words or of logic, instead of its having its seat in the heart. . . . The propositions may and must be used, and can easily be used, as the expression of facts, not notions, and they are necessary to the mind in the same way that language is ever necessary for denoting facts, both for ourselves as individuals, and for our intercourse with others. Again, they are useful in their dogmatic aspect as ascertaining

[1] *op. cit.*, pp. 99-101. [2] *ibid.*, pp. 95-96.

and making clear for us the truths on which the religious imagination has to rest. Knowledge must ever precede the exercise of the affections.[1]

Newman does not actually reject the structure of evidentialism, but he recognizes that the act of faith includes a supra-intellectual factor, which he calls the "illative sense".[2] It is this grasp of the importance both of the conceptual and the intuitive elements of religion that places Newman in the front rank of the architects of modern religious thought.

IV

The protests which Wesley and Coleridge had entered against the all-sufficiency of evidentialism ripened in the first half of the 19th century into a full-scale revolt against the prevailing methods of apologetics. Both the Evangelical and high church revivals had rediscovered whole areas of Christian truth for long eclipsed; and by now there was the added stimulus of the romantic revival in literature, with its emphasis upon the immanence of God in nature and man's faculties for perceiving it.

Few apologists questioned the validity of the older arguments; but apologetics is not primarily concerned with what may or may not be theoretically true: its business is with such arguments as are calculated to create a sufficiently persuasive presumption of the truth of religion and a cogent rationale of the Christian life. An argument, therefore, which ceases to make such an appeal must be removed from the repertoire. But we should only accept with caution the common view (derived from writers of the liberal school) that the reaction against evidentialism was an entirely healthy rediscovery of the true foundations of Christian faith. Some of the newer type of apologists tended to loosen their hold upon the historic foundations of the faith, as may be seen in the writings of Thomas Erskine, who makes a calculated attempt to reverse the customary methods of apologetics. It will be seen that as soon as the question of the relation of internal and external evidence was

[1] *ibid.*, pp. 116-17. [2] *ibid.*, pp. 343-45.

reduced to the level of discussions about the truths of theological propositions, back came all the difficulties experienced in the Deist controversy. Erskine's thesis is this: Suppose a traveller to have returned from China in the time of Archimedes, and amongst other tales he told he described a steam-boat which he had seen. Archimedes could have recognized the truth of the steam-boat story by the self-consistency of the data which the traveller supplied. He would then have possessed stronger evidence for the existence of the steam-boat than could have been provided by the testimony of any number of travellers.[1] Surely, then, in a system which purports to be a revelation from heaven, we may expect to find an evidence for its truth which shall be independent of all external testimony.[2] He argues that revelation presupposes some natural knowledge of God, which enables us to recognize it by its internal evidence. The doctrines revealed must be adequate to evoke a moral response: they must not only provide a picture of the perfection of God's moral nature, but must be adapted to human needs. There is in fact an intelligible and necessary connection between the doctrinal facts of revelation and the character of God as deduced from natural religion, in the same way as there is an intelligible connection between the character of a man and his most characteristic actions.[3]

There are unmistakable echoes in Erskine of the 18th century, and it is only fair to add that a somewhat richer understanding of the faith along Evangelical lines is to be found in his *Brazen Serpent*, 1831. The steam-boat simile has all the weaknesses of the 18th-century description of revelation. It is apt to this extent: that revelation is embodied in an actual life, and that the spiritual and moral effects produced by Christ are the chief evidences for His supernatural claims. But it was unfortunate that the growing fear of rationalism led to an attempt to cut the Gordian knot, to anticipate every subsequent attack upon sacred history by setting up a proof which was thought to be "wholly independent of the testimony of history". It was easy to forget that our knowledge of the historic Christ, and of the impression that He produced upon His immediate

[1] *Remarks on the Internal Evidence for the Truth of Revealed Religion*, 1820; 10th ed., 1878, p. 4.
[2] *ibid.*, p. 8. [3] *ibid.*, pp. 17-19.

followers, is dependent upon the historical documents, and indirectly upon the labours of scholars who evince the connection of these documents with the witness of the historic church.

More representative of the period of transition were John Bird Sumner and Richard Whateley. Though widely separated in many of their interests, they illustrate the transformation of Christian evidence writing which was henceforth to characterize English theology. They appear in part to be covering the same ground as Paley, and they have a firm grasp of the historic character of the Christian revelation, but their whole spirit is different.

The Evangelical Archbishop Bird Sumner wrote one of the most popular books of its type in his generation: *The Evidence of Christianity derived from its nature and reception*, 1824. The materials hitherto regarded as the principal evidences are here presented as but some amongst many strands in an inductive argument. The proof is intended to be cumulative, as in Butler's *Analogy*, but the stress is laid upon quite different inferences. The author begins by describing the historic origins of the Christian religion, and then goes on to the originality of the Christian doctrines, the agreement of the New Testament with subsequent Christian experience, the intrinsic wisdom of the Gospel dispensation and the originality of the Christian character. His exposition of the marks of authenticity in the personality and teaching of Christ is specially good. The traditional view of prophecy is accepted without question—the disciples could not possibly have engineered all the coincidences; on the other hand, in the first three-quarters of the book we find only two references of any consequence to miracles, and these are in footnotes.[1] He does not appear, however, to think of miracles as constituting part of revelation itself, and even the Resurrection and the miracles of the Apostolic age are no more than evidential.[2]

Whateley was renowned for his liberal scholarship as a member of the early Oriel school, and later as an ecclesiastical statesman as Archbishop of Dublin. He is one of the most attractive theological writers of the 19th century, who brings fresh light to every subject he touches. In his small volume,

[1] *op. cit.*, pp. 177, 184. [2] *ibid.*, pp. 258f.

The Christian Evidences, chiefly designed for the young, he shows himself a master of popular apologetic in the accepted framework of his time. Incidentally, Whateley prefers the term "superhuman" to "supernatural" in connection with Christ's miracles; for if nature is merely another word for that course of events that God has appointed, nothing that occurs can be strictly called "supernatural".[1] This approach was destined to have an important rôle in Christian thinking later in the century. He thought that the miracles of Christ must have had absolutely compelling evidence in order for the new religion to have won its way.[2] The internal evidence becomes a more and more valuable testimony to the Christian as he lives: for the fitness of Christianity does not mean that it does what we want it to do (like Islam, which promises plunder in this world and pie in the next) but that it has real insight into human needs.[3]

Whateley was also a keen polemical writer against what he believed to be illegitimate forms of historical criticism. He used not only his scholarly acumen but also the weapon of ridicule. His *Historic doubts relative to Napoleon Buonaparte* was published anonymously in 1819. The whole legend of Napoleon is a fantastic invention of the British press and of foreign correspondents whose very existence is not verified, and of politicians who cannot give the other party's game away for fear of exposing themselves. We ought to reject anything that is contrary to universal experience: well, what was ever more unique than the supposed career of Napoleon? The climax of the tract comes when Whateley solemnly recounts the story of the Napoleonic wars in the phraseology of the Authorized Version. We are told, he concludes, that people should use the same critical methods in every case. Men are prepared to accept contemporary stories such as this one, yet they reject the testimony of those who died for what they believed.

It must not be supposed, however, that Whateley was preoccupied with questions of historical evidence. In fact, his most telling appeal was made through other writings, notably his *Essays on some of the Peculiarities of the Christian Religion*, which created considerable discussion on its appearance in 1825. He later wrote a similar work on the teaching of St. Paul. The

[1] *op. cit.*, p. 35. [2] *ibid.*, pp. 43, 63. [3] *ibid.*, pp. 75, 96, 101.

appeal in these essays is to the intrinsic merits and novelty of Christian doctrines, and here, as in Bird Sumner, lay the creative apologetics of the future—no less objective for the fact that it addressed itself to man's whole spiritual insight.

Chapter Eight

THESIS AND ANTITHESIS

THE writers considered in the previous chapter exhibited new and profound insights into the character of Christian truth and certitude, but in what they rediscovered they saw no radical contradictions to the accepted principles of theology. Right through the 19th century, indeed, there were writers who simply set the older and the newer kinds of evidences side by side, without considering whether the latter did not presuppose a radically different idea of Christian assent from the former. But it would have been surprising if so radical a transformation of the materials of apologetics had come about without the synthesis being challenged; and between 1858 and 1865 a number of writings appeared in which inferences from the newer and older views were made to confront one another in the sharpest antitheses. They illustrate the parting of the ways from which a number of the characteristically modern attitudes to religious truth have developed, and they form a bridge between the 18th-century debate on the relation of revelation and reason and its counterpart in our own times.

I

The revival of the understanding both of the place of the intuitive aspects of human personality in religious faith and of the vital meaning of the creed had made it possible to say of Divine revelation—"It stands alone and speaks for itself. It receives light from no-where else; the source of its light is in itself and in itself alone." These words are not by Coleridge or Maurice but by Barth.[1] Barth, of course, means something

[1] *Revelation*, ed. Baillie and Martin, p. 46.

very different from what either of the former would have meant; and thereby hangs a tale. For the earlier writers, whilst holding that revelation needed no logical inference from miracles to evince it, none the less looked upon the act of faith as being made possible by the God-inspired reason in man working upwards from its contemplation of the lesser revelations in conscience and the world of nature. This, then, is the new thesis, that revelation has sufficient light of itself, and does not need to be accepted as a deduction from an elaborate system of proofs external to itself.

This whole approach was flatly challenged in 1858 by Dean Mansel in his Bampton Lectures. This work has generally been looked upon as a blind alley, and it suffered a certain notoriety by the use which Herbert Spencer made of it, but it did have the effect of forcing Maurice and others to think out the further implications of their position. Mansel could hardly have been popular in the 19th century, in view of his timely protests against the over-reaching pretensions of reason and natural theology. In some respects he is a striking forebear of the Ritschlians and Barthians by his attack upon intellectualism in theology.[1]

Mansel's contention is that before we could have an adequate critique of revelation, we should have to have a criticism of the possibilities of reason and a philosophy of the infinite with which to judge it.[2] Yet manipulate them how we will, the terms with which the philosophy of religion deals simply end in hopeless contradictions. For instance, we cannot think of consciousness without limitation and change; what then can we make of the idea of the eternal personality of God? The provinces of reason and faith are not co-extensive. "The highest principles of thought and action, to which we can attain, are REGULATIVE, not SPECULATIVE."[3] God must be thought of, Mansel tells us, exclusively in terms of personality, for that is the highest category we know; and the relation of the soul to God cannot simply be thought of as the relation of a being to the infinite, but as that of one person to another personal being.[4] Personal

[1] Cf. E. Bevan, *Symbolism and Belief*, p. 324.
[2] *The Limits of Religious Thought Examined*, 1858, 4th ed., e.g. p. 18.
[3] *op. cit.*, pp. 63, 93. [4] *ibid.*, p. 57.

religion had indeed been well understood since the time of Wesley, but few before Mansel had sufficiently articulated the distinction between the Biblical conception of the living, personal God, with whom man may have communion, and the scholastic metaphysics, which was still regarded by many as the quintessence of Christian thinking. It is unfortunate that Mansel did not work out the implications of this aspect of his thesis, but placed it simply within the old scheme of proofs from miracles and prophecy. He persists, moreover, in speaking of the acts of God—the Incarnation and Atonement—as "truths" to be accepted, which also tends to preserve the older rationalistic atmosphere.

Before coming to what Mansel has to say of the authentication of revelation, it is instructive to note his discussion of the miraculous. The course of Divine providence, he says, is represented in Scripture under the twofold aspects of general law and special interposition. But this has been discovered by philosophy to be irrational: God is unchangeable, and therefore He cannot be moved by man's entreaties. Here, Mansel urges, the rationalist mistakes a general difficulty of all human thought for a special difficulty of Christian belief. The really insoluble problem is how to conceive God as acting at all; not how to conceive His acting in this way rather than that. The creation of the world at any period of time, the establishment at any moment of immutable laws for the future government of the world; this is the real mystery. Further, if the condition of time is inseparable from all human conceptions of the Divine nature, what do we gain, even in philosophy, by substituting the supposition of immutable order in time for that of special interpositions in time? We are sometimes told that it gives a more elevated idea of the Divine wisdom and power to regard the Creator as having finished His work once and for all, rather than to represent Him as interfering from time to time. But both the terms of the simile are utterly incongruous: the world is not a machine and God is not a mechanic. The world consists of living and intelligent and freely acting persons, capable of personal relations with a living and intelligent, and freely acting ruler.[1]

[1] *op. cit.*, pp. 120-23.

The doctrines of revelation, therefore, must stand or fall by themselves and by the proofs given in Scripture; not as reasonable or unreasonable, but as Scriptural. The Incarnation, our central belief, is philosophically inconceivable, since infinite-plus-finite still leaves infinite.[1] Our Lord and His Apostles indeed appealed to reason in proof of their Divine mission; for the legitimate object of a rational criticism of revealed religion is not the contents of that religion, but its evidences.[2] The contents of revelation are still to be judged as part of the evidences; not in regard to their conformity with the supposed nature and purposes of God, but according to their adaptation to the actual circumstances and wants of man. Mansel admits that evidentialists had often erred in pressing one part of their case too far, but the crying need of the time, he believed, was the reassertion of the fundamental evidences of revelation.[3]

The climax of Mansel's argument is thus disappointing. He rejects the metaphysical presentation of theology in favour of the conceptions of a personal knowledge of God, and of truths which are regulative rather than speculative. Yet for the authentication of such a revelation he can see no further than the old external proofs; and although he modifies the definition of internal evidence so as to include the newer insights into the fulfilment of human needs, he still subordinates it to the external authority. The difficulties which arise for those who begin by denying the usefulness of conceptual reasoning regarding the metaphysical attributes of God are great. Thus, the judgment that a certain complex of phenomena is caused by a special interposition of God, i.e. that it is a miracle, rests upon a whole range of metaphysical presuppositions: yet judgments of this order are essential to Mansel's apologetic. Nor need his philosophical agnosticism have forced him back upon rationalistic evidentialism. He might have followed up his own clue regarding the personal relationship between man and God—towards the idea of a personal appraisal of Christ's person and work.

[1] *ibid.*, p. 118. [2] *ibid.*, p. 152. [3] *ibid.*, pp. 154-57.

II

Of those who were moved to controversy by Mansel's Bampton Lectures, none was so vehement as F. D. Maurice. Yet this was one of the tragedies of 19th-century theology, for Mansel and Maurice had more in common than either of them realized. They were both, in their several ways, in revolt against the sterile rationalistic theology which still dominated the schools of their day. To begin with, Maurice, despite his insistence upon the self-evidencing character of revelation, was fully alive to the dangers of that depreciation of the external evidences which was becoming fashionable at the time. Those who disparaged Paley were lacking in a quality which he possessed: his insight into the true foundations of Christianity.[1] But Maurice believed that he differed radically from Mansel both as to the way in which revelation was to be appropriated and as to its content. In the first case he did indeed differ from him: for whereas for Mansel the supernatural communication has to be received on the authority of outward evidence, for Maurice the nature of man is such that he can recognize the voice of God in revelation as in nature. But as to the content of revelation, it cannot be said that they did differ radically; and much of Maurice's eloquent denunciation appears to spring from emotion rather than from real understanding of his opponent. He believed that Mansel was denying our personal knowledge of God. He repeatedly confuses the question of metaphysical knowledge ABOUT God with personal knowledge OF God, when in reality Mansel had been striving to deny the former only, and to free the latter from extraneous ideas.

The whole body of religious and philosophical thought in Christendom both west and east testified, Maurice thought, to the fact that the conceptions of the infinite and absolute did mean something very real to the mind of man. The church, moreover, should come to the world not with a set of dogmas to be received on authority but with a Gospel of facts: an actual reconciliation between God and man, an actual Incarnation of the Eternal Son.[2] On Mansel's premises, à Kempis and

[1] *What is Revelation?*, 1859, pp. 448f. [2] *op. cit.*, p. 232.

all the mystics must be given up, since they admit a real knowledge of God.[1] Maurice is indignant with Mansel's contention that the doctrine of the Trinity does not make the abstract conception of the relation of the one and the many more intelligible.[2] Yet, in his own exposition of the Trinity, it is the light which the doctrine sheds upon personality human and Divine and upon personal relationships to which he draws attention. In suggesting a ground for the possibility of the Incarnation, it is the moral character of God and man to which Maurice appeals—not to any metaphysical considerations;[3] whilst man's knowledge of God is compared to a child's gradually coming to know and trust its parents.[4]

Maurice, then, was trying to say in other words very much what Mansel had said about the content of revelation: that it is a personal knowledge of God, a disclosure made by Him of His own good pleasure, not an act of human intellectual achievement. No more than Mansel was he interested in the purely metaphysical side of religious truth. The real contrast between them is to be seen elsewhere. Maurice indeed had no doubts in his mind about the necessity of the historic grounds of the faith; but revelation in history was no mere weighing of probabilities in respect of the supernatural proofs. The Bible itself pointed to a ground of certainty, not by merely stating dogmas but in the fact that it was a record of revelation in actual life. It testified how God had revealed Himself in the actual doings and sufferings of nations and in the doubts and struggles of individual hearts; all of which awakened echoes in our own experience.[5] We shall see later that Maurice had something constructive to offer also towards the understanding of the place of the Biblical miracles in revelation.

III

The insight into the personal character of Christian faith had thrown Mansel back upon the external proofs; whilst Maurice, like Coleridge, sought to exalt the inward appeal of

[1] *ibid.*, pp. 134-36. [2] *ibid.*, pp. 367f. [3] *ibid.*, p. 385. [4] *ibid.*, p. 390. [5] *ibid.*, p. 455.

revelation, though decrying any neglect of the historical data of Christian faith. But the position was not as simple as it appeared to Maurice; for if Christian truth is so luminous and the spiritual certitude so powerful, the time must come when men will question the function for present faith of the structure of historical credenda.

The lay theologian, R. H. Hutton, was keenly alive to this problem. Like Maurice, he came to the faith from Unitarianism, and cannot therefore be accused of having vested interests in traditionalism. He not only saw clearly that revelation could not rest its weight upon some supernatural bulwark external to itself, but realized that the problem for a thinking man of his day was the contrast between the seeming uncertainties of historical conclusions and the apparent intuitive certainty of religious ideas. Is it possible, Hutton asks, to do justice to the human element in religious history, without throwing impenetrable mist upon the absolute and Divine? Apologists, he found, had either abandoned the idea of revelation for that of inspiration—giving up the word which forces upon us the other and absolute side of the same fact, or they took refuge in positions vitiated by the same fundamental error, i.e. the "effort to fortify some reliable human base for a Divine infallibility—to slide in a false bottom into the abyss of Eternal Truth—to justify the exchange of the arduous duty of discriminating what God has told us of Himself, for some such (apparently) easier duty of discriminating what a given church or a given book states that He has told us."[1] Both of the lines of apology denied by implication the power of God to make Himself known to us; it is the grasp of the truth on us that men are willing to die for. The best analogy for revelation is the kind of avenues which a parent has to a child's convictions. "In all revelations proceeding from a higher to a lower mind, there is an intrinsic necessity that the reality revealed must be wider and more comprehensive than the modes of revealing", and the modes wider than the evidence that can be assigned for accepting revelation.[2]

Hutton was anxious to construct an argument for the Divinity of Christ which would be in a sense independent of

[1] *Essays Theological*, 1871, pp. 227-30.
[2] *op. cit.*, pp. 231-32.

the authority of church or Bible.[1] Whatever we may think of this kind of approach, it is worth noting that he was in advance of many orthodox thinkers of his time in recognizing some of the difficulties inherent in the idea of an historical revelation. He contends that the question is, not whether one should accept historical facts without historical evidence, but, "how far the belief in facts, for which there is more or less historical evidence, is legitimately shaken or strengthened by the tenacity with which they fasten on the conscience by their power of revealing the thoughts of many hearts."[2] Those who would receive the Gospels as religious myths and those who would suspend their judgment until they have weighed all the evidences are alike confused about the question of historical evidences, says Hutton. The idea of an impartial witness might be adequate to attest a simple fact, but useless as a witness to a complex moral and spiritual event; just as in a question of personal character one prefers the testimony of intimate friends.[3] There must none the less be satisfactory evidence that Christ did exist, that He made such claims as He did, and imposed a yoke which set men free from other yokes. We must also be satisfied that those wants which stirred antiquity were not only adequately answered, but that men's characters were fortified and strengthened by Christ's Incarnation. These two parts coalesce into an historical faith which is something far more than assent to historical testimony.[4]

We have here an adumbration of the modern conservative position in regard to the relation of faith to history: that there is a reciprocal relationship between faith and historical evidence. A most interesting corroboration of the same line of thought is to be found in the fragments of G. J. Romanes, which Gore published under the title *Thoughts on Religion*, 1894. All the parts of the human mind, he says, are involved in faith: the intellect, the emotions and the will. This is a matter of fact, whether there be a God or Christ or not.[5] If there be a God, the fact is certainly of the nature of a first principle: if He is knowable, therefore, it must be by intuition, not by reason, like other first principles.[6] Although God might give an objective revelation of Himself, even this would not give

[1] *ibid.*, p. 235. [2] *ibid.*, p. 236. [3] *ibid.*, pp. 237-38.
[4] *ibid.*, pp. 243-44. [5] *op. cit.*, p. 131. [6] *ibid.*, p. 146.

knowledge of Him save to those who believe the revelation to be genuine. It is doubtful whether it is logically possible for any form of objective revelation of itself to compel belief in it.[1] Romanes finds a good deal of objective prima facie evidence which might justify the act of faith in the Christian religion. The religious experience of Christians can to some extent be objectively estimated by reference to its quality, whilst a great deal has recently accrued to the Christian evidences by the findings of Biblical criticism: the genuineness of the chief Epistles of St. Paul and the first century origin of the Synoptic Gospels.[2] But it still remains that the only thing for a man to do is to "try the only experiment available—the experiment of faith". If Christianity be true, the verification will come, not indeed mediately through any course of speculative reason, but immediately by spiritual intuition. Only if a man has faith enough to make this venture honestly, will he be in a just position for deciding the issue.[3] The evidences of design in nature and in revelation are sufficient to arouse serious attention, but not to convince. Paley's writings afford an excellent illustration of the identity of the two kinds of teleology. But he makes the mistake of supposing that the appeal to reason is alone sufficient.[4]

Hutton and Romanes, then, were amongst those who carried on the approach laid down by Coleridge and Maurice. God's revealed truth must in an important sense be self-authenticating, for it is *sui generis* and cannot be proved by something that is less than itself. But revelation has come by the Word Incarnate, and its acceptance involves the belief in the occurrence of certain events in past time. The tide of historiography was running hard against belief in the unique significance of events, let alone the miraculous; so it was with brave perseverance that conservative apologists went on contending that a fully personal apprehension, together with moral presuppositions, was a legitimate and reasonable manner in which to approach the New Testament.

[1] *op. cit.*, p. 147.
[2] *ibid.*, pp. 155-57.
[3] *ibid.*, pp. 167-68.
[4] *ibid.*, pp. 178-80.

IV

But for the moment we must turn to a pair of opponents who moved in a very different sphere. Both men believed in a neat world of historical knowledge, where things are proved or disproved entirely by rational processes, in the old sense. One of them held that religious truth was completely separable from historic truths; the other held that religion stood or fell by historic demonstration.

To some, whose minds had been seized by the idea of the self-authentication of religious truth as a controlling doctrine, the theology of both Maurice and Mansel appeared to be hopelessly compromised by its connection with historical data. The advance of historical criticism made the Deist ideal of an independent, self-sufficient body of religious truth again attractive to many thinking men. In this spirit, Professor Baden Powell not only attacked the possibility of establishing that any event was miraculous, but attempted to draw away religious truth altogether from the sphere of historical controversy. "When," he says, "a reference is made to matters of external fact (insisted on as such) it is obvious that reason and intellect can alone be the proper judges of the evidence of such facts. When, on the other hand, the question may be as to points of moral or religious doctrine, it is equally clear, other and higher grounds of judgment and conviction must be appealed to."[1] Yet we continually find the professed advocates of an external revelation nevertheless making their appeal to conscience and feeling, and the professed upholders of faith and internal conviction regarding the external facts as not less essential truth. It was absolutely wrong to approach critical questions with the spirit of a "believing disposition"; as well might we decide the question of Caesar's landing in Britain by such means. By the introduction of such motives the evidentialists had, he believed, given away their own cherished position; whilst high church apologetics had done likewise—not only by the substitution of the appeal to ecclesiastical authority in place of the examination of Christian origins, but by the conjoining of the proof from miracles with that from the internal evidences.[2]

[1] *Essays and Reviews*, 5th ed., p. 97. [2] *op. cit.*, p. 122.

In the somewhat confused state of apologetics in the middle of the 19th century there was some ground for these strictures. Apologists had continued to shovel in new and diverse evidences for the truth of Christianity, often into the formal framework of evidentialism, failing to see that the older scheme had been dislodged in principle, and that words had changed their meaning. New insights regarding the personality of Christ, the significance of His redemptive work, and the mission of the Spirit, had been packed into the older scheme and styled "internal evidences". Hence the impression was created that the historic Gospel was being established on purely subjective judgments; whereas the new arguments largely turned upon the fuller understanding of the historic facts, and were meaningless without them.

Baden Powell put forward a radical solution for the problem of the relation of faith to history, which has had an immense influence in modern times: continental liberals, catholic modernists, English modernists and even some of the Barthians have all to some degree espoused it. He contemplated the evacuation by religion and theology of all territory, where the investigations of natural science might hold sway; and this, of course, included the study of history, as we see in his admission of the so-called scientific judgment against the miraculous. "We must recognize," he says, "both the due claims of science to decide on points properly belonging to the world of matter, and the independence of such considerations which characterizes the disclosure of spiritual truths, as such."[1] This solution—of abandoning nature to mechanical causation whilst retaining the conscious experience of man for the sphere of religion—was fraught with difficulties, as we shall see. Furthermore, Christianity is deeply concerned with history as the sphere of Divine activity; and it is not surprising, therefore, that the retirement into religious subjectivity, which *Essays and Reviews* seemed to many to characterize, should have produced that sharp reaction into evidentialism which we are now to consider.

[1] *op. cit.*, p. 127.

V

J. B. Mozley's Bampton Lectures of 1865 are most commonly cited for their refutation of the pretensions of the inductive philosophy; but for the historian of Christian thought, the chief interest of the work lies in its representation of the traditional scholastic view of the nature and function of miracles. This position is asserted with all the vigour and seeming logical cogency which often characterizes the revival of a position that has become archaic.

Miracles, says Mozley, are the necessary guarantees and vouchers of Divine revelation. Our reason cannot prove the truth of revelation, for it is by definition beyond our reason. There must be, then, some sign to distinguish it as a true communication from God, which can be nothing else than a miracle.[1] The evidential function of a miracle is based upon the argument of design, and consists in the coincidence of the miracle with the word of the messenger: the greatest prodigy standing by itself would prove nothing. This teleological aspect also acts as a bulwark against the possibility of the natural explanation of miracles: for even if the question were to be raised, whether Christ's Resurrection was referable to the laws of nature, the coincidence of this singular event with the bestowal of Christ's revelation would put the matter beyond any shadow of doubt.[2] If a person of evident integrity asserted that he had existed before his natural birth from all eternity in a state of glory with God; that he was the only-begotten son of God; and all he did was to make the assertions, the inevitable conclusion would be that he was disordered in his understanding. Miracles alone are the complement of the truth of such announcements.[3] Internal evidence cannot *ipso facto* prove what is beyond reason. The idea of an incarnation has approved itself to mankind, appearing in many religions; and the Christian doctrine appeals to every lofty aspiration of the human heart; but is this a proof that it has actually been enacted? The evidence of the fruits of Christianity in history is no substitute for the miracles of Christ.[4] The person whose present faith does not depend on miracles is not absolved from

[1] *Eight Lectures on Miracles,* 1895 ed., p. 5. [2] Pref. to 2nd ed., p. xvi.
[3] *op. cit.,* 1895 ed., pp. 10-11. [4] *ibid.,* pp. 11-14.

their proof, for the doctrines which he believes come from the very same witnesses as do the miracles: if the corpus of Christian tradition has been mistaken with regard to facts, how can we trust it with regard to doctrines?[1]

Although in respect of either the natural or the spiritual world, contends Mozley, a miracle is an anomaly, yet in respect of revelation it becomes part of the universe like any tool of art or husbandry, which by itself is an eccentric and unmeaning thing, but in exact order and place as the medium between the workman and his material; so miracle is in perfect order and place as the medium between two worlds.[2] Mozley is quite emphatic that religion must have a strictly rational basis. Thus the belief of the Mahomedan is in principle irrational, because he accepts the prophet's own assertion; whereas the Christian belief is at least rational in form.[3]

Mozley combines this position with a kind of radical empiricism. The difficulty of belief in miracles, he says, arises from their unlikeness to the order of nature. To define this order as "recurrence of physical events of which we have had experience" omits the main point; for the order which we assume in all our plans in life is not a past but a future. How do we justify our expectation that the future will resemble the past?[4] Our first impulse is to say that the expectation is self-evident. But "self-evident" means that of which the opposite is self-contradictory. Though the fact that the sun rose today would be contradicted by the fact that it did not rise today, it is in no way contradicted by the fact that it will not rise tomorrow. Nor do the repetitions of a natural fact show the existence of a permanent cause which will produce results over and above these particular effects. In fact, all professed reasons for the expectation of uniformity turn out to be merely restatements of the expectation itself. The ground is therefore gone upon which it could be maintained that miracles, as opposed to the order of nature, are irrational.[5]

The hazards attendant upon any modern attempt to con-

[1] *op. cit.*, p. 16. [2] *ibid.*, p. 18. [3] *ibid.*, p. 24. [4] *ibid.*, pp. 26-27.

[5] *ibid.*, pp. 35-38. Mozley's lectures began an Indian summer for evidentialism; e.g. J. J. Murphy, *Scientific Bases of Faith*, 1873; C. A. Row, *Supernatural in the New Testament*, 1875.

struct such a scheme of proof as Mozley's are illustrated by the appearance in 1884 of Walter Cassel's *Supernatural Religion.* This anonymous book caused some fluttering in the dove-cotes, because a tale went round that it had been written by a very eminent scholar. The work begins by adopting Mozley's conclusion that miracles alone could prove revelation, and then, by a lengthy examination of the early Patristic evidence for the origin of the New Testament books, alleges that the evidence for their reliability is wholly insufficient. J. B. Lightfoot, in a volume of essays on the work, exposed the shallowness of much of its scholarship; but *Supernatural Religion* has none the less reinforced the lesson that the basis of Christian certitude envisaged in the 18th century is incommensurate with modern needs.

In this chapter we have heard a babel of tongues, but certain positions were becoming clearer. If we were to go the whole way with J. McLeod Campbell[1] that revelation is light and therefore has the self-evidencing nature of light, there still remain vital alternatives. There was a tendency, inherited from scholasticism and the Illumination, and heightened by the revived interest in the philosophy of religion, towards identifying religious truth with "knowledge" in the philosophical sense. Baden Powell and Mozley both represent this tradition albeit in different contexts. At the beginning of the present century, H. M. Gwatkin noticed that many theologians were still troubled by the dilemma as to whether to present the truths of revelation as self-evident or beyond the reach of unaided human reason.[2] The 19th century saw a deep enrichment of the philosophy of religion, but the lesson still holds that belief in revelation is in jeopardy when this kind of knowledge is seen as something distinct from God's personal approach to man. Fortunately, there were those for whom the new religious insights led to a fresh apprehension of the significance of the acts of the Incarnate Christ. Mansel, Maurice and Hutton stand in this tradition; and in 1866 Westcott's *Gospel of the Resurrection* appeared, in which he expounded with really fresh vitality the meaning of the crowning historical event of the Incarnation.[3] There was thus being reasserted a view of

[1] *Thoughts on Revelation,* 1862, p. 12. [2] *Knowledge of God,* I, p. 31.
[3] Cf. also J. J. S. Perowne, *Immortality,* 1869, p. 97.

revelation consisting in two poles—the objective and subjective: in the words of F. W. Robertson, "Christ is the voice of God without the man—the Spirit is the voice of God within the man."[1]

[1] *Sermons Preached at Brighton*, First Series, No. 1, 1847.

Chapter Nine

THE RE-BUILDING OF APOLOGETICS

I

THE internal conflicts described in the foregoing chapter were some of the growing-pains of a new apologetic that was slowly but surely rising to replace evidentialism.

Too much is heard of those who waged unsuccessful warfare in the name of religion against the legitimate work of natural science, and too little of those who gladly accepted what they believed to be of genuine truth in the new scientific attitude to the universe. Frederick Temple accepted the theory of organic evolution, and turned it to good effect, claiming that Paley's argument about the watch gained in force by the new insight into nature.[1] A. B. Bruce, the important Scottish theologian, contended that the objectionable thing for theology was not the fact of evolution but the inferences which were drawn from it—that all the higher categories of nature were simply developed out of the lower by mechanical operation.[2] To confuse different categories, explaining the higher by the lower, is an abuse of scientific method.[3] The so-called Theistic philosophies of the 19th century, it was urged, were like Spinoza come to life again—for their common assumption was a mechanistic view of nature. Spinoza's argument was based upon the fallacy of beginning with a meaning of the term "nature" not very different from the scientific usage—a system of observed uniformities—and then assuming that the observed uniformities, or necessities as he would call them, belonged equally to nature in the sense of the whole of reality including God and man. But if nature be understood in the wider

[1] *The Relations between Religion and Science*, 1884, p. 112.
[2] *Miraculous Element in the Gospels*, 1886, p. 34.
[3] R. H. Hutton, *Essays Theological*, pp. 49-51.

sense, what right have we to say that miracles are contrary to it?[1]

Apologists like Bruce had no illusions about the immanental philosophies of Theodore Parker, F. W. Newman, Fiske and Martineau. As they are not grounded in a doctrine of Divine transcendence, the world is not only God's dwelling place but His prison.[2] These systems were an object-lesson in the consequences of denying the supernatural: their final conclusion could only be the destruction of personal religion. They denied the freedom of the Divine personality, and the same arguments from the analogy of physical process would equally reduce the free and responsible nature of man to the status of an automaton. Further, the Theistic systems, like Deism, suffered from a defective appreciation of the human situation. In their assumption that this is on its way to becoming the best possible of worlds, they overlooked the profound disequilibrium of man, in his inner self and in his relations with God. Sinful man cries out for a way of escape from the deadlock in which he finds himself, and the Divine answer must seemingly be of a supernatural character. Intervention would only imply imperfection in God's work on the crude theory of nature as the work of an artificer, not on the Christian view of man as responsible personality.[3]

II

In the third quarter of the century, the leading apologists showed a clear understanding of the abstract character of scientific generalization and of the partiality of its approach to reality. Hutton, arguing that the scientific view of the universe presents a spectacle of "incredible incoherence" without the Theistic nexus, points to the abstract character of the world as described by science. It is like dry colours scraped off a picture, which has indeed been etched out of actual existence, but which no power could ever constitute into it again.[4]

[1] J. H. Bernard, art. "Miracle", Hastings, *D.B.* III, 380-81. He cites Augustine, *De Civ. Dei*, XXI, 8.

[2] *Miraculous Element*, p. 20.

[3] *H.D.B.* III, p. 381; cf. H. Bushnell, *Nature and the Supernatural*, chs. VI, VII, VIII.

[4] *Essays Theological*, p. 46.

A law of nature, observes Westcott, can mean nothing else than the law of the human apprehension of phenomena. We are forced to regard things under conditions of time and space, and the consequence is that phenomena are grouped together according to certain rules.[1] The antecedent likelihood of a miracle proceeds from a comprehensive view of all nature, moral and physical. But the necessary condition of all scientific enquiry is to put out of sight the indeterminate element in nature, and thus to unfamiliarize the mind with those aspects of the world in which the miracle finds its proper place.[2] In rebutting Baden Powell, Westcott argues that to affirm that miracles are unnatural is to constitute general laws of observation into a fate superior to God, and the denial of His personal action in the physical world involves the denial of His action on the hearts of men.[3] Frederick Temple, answering the same opponent, maintains that the so-called principles of physics are indispensable postulates, not indeed of observing with the senses, but of comprehending with the understanding whatever happens. But it does not follow that events cannot happen, or affect our senses, without being susceptible of such explanation. It is not the case that there is a science of abstract physics corresponding to the science of mathematics and sharing in the same character of necessity.[4]

It was very difficult at this time for theologians to win recognition for this analysis. Even the study of history was drawing into the family circle of the natural sciences. Apologists were obliged to concentrate upon the one unassailable bulwark of the spiritual view of the universe, the transcendental element in human personality, man's experience of volition and all that goes with it. To reduce history, it was argued, to processes of causal reactions of a mechanical kind acquired verisimilitude only by putting history through a sieve of a certain mesh, which did not register the activity and experience of human wills. However inconceivable in theory, says Mozley, it is a fact that physical laws are suspended whenever an animate being moves part of its body.[5] The autonomy and responsibility of human personality is never doubted in practice. Nature never made a gun, nor pulled the trigger—the murderer alone is

[1] *Gospel of the Resurrection*, 3rd ed., p. 25. [2] *op. cit.*, p. 46.
[3] *ibid.*, pp. 28, 38. [4] *op. cit.*, p. 17. [5] *Bampton Lectures*, p. 129.

hanged.[1] Admittedly, the analogy between human volitions and miracles is not complete. Human free will does not violate the idea of law, says Bernard, for it represents a continuity of physical sequence: but it does force us to recognize that there is an intrusion of spirit into the physical order.[2]

III

Human freedom, our most apt analogy for the miraculous, is exercised within the structure of the physical universe: laws of matter and motion are overlaid by what, in the theological language of the time, was called a "higher law of human freedom". It was an easy step from this to the plea, first, that miracle itself is "natural", since it represents the highest of the spiritual forces at work in the world; secondly, that miracle is worked according to "law", the rational and moral law governing God's action; and thirdly, that miracle does not infringe the concept of cause and effect, since it is but the proper result of God's direct action. In the 18th century, when the prevailing idea of God's relation to the world was Deistical, it had not seemed wrong to speak of miracle as a "violation" or "abrogation" of the laws of nature. In the 19th century, however, there was an increasing appreciation of the intricate harmony of the natural order, a growing conviction of the immanence of God, and a sense that the orderliness of nature reflects the mind and purpose of God. Under these changed circumstances, it was incumbent upon apologists to seek for a mode of representing the miraculous facts of Christian belief in a way which might preserve the essence of the supernatural initiative and yet bring them into an intelligible relation with the rest of God's activity in the universe.

We shall be repeating constantly the terms "nature", "law" and "cause". It has not always been sufficiently realized that in each case there is a distinctively theological and a scientific usage. In theology, the nature of a thing is the function or end for which God has created it, and hence derivatively it denotes the form and attributes of the thing. The most that the term can mean to science is, a system of observed uniformities.

[1] Bushnell, *op. cit.*, p. 23. Cf. Temple, *op. cit.*, Lc. III.
[2] *H.D.B.* III, p. 380. Cf. Bruce, *Miraculous Element*, p. 67.

Similarly, the theological concept of a law of nature, whether it be thought of as imposed or immanent, is teleological in character, and covers a different range of ideas from that of "observed regularity". Finally, the various theological ideas of causation include far more than the bare notion of "invariable antecedents". It is perhaps to be regretted that science has preserved these terms from another world of thought, using them in a purely metaphorical sense. Criticism, perhaps rightly, has been directed against the apparent confusion by some apologists of the philosophical and scientific usages of these terms; but it ought to be appreciated that the theologian has a perfect right to the terms in the non-scientific sense for his own purposes.

Archbishop Trench represents the best theological feeling of his generation in his disowning of the charge that miracle is "unnatural". A miracle, he says, is to be regarded as an example of a lower law being put out of action by a higher. We find such a superseding of law throughout nature: "mechanic by dynamic, chemical by vital, physical by moral; yet we say not, when the lower thus gives place in favour of the higher, that there was any violation of law, or that anything contrary to nature came to pass; rather we acknowledge the law of a greater freedom swallowing up the law of a lesser."[1] A miracle is simply analogous to a man lifting up his arm, against the law of gravity. "The distinction indeed," says Trench, "which is sometimes made, that in the miracle God is immediately working, and in other events is leaving it to the laws which He has established to work, cannot be at all admitted: for it has its roots in a dead mechanical view of the universe, altogether remote from the truth."[2] This conception of continuous creativity was to receive strong confirmation in more recent philosophy—the very idea which Baden Powell poured scorn upon in the name of the scientific thought of his day. This idea of the immediate action of God throughout nature is certainly that of the Bible, even though the Aristotelian distinction of causation has its philosophical uses. Miracle in itself, says Trench, though not a greater, is a different manifestation of God. In the miracle, the

[1] *Notes on the Miracles of Our Lord*, 1862; 7th ed., p. 17. Cf. Westcott, *Gospel of the Resurrection*, p. 30.

[2] *op. cit.*, p. 11.

power which works in nature steps out from its concealment. At the same time there is in miracle an extraordinary Divine causality, and the introduction of powers of God other than those which have always been working.[1]

Some attempts were made to go beyond the position represented by Trench. The best known of these was Charles Babbage's *The Ninth Bridgewater Treatise*, 1837. This volume was not one of those commissioned by the Duke of Bridgewater, but bears its title on account of its author's desire to supplement the eight treatises! Butler had suggested that if we had all the requisite knowledge even the Incarnation might appear "natural". But Babbage had an analogy to hand which fired his imagination to rationalize this idea. He had been commissioned by the government to superintend the construction of a calculating machine; and from the contemplation of his own ingenuity, he conceived the idea that for God to have foreseen the necessity for miracles, and so to have arranged the mechanism of nature that at the required moments such and such would occur, "assigns a far higher degree of power and knowledge to the Deity" than could have been exhibited by sporadic interventions in nature.[2] As an eirenicon with science, Babbage's simile of the calculating machine which can meet strange eventualities is a failure, for unless miracles are to be regarded as periodically recurring phenomena the hypothesis serves no useful purpose. On its theological side too it has received severe treatment. It has been urged that the theory does not even fit the miracles that it is meant to rationalize. Most of the Gospel miracles are represented as having been worked by Christ in response to personal faith in Himself; they do not at all resemble a set of anomalies cropping up in nature. It has also been said that the simile proves too much; it saves miracles at the cost of their miraculousness—an atheist could believe in them on Babbage's hypothesis.[3] Finally, the simile is repugnant to all those who are influenced by the belief in Divine immanence.[4]

[1] *op. cit.*, p. 13. [2] *op. cit.*, p. 94. [3] Bruce, *Miraculous Element*, p. 51.
[4] Bernard, *H.D.B.* III, p. 381. Mozley, *Bampton Lectures*, pp. 127-28.

IV

Bushnell's *Nature and the Supernatural*, 1858, is the most characteristic work of the newer apologetic. In its attitude to miracles it stands in the line of Trench and the (later) *Lux Mundi* school. Its thesis is the fact of the spiritual hierarchy in the universe. The scientific verdict on reality is insufficient, for the real system of God, he says, consists of two parts: nature, and a higher and more inclusive system, the supernatural; and it is no more incredible that the one should act upon the other than that one planet or particle in the department of nature should act upon another.[1] The supernatural is erected by God upon nature, ruled and marshalled under its own laws, and able continually to vary the processes of nature. Indeed, the spiritual realm is much more of a system than the natural order, for it is closer to God, and contains within itself the ends for which the other exists. Characteristic of the supernatural realm is free, responsible personality: nature is but the platform on which God has established His kingdom of minds or persons, every one of whom has power to act upon nature.[2] The disorder brought into creation by evil, he urges, both proves the incompleteness of nature as a self-sufficient and self-explanatory order, and also provides the justification for the peculiar supernatural intervention of God. Christianity, as a supernatural intervention, works to repair what the laws of nature would penally bring about if left to themselves.[3] Nevertheless, Bushnell does not go very far in helping us to see how the actual miracles of the New Testament effect the work of recreation.

We know, he says, that moral laws and purposes become immutable to a man in proportion to his sincerity. Hence all God's supernatural acts will be dispensed by immutable, universal laws. Because God's ends never vary, a supernatural event, never known to occur but once, takes place under an immutable and really universal law.[4] It must be obvious that Bushnell no more than Babbage presents a rationale of the miraculous which can make contact with the categories of natural science. His characteristic expression, "the law of the end",[5] is unequivocally teleological. Although he conceives the

[1] *op. cit.*, p. 7. [2] *ibid.*, p. 34. [3] *ibid.*, p. 22.
[4] *ibid.*, pp. 173, 183, 185. [5] *ibid.*, p. 352.

higher strata of existence as a "system", he does not, like Henry Drummond in his *Natural Law in the Spiritual World*, think of the supernatural as a realm characterized by a system of imposed or inherent necessities. On the contrary, Bushnell speaks of the supernatural as a realm in which the law of cause and effect does not apply. In this curious language he clearly intends us to regard the supernatural as characterized by personal freedom. But the book makes a good beginning towards the consideration of miracles from the standpoint of personality and the work of redemption.[1]

V

Frederick Temple's treatment of miracles in relation to the reign of law stands somewhat apart from the attitude of the writers considered above. The ideas which he advanced had been familiar on the continent since Schleiermacher, but Temple was one of the first in England to perceive the long-term effects which science was to bring about in the concept of the miraculous. His statement of the relation of scientific thought to the miraculous is as decisive as that of Tennant forty years later. He writes: "If a miracle were worked science could not prove that it was a miracle, nor of course prove that it was not a miracle." To prove it to be a miracle would require, not a vast range of knowledge, but absolutely universal knowledge. To assert an event to be a miracle means we cannot explain the event otherwise than by reference to a will like our own.[2] In fact, he claims, the question of miracles is precisely parallel to the controversy regarding human free will. It is necessary to assert the miraculous in order to vindicate the absolute supremacy of the moral law over the physical—the miracle being a breach of natural uniformity, such as every man's conscience claims for the autonomy of his own conduct.[3] Moreover, just as moral law is often kept unbroken, despite

[1] Cf. Bruce's criticisms, *Miraculous Element*, p. 59. A number of other works carried on the type of theses propounded by Babbage and Bushnell: the Duke of Argyll's *The Reign of Law*, 1866; G. H. Curteis' *Scientific obstacles to Christian Belief*, 1885, and W. Arthur's *On the Difference between Physical and Moral Laws*, 1883. These works contain much that is suggestive, but add little to the apologetic value of miracles, nor to the understanding of their doctrinal significance.

[2] *The Relations between Religion and Science*, pp. 30-31.

[3] *op. cit.*, pp. 193-94.

our personal freedom—i.e. given certain conduct there will follow certain consequences—so it is possible that "the intervention which has apparently disturbed the sequence of phenomena is, after all, that of a higher physical law as yet unknown."[1]

There is no ambiguity here: Temple does mean physical law as yet undiscovered. He instances faith-healing, the immense power of mind over body, as yet scarcely understood but none the less probably falling within the domain of science. Revelation, he says, is not bound by the scientific definition of miracles: for if all the Biblical miracles happened exactly as they are told, and if science were some day able to show that they could be accounted for by natural causes, this would not in any way affect their character, as regards the revelation which they were worked to prove or of which they form a part.[2] Theologians in the 19th century were not unnaturally slow to realize the implications of scientific theory: Temple's lectures mark a definite point of advance. To many it seemed that the evidential value of the miracles was given away even by the speculative hypotheses about "higher laws".[3] But by degrees it came to be realized that apologetics must be adapted to the possibility that natural causes were associated with the miracles. Bruce holds that if natural explanations could be postulated for Our Lord's miracles of healing, it would militate against the evidential use of them, but the cures themselves would still remain integral to revelation, as illustrating the compassion of the Son of Man.[4] This is a foretaste of things to come. Several English apologists have looked with favour upon Rothe's hypothesis. According to this treatment, miracles are divided into "absolute" and "relative". In the absolute miracles, such as the feeding of the multitude, there is no conflict with the order of nature: a new thing is simply added, which from the instant of its creation obeys the laws of nature. In the case of relative miracles, such as the drying of the Red Sea, God providentially disposes materials and forces already in the world.[5]

[1] *ibid.*, p. 195. [2] *ibid.*, p. 195.
[3] Mozley, *Bampton Lectures*, 1895 ed., pp. 115f.
[4] *Miraculous Element*, p. 54.
[5] Bruce, *Miraculous Element*, p. 60; Lonsdale Ragg, *Evidences of Christianity*, 1905, p. 44. For all we know, this may be a perfectly true analysis of the ways in which God operates upon the world; but to argue that the creative miracles are not interruptions of the pattern of nature looks like a sophism.

A modern author or playwright may describe events which did not or could not happen. But, if he is to catch men's imagination, there is a certain kind of conformity with human experience to which he must adhere. The problem facing the Christian apologist is not wholly dissimilar from this. Granted that the Gospels contain events outside the pattern of ordinary human experience, how could they be made to appear congruous and acceptable? The mid-Victorian apologists developed two kinds of approach.

First, it was argued that miracles were analogous to the acts of human volition. Though some of the outlying hypotheses were quickly discarded, the main position was well constructed. The appearance in the universe of responsible human personality indicates a hierarchy of being, and points to a teleological view of the world process as a whole. Personality, in so far as its moral character is realized, is not characterized by caprice but by consistent obedience to the laws of moral demand. Thus, in the combination of freedom over the physical realm and obedience to a higher moral law, which characterize human life at its best, we have an analogy in microcosm for the supernatural activity of God in the world. Secondly, attention was focused upon the character and significance of Christ's miracles: their moral ends, their part in His redemptive work, their demonstration of the nature of the Incarnate person, and their prophetic symbolizing of the work of Christ in His church. We shall be concerned with this approach in the remainder of this and in the following chapter. On one thing these apologists were clear—the fact that revelation consists in a unique cycle of historical events does not mean that they can be presented simply in their stark differentiation from the rest of human experience. These events must be related to the rest of man's moral and spiritual experience, and an outlook on life must be fostered which will enable man to recognize and to surrender to God's revelation in Christ. Some neo-protestants, in their rejection of natural religion, are impatient with all this; but the Victorian apologists had a wider and wiser view.

VI

When we turn from theoretical arguments to our apologists' presentation of the evidence for the Gospel miracles, the first thing which strikes the modern reader is the comparative innocence with which questions of historical criticism are handled. The leading continental critics of the time are simply treated as members of the enemy camp, along with Spinoza, Woolston and Hume. Little was it dreamed that some of the principles which these critics brought to the study of the Gospels, albeit crookedly, were destined to play a part in constructive apologetics. On Schleiermacher's theory of "relative miracles", either Our Lord can no longer be regarded as one who commands nature in a way different from other men,[1] or He was like a European disingenuously frightening natives by predicting an eclipse.[2] Paulus had argued that most of the Gospel miracles could be explained as this misunderstanding or misrepresentation of natural events. This explanation breaks down because it is too far-fetched, says Bruce.[3] What he fails to recognize is that the explanation which breaks down as a basis of reconstruction for the whole Gospel narrative may none the less be plausible in the case of certain particular miracles. But Strauss was the real *bête noire*, for George Eliot's translation of his first *Life of Jesus* had reached a large public in this country.

The point generally urged is that, for the process of myth-forming to have taken place, a very late date must be assigned to the Gospels. But not only was the interval between the Ascension and the earliest canonical writings insufficient for a human Jesus to have been transformed into a supernatural Christ; within the period in which the New Testament itself was written, between 1 Corinthians and the Fourth Gospel, we do not in fact find the supernatural interpretation of Christ growing.[4] There was one period in the 19th century when all too little attention was given to the external relations of the New Testament, the authorship, date and place of composition,

[1] Trench, *op. cit.*, 7th ed., p. 74.

[2] Heurtley, *Replies to "Essays and Reviews"*, p. 165.

[3] *op. cit.*, p. 86.

[4] Bruce, *ibid.*, p. 91. Cf. Bernard, *H.D.B.* III, p. 392; Bushnell, *op. cit.*, p. 233; Principal Tulloch, *Lectures on M. Renan's "Vie de Jésus"*; Liddon's Bampton Lectures also contain many detailed criticisms.

and the occasion of these writings in the life of the early church. Paley had made an outstanding attempt to illustrate the combined witness of Acts and Epistles in his *Horae Paulinae*; but we have to wait until we come to Lightfoot, Westcott and Hort to see this vital department of apologetics tackled with adequate capability.

In the second half of the 19th century the Old Testament miracles were rapidly becoming an embarrassment to apologists. Trench had been cautiously conservative about these miracles. He is anxious to show that the Old Testament is no mere epic of fabulous stories; its miraculous element is kept within strict bounds. Many of the plagues of Egypt were the natural plagues of the land. Nor are the reports of miracles scattered abroad like the ecclesiastical miracles: they appear at specific junctures. There is a notable absence of wonder-making too; Abraham, David and Daniel have no miracles ascribed to them.[1] Bernard represents the troubled attitude of a conservative scholar after the controversies of the eighteen-nineties concerning higher criticism. He cannot feel the same confidence about the miracles of the Old Testament as about those of the New. They are contained in ancient books whose origin is often uncertain.[2] But since the Old Testament is a preparation for Christ, it ceases to be *a priori* improbable that, at exceptional crises in the history of the Hebrews, special manifestations of Divine power might be vouchsafed. The Old Testament miracles stand out chiefly as tokens of God's providence, and none of the Exodus miracles need have involved a breach of the natural order. Prophecy is another characteristic of Old Testament miracles, by which men were led to see the finger of God in these events. Some miracles, such as those of Elijah and Elisha, are not on a high moral level; whilst others, such as the sun standing still at Beth-horon, are poetical.[3]

VII

When we look at the treatment of the Gospel miracles, we find that a profound change is taking place. For a series of events, once regarded as the central proof of Christianity, to

[1] *Notes*, 7th ed., pp. 14, 47. [2] *H.D.B.* III, p. 392.
[3] *H.D.B.* III, pp. 392-93.

have become matter requiring justification was indeed a serious turn of events. Many Christians have come to believe that the seeming loss is no loss at all, but a shifting of attention to wider and more appropriate grounds of certitude. Be it so, none can doubt the gravity of the revolution that was taking place. The apologists with whom we have been concerned in this chapter did not regard the miracles as an embarrassment to the establishment of the general historicity of the Gospels. What we do find is that they are obliged to treat the miracles as part of the whole story of Christ, the truth of which they are endeavouring to sustain.

Bushnell is frankly antagonistic towards the new historical criticism, yet he grants that the times have changed since the days when miracles could be used, not only to prove the truth of doctrine, but even the truth of the Gospel history itself: now they are a heavy burden on its credibility.[1] He therefore concentrates upon the unique personality of Christ as portrayed in the Gospels. Since Christ is superhuman, nature will have a special relation to Him. The difference between the effects produced by Christ upon nature and those produced by ordinary men may be likened to the different results achieved by a man and an animal on the keyboard of an organ.[2]

The mid-Victorian apologists introduce us to a familiar modern argument. It is urged that to expurgate the miracle stories from the New Testament documents renders it impossible to reconstruct a consistent, intelligent historical picture of the life of Christ. The four Evangelists, says Liddon, concur in representing a Christ whose life is encased in a setting of miracles. The Christ of dogma is the Christ of history: He is the Christ of the only extant history which describes the founder of Christendom at all. As the Gospel narratives stand, they present a block of difficulties to humanitarian theories; and these difficulties can only be removed by mutilations of the narratives so wholesale as to destroy their substantial interest, besides rendering the retention of the fragments a purely arbitrary procedure.[3]

One characteristic of the Gospel miracles begins to be alluded

[1] *op. cit.*, pp. 191, 232. [2] *ibid.*, pp. 196, 245.
[3] *Bampton Lectures*, pp. 159-61. Cf. Lyttelton, *The Place of Miracles*, p. 44.

to at this time. The miracles of Jesus appear to have been conditioned in some way by human faith, and they are represented as having been wrought at great personal effort to Our Lord—not wrought simply in the fullness of Divine power. Hence these narratives stand in a class by themselves.[1] Thus also Bruce believed that it was possible to evince the Apostolic origin of the Gospels on a "moral" criticism, which he places above the purely historico-critical questions in importance.[2] Nevertheless, he is one of the earliest conservative apologists to seek to establish the historical character of the Gospel miracles with something approaching critical technique. The history of criticism, he says, is instructive: whenever the miraculous is not involved, little doubt is expressed regarding the Apostolic testimony to it.[3] Yet the miracles wrought on the sabbath must be received as is the story of the cornfields, Mark 2: 23f., since, as critics recognize, no one would have dreamed of inventing the latter.[4]

The growing prominence of the Synoptic Problem led Bruce to attempt to discover the probable place of miracles in the primary source. The hypothesis that the "Logia", ascribed by Papias to St. Matthew, underlay the Synoptic tradition might suggest that the original Gospel was only a collection of Christ's sayings. But, contends Bruce, the work may well have been a collection of Christ's sayings presented in their context; in which case it almost certainly contained miracle stories which are bound up with so many of the sayings, e.g. those on faith and on the sabbath.[5] He gives a careful analysis of the way in which the different types of miracles are corroborated in each of the Synoptic Gospels. He does not, however, consider to what extent the first and third Gospels really represent independent corroboration of the Marcan material. But he allows that individual miracles may be considered doubtful on account of the seeming lack of attestation. How, for instance, did the Johannine story of the raising of Lazarus come to be omitted from the Synoptic tradition if it really took place?[6] The general summaries of miracles in the Synoptic Gospels show that the Evangelists did not invent miracles to fill out their narrative;

[1] Westcott, *Characteristics of the Gospel Miracles*, p. 45. Bernard, *H.D.B.* III, p. 389.
[2] *Miraculous Element*, pp. 110f.
[3] *op. cit.*, p. 84. Cf. Liddon, *Easter Sermons*, I, p. 78; E. H. Perowne, *The Godhead of Jesus*, 1866, p. 11.
[4] Bruce, *op. cit.*, p. 119. [5] Bruce, *ibid.*, pp. 103f. [6] *ibid.*, p. 131.

indeed, a number of the miracle stories have survived simply because of some special word spoken by Jesus on the occasion. Strauss had argued that we could trace a steady increase in the miraculous element from St. Matthew through St. Luke to St. Mark. Bruce invokes the priority of St. Mark to show the hollowness of this assertion.[1] The older harmonizing methods had given the impression of special pleading; the discrepancies are due, he says, to simple men combining their sources without modern literary skill; in other words, the discrepancies show the good faith of the Evangelists and the variety of the testimony which is offered for the miracles.[2]

[1] *ibid.*, pp. 131-35. [2] *ibid.*, p. 137.

Chapter Ten

THE RE-INTERPRETATION OF MIRACLES

I

If the purpose of the Biblical miracles was not after all to provide independent proofs of revelation, it was natural for search to be made as to whether their real significance had not heretofore been overlooked. Miracles are a prominent and integral part of the story of Jesus as it has come down to us, and they must therefore have been in the forefront of the church's first proclamation of the Gospel. Many of the most active Christian minds in the 19th century found their answer in the idea, well known to the Fathers, that the miracles of Christ were actually vehicles of His revelation, and prototypes of the characteristics of the church. Wesley, as we saw, retorted to the enemies of "enthusiasm" that the New Testament miracles give a positive presumption that there will be spiritual wonders in the church's life. The reinterpretation of miracles was made possible by the great development that had taken place already in the idea of revelation. In the Illumination theology, the relations of God and man were primarily thought of forensically, and revelation was summarized as a republication of the religion of nature. But now the dominant interests were soteriology, the Incarnation, and the dispensation of grace. In the new atmosphere, it was not difficult for the miracles to be thought of as acts which exhibited and accomplished sacramentally the Saviour's lordship over nature and over the powers of evil within and around man.

Archbishop Trench devotes the greatei part of his work on miracles to the exegesis of their religious significance. He examines first the principal terms by which the supernatural acts of Christ are described in the New Testament; a procedure obvious enough to the modern student, but a welcome novelty in Trench's day. The term *teras*, "wonder", touches only the outside of the matter: the ethical meaning of the miracle would be wholly lost were blank astonishment all that it aroused.[1] But it is profoundly characteristic of the New Testament that *teras* and its association is never used except in conjunction with some other term—*semeion* or *dunamis*. The synonym *thauma*, though common in the Fathers, never appears in Scripture, whilst *thaumasion* appears only once, Matt. 21: 15. The term *paradoxon*, also common in the Fathers, appears only in Luke 5: 26. The Gospel writers almost go out of their way not to stress the thaumaturgic element in the miracles, and it is unfortunate that the two common words in our own speech, "wonder" and "miracle", bring out only the superficial meaning. The word *semeion*, "sign", is meant to indicate more clearly the purpose of the miracle. The rendering of this word in English (in the A.V.) by "miracle" was unfortunate, and in John 6: 26 it made nonsense of the passage. The miracles were a manifestation of God's will to restore nature's true ends. So we see Our Lord "walking on the stormy waves, or quelling the menace of the sea with His word; incorporating in these acts the deliverance of man from the rebellious powers of nature, which had risen up against Him." Similarly, on the multiplying of the loaves: "The original curse of sin was the curse of barrenness . . . but here this curse is removed, and in its stead, the primeval abundance for a moment reappears."[2]

Trench vigorously criticizes the attitude of most evidentialist writers to the miracles: their aspect of power had been stressed to the almost total exclusion of their ethical significance.[3] Apologetics since Grotius had partaken in the general depression of the times: it had been thought that Deism was best refuted by reducing Christianity to a sort of "revealed Deism"; and large areas of truth, relating to the redemptive work of Christ and the spiritual life of believers, were cast away.[4] Miracles had been rent away from the person and revelation of Christ—like seals torn off a document they once rendered valid—and had been given an exaggerated position in an attempt to produce objective demonstration of revelation. Miracles, he says, belong to the very idea of a redeemer; and

[1] *Notes*, 7th ed., p. 2.
[2] *ibid.*, p. 33.
[3] *ibid.*, p. 33.
[4] *ibid.*, pp. 90f.

the fact that they are now seen in a wider context does not mean arguing in a circle, but receiving the total impression which revelation is calculated to make upon us.

As we have seen, F. D. Maurice was brought face to face with the issue of miracles in his violent reaction to Mansel. He saw the miracles as the manifestation of Christ's glory—"unveilings or manifestations to the whole man, of the nature, character, mind, of the Son of Man; and therefore, . . . of the nature, character, mind, of the Father who sent Him."[1] He accepts the belief in demon possession, and therefore regards the exorcisms of Christ as manifestations of His warfare against evil.[2] It was the worst superstition which connected evil with the will of God or with the man himself. Christ separated the man from the evil which possessed him. In his *Discourses on the Gospel of St. John*, 1857, Maurice amply illustrated his thesis. This Evangelist employs the term "sign" for the miracles of Christ: of what were they the signs? In the story of Cana there is nothing that we usually associate with the idea of miracle; no effort to produce a sensation, nor was the act done to produce conviction. But Christ "manifested forth his glory"—He proclaimed the universe to be His own realm, and blessed the marriage as a fundamental part of this order.[3] In the cure of the nobleman's son, Jesus blessed the relationship of father and son; whilst the restoring of sight to the blind man represents Christ's bringing light which enters into men and condemns them. We even feel that it is not a violation of nature for Him to raise the dead, for He teaches that nature is not men's master.[4]

II

No one laboured so ardently to establish the reinterpreted view of miracles as Westcott. "The miracles," he tells us, "are all faint reflections of the glory of the Incarnation. That is the miracle of miracles to which all others point."[5] They are in reality a treasure, rather than a bulwark, of the faith. In meaning, as well as in time, they lie between the Incarnation

[1] *What is Revelation?*, p. 57. [2] *op. cit.*, pp. 73f.
[3] *op. cit.*, pp. 63-64. [4] *ibid.*, pp. 140, 273, 176.
[5] *Characteristics of the Gospel Miracles*, 1859, p. 3.

and the Ascension: they look back to the coming of God to man, and forward to the bringing of man to God. They become an evidence of his faith to a Christian who understands them rightly.[1] We shall meet this argument again. It attempts to bring the persuasion of miracles into an intelligible relationship with the living faith of the believer.

A more cautious approval must be accorded to the further step of attempting to probe the significance of each particular miracle. Although the acts of Christ are symbolic both in what they teach and in what they accomplished, we must beware when we approach the gateway to the wonderland of allegory through which writers with less caution than Westcott plunged. Here are some instances of Westcott's own interpretations. The creative nature miracles he designates as follows: The turning of water into wine—"Christ the source of Joy"; The feeding of the multitudes—"Christ the source of sustenance"; The walking on the sea—"Christ the source of strength".[2] The "miracles of providence" are thus interpreted: The first miraculous draught of fish—"The formation of the outward church"; The stilling of the storm—"The defence of the church from without"; The coin in the fish's mouth—"The support of the church from within"; The second draught of fish—"The church of the future".[3] Thus, "We see the perils, nay even the schisms, of the outward Church, imaged in sinking ships, and breaking nets."[4] The cures throw light upon the Incarnation itself, and the power of Christ in the church, and they prefigure the different modes by which men are brought into union with God. We find three classes of cures: those brought about by the faith of the sufferer, those by the mediation of friends, and those by the spontaneous mercy of Christ; from which we have lessons in faith, intercession and love. The Gospel without miracles would be like a church without sacraments.

In another work, Westcott applies the same principles of interpretation to the appearances of Christ after the Resurrection. The various appearances each show something of the way in which Christ's presence is offered and realized. The Gospels supplement one another in their descriptions of the risen Christ.

[1] *op. cit.*, p. 7.
[2] *ibid.*, p. 10.
[3] *ibid.*, pp. 20-21.
[4] *ibid.*, p. 23.

St. Luke shows the signs of His abiding humanity; St. John, the signs of His majesty. In this composite witness we have the assurance of Christ's personal Resurrection, that He was wholly changed yet wholly the same.[1] The bodily Resurrection is the miracle essential to the creation of faith in His abiding Divine-human personality. In the Ascension, the physical elevation was a parable, the change involved being primarily one of state: but "from the necessities of our human condition, the spiritual change was represented sacramentally, so to speak, in an outward form."[2] This view—that the bodily Resurrection and Ascension took place for man's sake—is integral to the reinterpreted view of miracle.

As the 19th century proceeded, a picture was gradually assuming shape in the minds of many educated Europeans: that of the non-miraculous "Jesus of history". It was thus necessary for orthodoxy to reassert both sides of its own equation: the religion of grace, and the supernatural Christ. He who had performed such acts as are recorded of Him could alone work the moral miracle of regeneration. It is against this background that A. B. Bruce set the reinterpreted view of miracles. Like that of many men of his generation, his theological outlook was an interesting mixture of old and new. He accepted many of the principles of higher criticism, and expounded a kenotic Christology far in advance of his time; yet of miracles he could speak in 1881 as if the debate with evidentialism was still a living issue.[3] Bruce believed it to be an imperative task for the apologist to make the relation between revelation and the miraculous "more intimate and vital".[4] His position is that God has revealed Himself in history, not merely by words, but by deeds; and that among these acts, the miracles of Christ are of the essence of a revelation which is a dispensation of grace.[5] Granted that miracles are not very consequential to a revelation which is merely a didactic instrument of righteousness, as Matthew Arnold conceived Christianity to be, the case is very different with a revelation of grace made by acts rather than by words.[6] Miracles are the heart and essence of revelation. Not that grace cannot be manifested

[1] *The Revelation of the Risen Lord*, 1881, p. 68. [2] *ibid.*, p. 180.
[3] *Chief End of Revelation*, p. 166. [4] *op. cit.*, p. 164.
[5] Cf. Matt. 11: 5. *ibid.*, p. 169. [6] *ibid.*, p. 175.

without them, for it is so manifested in the moral order: but the maximum of gracious possibility cannot be manifested without miracles.[1]

All these writers so far considered had before them the labour of clearing away the vast earthworks of exegesis with which the theologians of previous generations had surrounded the Gospel history. It required courage to pull down the edifice of apologetics which had become so venerable, and to create new habits of thought. It is not surprising to find at this stage different approaches to the reinterpretation. There was a genuine attempt to go back to the New Testament to find out what the miracle stories meant to those who told them, to understand their significance in relation to Christ's person and work, and to appreciate how the symbolism of the miracles fits into the thought-patterns of the Judaeo-Christian world. This method has gone on bearing fruit down to our own day. Side by side with this development there runs, as though by a shorter cut, a purely theological exegesis of the Gospel stories. There is in this respect a considerable difference in depth between the various interpretations that are offered.

In the first place, the miracles of Christ were described as acted parables. As the Hebrew prophets performed symbolic acts foretelling the judgments of God, so Christ performed supernatural signs betokening the various aspects of His redemptive work. At one time this view was held by some scholars along with evidentialism, e.g. by Whately.[2] It is to be regretted that the parabolic method of interpretation should have gone to earth in a warren of Victorian homiletics.[3] It is perfectly reasonable to hold that the miracle of Cana is intended to symbolize the supersession of the Law by grace, that the feedings of the multitudes are recorded as types of the Eucharist, and that the healings are outward signs of the regeneration brought about by Christ. But the allegorization of the details of the miracle stories indulged in during the 19th century is open to the same kind of objection as the similar treatment of the

[1] A. T. Lyttelton, of the *Lux Mundi* school, carried the reinterpretation of miracles on into the Apostolic age. *The Place of Miracles in Religion*, 1899.

[2] *Sermons*, 1835, p. 228.

[3] Trench's *Notes*, F. W. Farrar's very popular *Life of Christ*, 1874, J. Laidlaw's *Miracles of Our Lord*, 1890 and W. M. Taylor's *Miracles of Our Saviour*, 1891, all contain a wealth of material illustrating this homiletical method.

parables. Just as we have come to think of the parables, not as a web of allegory, but as each containing a central point of Christ's teaching with a minimum of explanatory symbolism, so in the case of the miracle stories the allegorization should be rigorously pruned, in order that the central meaning may be allowed to speak for itself. One would suggest also that preaching and devotional writing would gain in realism if the same discipline in exegesis were applied to them as is demanded in theological research.

Nevertheless, some very useful comparisons were drawn between the physical miracles of the Incarnate life and the spiritual miracles wrought by Christ in the church. This too was a Patristic method of interpretation. It was not suggested that the spiritual miracles could be used in the old evidentialist way, but it was contended that they are real miracles, and they offer a striking presumption for the truth of Christianity. It also came to be suggested that the unity of ethos between the Gospel miracles and the spiritual miracles helped to reveal the purpose behind the former, and so to make them seem more credible.

III

But the theological reinterpretation penetrated to a deeper level: it entered the field of Christology itself. The theology of the evidentialists had been singularly innocent of Christology. Christ's performance of miracles had been regarded as evident proof of His Divine mission, and was not conceived of in any other light than as a necessary function of His mission to reveal Divine truths. But with the coming of the view of revelation as consisting in the person and acts of Our Lord, interest became aroused in the relation of His miraculous powers to the human nature assumed at the Incarnation. This was the beginning of the groping after a historical Jesus who should be in some sense psychologically intelligible, which was to ripen into the revolution of Christological thinking in England that followed the publication of *Lux Mundi*.

One of the first steps was the reassertion of the Patristic belief that the performing of physical miracles was a perfectly "natural" activity for a Divine-human person. Just as free moral acts, superimposed upon the lower spheres of natural life, are the characteristic activity of human personality, so, gracious, supernatural acts were the normal accompaniments of the life of the God-man, Christ. This is one of the positions taken up by R. I. Wilberforce in his *Doctrine of the Incarnation of Our Lord Jesus Christ in its Relation to Mankind and to the Church*, 1848. This work is an exposition of the Patristic approach to Christ's person, unruffled by the storms of historical controversy which were already gathering. Yet the author makes no attempt to placard the miracles as peculiarly demonstrating Christ's Divinity. This is a noteworthy fact—that the faith of the Tractarians, so rich in religious insights, was not linked with any special emphasis upon what had but recently been invoked as the master-proof of supernatural revelation. Indeed, it can only have been the Tractarians' grasp of the teleology of the whole Christian economy that enabled them to allow the miracle apologetic to slide gently into the background. They, like the Evangelicals before them, had other evidences to stress.

Wilberforce begins his exposition of the person of Christ from the standpoint of His humanity. This method shows considerable originality at this time, and foreshadows the Christological preoccupation of a much later date. His exposition of the ways in which Christ was constituted to be the "Pattern man" is masterly, and contains an attempted vindication of the conception of "human nature", dissociated, as he believed, from a false realism.[1] Since Christ was the pattern man, the sinless second Adam, His humanity possessed in itself powers of which our fallen manhood can scarcely dream. His manhood also provided a perfect medium through which the power of God could operate. Virtue proceeded out of Him, we read; people wished simply to touch Him; which shows clearly that it was His very humanity that was the vehicle of this power.[2] Wilberforce thus pointed the way to an aspect of the church's teaching about Christ's person which was later to provide one important basis for modern theology. For the idea that Christ's miracles were grounded in His perfect humanity, or mediated through it, was to provide the means of bypassing the difficulty that arose when it was no longer possible to assert categorically that the Gospel miracles were beyond the powers of nature to produce.

[1] *op. cit.*, pp. 35f. [2] *ibid.*, pp. 93f.

Westcott went further. He held that the miracles of Christ threw light on the Incarnation. They were not wrought by limitless Divine power, but by Christ's two natures together: not by His Divine power only, for then they would have ceased to contain any element of instruction for men; and not by His human nature only, for then they would have been emptied of their special promise. Christ's cures, Westcott believed, were the outcome of inward struggle, of effort and suffering in the depths of His being, just as His whole redemptive life was accomplished by suffering.[1]

IV

From Wilberforce, and even from Westcott, we take a very long jump into the characteristically modern Christological atmosphere when we come to Sir J. R. Seeley's *Ecce Homo*, 1866. Amongst other innovations, the work contains a novel view of the relation of Christ's miracles to His person. Seeley attempts to see the significance of Christ's miraculous powers in relation to the development of His mission and conquest of evil. Many tentative reconstructions of the life of the so-called "Jesus of History" had already appeared abroad, but *Ecce Homo* is one of the first serious efforts in England to understand Christ's life from within, as it were. The book nevertheless has strong links with the past. Religion is envisaged primarily as a buttress for morality; and the directly religious and eschatological language of the New Testament is moralized. On the words, "He shall baptize with fire" the author comments: "Moral warmth does cleanse."[2] Clearly not a Barthian Christ!

Seeley believed in the Gospel miracles,[3] and the crux of his argument is reached in the discussion of Christ's temptations. We are to conceive of Christ here for the first time becoming conscious of the possession of miraculous powers, powers which conferred certain obligations in respect of their exercise. His victory consisted in declining to use them for His own personal advantage, or to establish His Kingdom by power, and in consecrating them solely to beneficent ends.[4] Seeley does not present the miracles as direct proofs, but he does present them

[1] *Characteristics of the Gospel Miracles*, pp. 44-45. [2] *op. cit.*, 5th ed., p. 8.
[3] *ibid.*, p. 10. [4] *ibid.*, pp. 12-16.

as an undeniable element in the success which Christ's earthly mission achieved. Christ professed to work miracles, and was believed by His followers really to work miracles, and it was mainly on this account that they conceded to Him the pre-eminent dignity and authority which He claimed.[1] But supernatural power alone could not have procured the kind of ascendency which Christ wanted. The appeal of His miracles lay in their moral character. "This temperance in the use of supernatural power is the masterpiece of Christ."[2] Here is a moral miracle superimposed upon a physical one: it is this combination of power and goodness, the victory within Christ's person of the latter over the former, to which Seeley points as the hall-mark of Christ's Divinity, and the strength of the Lord's appeal both then and now.

Thus to have set the Gospel miracles within the drama of Christ's personal life was a notable contribution to the awakening of interest in Christology. Had this writer not been so fettered by a moralistic view of religion, that echoed the thought of the Illumination, he might well have gone on to an understanding of the place in redemption of these supernatural acts. We can see how fruitful the reinterpretation of the miracles could become if we look at a later writer who combined modern critical studies with the full traditional Faith. A. J. Mason, like the *Lux Mundi* school, accepted the full personal Deity of Christ, whilst envisaging His possession of true manhood in its psychological as well as its physical aspects. He points out that Christ's miracles had generally been regarded as exhibitions of His Divine nature, in contrast with His sufferings, which were regarded as exhibitions of His human nature.[3] But, if we try to put ourselves back into the place of the disciples, we do not find that their immediate deduction from the miracles was that their Master was possessed of the nature of Deity. On the contrary, Jesus' miracles are represented in the Gospels as showing Him to stand in a unique relationship to God. The more Jesus' power was exhibited, "the more the disciples felt that it told them of a unique connection between their Master and God. . . . It did not exactly strike them that He was Himself possessed of the Divine attributes, for this they

[1] *ibid.*, pp. 42-43. [2] *ibid.*, p. 37.
[3] *The Conditions of Our Lord's Life on Earth*, 1896, p. 85.

did not recognize at first and only came to believe it distinctly after His Resurrection."[1]

On this view, the miracles are in line with the whole of the Incarnate life, for Jesus teaches that His every action reflects the Father who sent Him.[2] The Gospels recognize the limitation of Christ's power—as by the faithless Nazarenes; and the term *exousia*, authority, does not mean that He had boundless power within; in John 10: 18 even the Resurrection is spoken of as an *exousia* derived from the Father.[3] The idea of Christ's *exousia* is closely bound up with the descent of the Spirit. The significance of the fact that no miracles are attributed to Christ before His baptism is that they were not thought of as exhibitions of His own nature. He returned "full of the Spirit", we are told; and the passage from Isa. 61 which St. Luke represents Jesus as reading at Nazareth speaks of the powers of the Messiah as being exercised in virtue of the Spirit.[4] Finally, Mason held that Christ's miracles were a measure of the depth to which He entered into human experience, especially human suffering. Jesus' miracles were not different from those of prophets before or Apostles after Him. They were above all achievements of faith and prayer. They were thus powers which might be bestowed on other men, not just powers of the Logos Himself.[5] Jesus did not heal right and left by a mere fiat of Divine power; it cost Him great effort. He took our nature and identified Himself with it at all its depths.

V

In the Scholastic view of miracles, the physical aspect had predominated. The background to the discussion since the 17th century had been the Newtonian cosmology, and the kind of commonsense epistemology that was taken for granted along with it. It was assumed that we knew just what a miracle was, and that if one could be observed, cognizance could be taken of it just like any other physical event or process. The idea of value-judgment belonged only to the doctrines which the miracles attested. In the 19th century, however, two simultaneous developments were shifting the interest away from the

[1] *op. cit.*, p. 87. [2] *ibid.*, p. 90. [3] *ibid.*, pp. 96-101.
[4] *ibid.*, p. 103. [5] *ibid.*, p. 106.

physical aspect of miracles to their interpretation. First, revelation was coming to be thought of as consisting pre-eminently in the person and the acts of Christ, and secondly, this appeal of God to man was being thought of more and more as by its very nature self-authenticating. So, as miracles came to be conceived of as revealing acts of Christ, the question was raised whether they did not acquire their credibility partly on account of their being an element in the whole revelation made by God.

That the significance of facts or events lies in the combination of the material fact plus its interpretation is part of the fundamental structure of human experience. We have the physical event of Caesar's crossing the Rubicon, and its meaning for history; and we have the pigment composing a Raphael Madonna, and its significance for the beholder, as different illustrations of this principle. It holds good also of the life of Christ, where the events are discerned by faith to be of eternal and universal significance for man. This truth was partly obscured so long as it was thought that the Gospel miracles could be understood purely by reference to their physical character. Further, so long as they were defined in this way, the chief emphasis in the matter of their convincingness was bound to be laid upon the weighing of historical probabilities. A miracle, of course, is a peculiar case, because its most obvious characteristic is its physical non-conformity, which raises many peculiar problems of evidence. But a miracle wrought in the context of revelation must have as its breath of life some special significance for man; and this significance may turn out to be a factor even in the apprehension of the evidence for the outward event itself. The Crucifixion of Our Lord is an event in which the combination of physical circumstance and interpretation by Christian faith is supremely illustrated. But so too is the Resurrection. The most rationalistic evidentialist knew that he was dealing with a fact of infinitely greater significance than the mere resuscitation of a man. What he did not realize was that, in contrast to the Crucifixion, the Resurrection is simply incredible without its meaning for Christian faith. Here, fact and significance are inseparable, whether we are dealing with the New Testament evidence or with the meaning of the Resurrection for religion.

This was a discovery of 19th-century theology, and to some writers it was such a joy to be able to speak of the miracles as a unique sign-language of God that they would skate over some of the historical problems even where the ice was rather thin. George Macdonald, to whom Dr. C. S. Lewis is much indebted, delights to write of the miracles as God's direct speech to man. They are one of the modes in which Christ expressed His unseen life—every one of His words and actions being necessary to understand what He tells us of God.[1] Surely God will speak the clearest, grandest word of guidance which He can utter intelligible to His creatures.

> It is but natural [he says] to expect that the deeds of the great messenger should be just the works of the Father done in little. If He came to reveal His Father in miniature, as it were, . . . to tone down His great voice . . . then the works that His Father does so widely, so grandly, that they transcend the vision of men, the Son must do briefly and sharply before their very eyes.[2]

It cannot be denied that Macdonald has put his finger upon what must ultimately be the justification of belief in the Gospel miracles along with the historical evidences: their power to reveal, and their congruity with the whole person and work of Christ.[3]

[1] *The Miracles of Our Lord*, 1884. [2] *op. cit.*, pp. 2-3.

[3] Cf. Westcott's careful analysis of the subjective appeal of the miracles—the subtle signs calculated to force upon us the belief that God is working personally in these events, even though other explanations of the same events may be conceivable. *Gospel of the Resurrection*, 3rd ed., pp. 41f.; *Gospel of Life*, 1892, pp. 206f.

Chapter Eleven

THE ENGLISH "PROGRAMME OF MODERNISM"

I

We pass from the period characterized by tentative reconstruction of the purpose and place of miracles to the epoch in which the principles of higher criticism are recognized as the primary tools of investigation. Broadly speaking, two approaches to the investigation and two types of theology have emerged, of which the more radical will first be considered.

The distance between the writers of *Essays and Reviews* and what in England came to be known as the "Modernist" movement is bridged by the work of Percy Gardner and E. A. Abbott. Neither was an amateur at his trade. Gardner was a notable student of archaeology; whilst Abbott, in his study of the miracles alleged to have been wrought at the tomb of St. Thomas of Canterbury, had exposed some striking facts about the strength and the weakness of the evidence for miracles. Like Baden Powell they regarded the belief in miracles as no mere otiose question but as a positive menace to Christianity in the modern world.[1] But far more than had the Professor of Mathematics, they were able to draw upon the ever-increasing knowledge of comparative mythology and documentary criticism.[2] Nor must we forget the softening-up barrage kept up continuously by literary figures of the period such as Samuel Butler and Mrs. Humphry Ward. Never, it was believed, was the task more urgent of reconstructing Christian belief in the light of modern knowledge. That this remarkable endeavour did not produce a generally acceptable synthesis was not due

[1] See esp. Abbott's Preface to *Oxford Sermons*, 1879.

[2] Cf. Abbott's withering attack on Newman in his *Philomythus*, 1891.

to any lack of courage or learning. The limitations from which the modernism of the first quarter of the present century suffered were due to prematurity. An attempt was made to precipitate a synthesis before the true character of scientific thinking was properly understood by theologians—and at the time when the Newtonian cosmology and even the Newtonian mechanics were to be modified. Religious thought, moreover, was still too much under the influence of the rationalism of the two preceding centuries. The newer "Biblical theology" has shown that the Scriptures can only be justly understood and appraised by their own categories.

At the beginning of the century, however, it was considered to be a matter of life or death for Christianity to enquire into the connection between the Biblical miracles and the fundamentals of the Faith in the light of the secular thinking of the day. The investigation was carried out in the conviction that the Christian beliefs about the person and work of Christ would remain intact, whatever disclosures were made as to the unhistoricity of the miracles.[1] Unfortunately the assumptions and methods of contemporary historians derived from positivism, so that, in the consideration of miracles, the prisoner was not at the bar but already on the way to the scaffold. A century of German Biblical scholarship had already produced an astonishing range of non-miraculous reconstructions of the Gospel history; for the German scholars, whilst disagreeing about practically everything else, had been unanimous in their rejection of the miraculous element.[2] Again, despite the battering given to the argument by Mozley, most modernists clung to the *a priori* presumption against miracles from natural uniformity. "The whole tendency of modern science," writes Glazebrook, "is to confirm that belief in the uniformity of nature which raises a strong presupposition against the accuracy of each record of a supposed miracle."[3] There is little doubt as to what these writers had in mind when they thought of nature. Sanday explicitly identifies the term "nature" with "the laws of matter and motion",[4] scarcely an adequate basis for a Christian philosophy. If it be replied that what was

[1] Major, *English Modernism*, ch. X. Gardner, *Historic View of the N.T.*, pp. 160-61.
[2] C. J. Wright, *Miracle*, 1930, p. 6.
[3] *Faith of a Modern Churchman*, 1917, p. 67. Cf. Major, *op. cit.*, ch. X, sec. IV.
[4] *Form and Content*, p. 99.

at stake in the expectation of uniformity was a rational philosophy of the universe, it must be pointed out that this is not a scientific discovery but a philosophical and religious belief.

The bounds of nature's powers are imperfectly known, and many alleged miracles may well have really taken place, but as unusual natural occurrences. Our Lord's healings seem to fall within this class, and so do such psychopathic phenomena as visions and voices.[1] Therefore it was believed that the Biblical evidence for miracles would yield to one of two treatments: a recorded event was either a violation of nature and therefore incredible, or a natural phenomenon brought about by unusual forces and might be credible.[2] Traditional apologists had always appealed to some transcendental or moral factor when presenting the case for the Biblical miracles. Even Paley writes about the moral probability of God's revealing Himself to man. The modernists, on the other hand, sought to evaluate the evidence without any such factors of interpretation. Kirsopp Lake believed himself to be studying the evidence for the Resurrection "without transcending the boundaries of historical research." Spiritual experience could not guarantee the historical Resurrection: it could throw light upon the meaning of events which were historically vouched for by other means.[3] The general argument that there are excellent reasons why miracles should have happened "stultifies any investigation of evidence", claims J. M. Thompson. Presuppositions there must be, but only such as are appropriate to the subject, viz. the relative value of documents, the trustworthiness of witnesses, and the general rules which govern the formation and transmission of evidence.[4]

With such a method in itself fatal to miracles, the modernist found himself in an uneasy position with his historical enquiry. The pursuit of scientific historiography demanded the practical exclusion of occult causes; yet this was the very point which he

[1] Gardner, *Historic View of the N.T.*, p. 145. Sanday, *Life of Christ in Recent Research*, p. 213.

[2] Major, *English Modernism*, ch. X, sec. III. J. M. Thompson, *Miracles in the New Testament*, 1911, pp. 2-4.

[3] *Historical Evidence for the Resurrection*, 1907, pp. 1-4. Cf. P. Gardner-Smith, *Narratives of the Resurrection*, 1926, pp. xxiii-xxvi; L. A. Reid, *Preface to Faith*, 1939, p. 63.

[4] *op. cit.*, pp. 5-7.

claimed to be investigating. Thompson claims to assume that miracles are both possible and capable of attestation; yet he confesses that to admit a miracle is in practice intellectual suicide. In order not to appear dogmatic, the enquiry was cast in the form of an investigation into the credentials of the miracles, whereas in fact it was concerned with the rather different task of elucidating the causes which had produced the miracle stories. It is this tension which gives that slight touch of apparent disingenuousness to so much work of high scholastic value.

If the value-judgments which the New Testament itself passes upon the person and work of Christ are excluded, the attempt to make the miraculous interpretation of any event appear more probable than a score of natural alternatives is a sheer impossibility. Then, as Lecky said, "Men are prepared to admit almost any conceivable concurrence of natural improbabilities rather than resort to the hypothesis of supernatural interference."[1] Taken out of their actual historical context in the proclamation of the Gospel, the New Testament miracles were exposed to every kind of superficial comparison with mythopoeic tendencies at large.[2] We are referred to the general low level of education among the early Christians, and to the conditions of enthusiasm and imagination in which the Gospel first spread.[3] Comparison with heathen stories shows not so much the superiority of the Scriptural records as the general tendencies at work, whilst the Old Testament is seen as a formative influence continually operating: Christ raises a widow's son at Nain near Shunem, where Elisha performed a similar miracle.[4] The Apocryphal Gospels, Rabbinic and heathen sources all go to show that the Gospel emanated from a society in which the myth-making tendency was at work, and the process can even be seen at work amongst the critically separable documents of the Gospel tradition.[5]

The attempt to study the evidence for miracles independently

[1] *Rationalism*, I, p. 156.
[2] Abbott, *Oxford Sermons*, p. xxxvi; *Kernel and Husk*, pp. 15, 165.
[3] Henson, *Creed in the Pulpit*, 1912, p. 89; Barnes, *Rise of Christianity*, 1947, p. 62.
[4] J. E. Carpenter, *First Three Gospels*, 1890, pp. 194f.; P. Gardner, *Historic View of the N.T.*, 1901, pp. 156-57.
[5] Major, *English Modernism*, 1927, ch. X, sec. VII.

of the interpretative element arose from presuppositions regarding the character of history of far wider consequence than the present subject. The prevailing attitude towards history in the 19th century bears some analogy to, and some genitive connection with, the established cosmology. In the Newtonian cosmology, there is matter in time and space and there are secondary qualities, like colour, existing within the mind of the beholder. It was thought that history likewise consisted, first, of material facts, and secondly, of the film of interpretation imposed upon them. History as it comes down to us was—to use a chemical analogy—a mixture, not a compound; and the elements of interpretation could be dissolved away so as to leave us with the true historic facts. It was believed further that these bare facts were our true interest in history. But it is very doubtful whether most of the known facts of history would be worth having were it not for the value-judgments attached to them at the time and in subsequent ages. Nowhere is this seen more clearly than in the case of Our Lord's person and work. The "Historical Jesus" was sought for so very diligently: yet He seemed a strangely unattractive figure in the hands of many who thought they had come closest to Him. Without the faith which the men of the New Testament held, the miracles they record would be not only incredible but without importance for us. The modernist attempt to reach the "facts" of sacred history, and thence to make a fresh evaluation of them, achieved little save to clear away some of the relics of evidentialism. Further progress awaited the rise of a Biblical theology which studied record and interpretation together, and tried to evaluate Scripture as the expression of a living faith.

II

With the premises and technique described above, the modernist turned to the Scriptural evidence for miracles. It was believed that the miraculous element in the Old Testament might be reduced to (1) a providential deliverance from Egypt; (2) folklore stories of Elijah and Elisha; (3) the psycho-physical abnormalities of the canonical prophets, and (4) "literary miracles" such as those of Jonah, Daniel and Joshua 10: 12.[1]

[1] Sanday, *Life of Christ in Recent Research*, 1907, pp. 211-12.

The most complete analysis of the New Testament evidence viewed in the modernist way is provided by J. M. Thompson's *Miracles in the New Testament*, and we shall broadly follow its argument.

We begin with St. Paul, whose Epistles form our earliest sources of information. The Apostle unquestionably believed himself to possess miraculous powers, but unfortunately he has left no record of the feats which he believed to be miraculous.[1] The gifts of prophecy, tongues and healing, of which we hear much, may be entered as illustrations of familiar phenomena of the psychology of religion. St. Paul, says Thompson, typifies the attitude of indifference in the early church to the events of Christ's life, which tells against the accuracy of the Gospel tradition.[2] Turning to the Acts, Sanday and Thompson agree in ascribing the whole of the book to St. Luke. In the second half of the work, composed of the writer's own observations or those of other travel-companions of St. Paul, we have, says Sanday, as good testimony as can be afforded by any eye-witness.[3] But here again, there is nothing more than the phenomena of prophecy, visions, faith-healing and exorcisms. Eutychus (Acts 20: 7-12) probably suffered from no more than concussion; whilst the earthquake at Philippi (Acts 16: 16f.) was a natural event.[4] As with the Pauline Epistles, where we come to close quarters with the witnesses "there is not a single credibly attested miracle".[5] For the first part of the Acts, the author was dependent upon various Palestinian sources, and there is a greater element of miracle—though even here there is nothing that might not be explicable by natural causes. There are different recensions of several stories, which point to the fluidity of this part of the tradition (e.g. Acts 5: 19=12: 6; Acts 4: 31=2: 1f.).

Sanday and Thompson admit that in the Synoptic Gospels we are still on solid ground. Yet, "the Gospels, good as their credentials are, stop short of evidence that is absolutely at first hand."[6] Assuming the Marcan authorship of the second Gospel, we are at once struck, Thompson says, by the uneven distribution of the miracles. The nature miracles, except the cursing of

[1] Sanday, *op. cit.*, p. 215. [2] Thompson, *op. cit.*, pp. 13-20.
[3] *op. cit.*, p. 212. [4] Thompson, *op. cit.*, p. 123.
[5] Thompson, *op. cit.*, p. 123.
[6] Sanday, *op. cit.*, p. 213. *Form and Content*, p. 103.

the fig tree, and all the cures fall outside the Judaean ministry. The miracles belong to Galilee, to the times of enthusiasm, to the period of the ministry which St. Mark himself did not witness.[1] With regard to the character of the Marcan miracles, we have, first, phenomena of the vision type at the Baptism, Temptation and Transfiguration. The twelve cures are different modes of faith-healing; exorcism, for instance, is a primitive kind of psycho-therapeutics.[2] The nature miracles show some signs of first-hand evidence, but they may be explained like similar miracles elsewhere. The storm on the lake subsided naturally; Jairus' daughter may have been suffering from a cataleptic trance; the walking on the lake may represent some psychical experience of the disciples; whilst the feeding of the multitude may represent the institution of the Agape or Eucharist.

In the material common to SS. Matthew and Luke, Thompson holds that the story of the healing of the centurion's servant (Matt. 8: 5=Luke 7: 2) was told chiefly for the sake of the saying on faith; and he adds that if the incident really happened it must have been a coincidence—he discounts the notion of spiritual power being exercised at a distance.[3] The modifications of Marcan material made by SS. Matthew and Luke represent simply literary or theological interpretation, rather than fresh original testimony.[4]

Of the miracles peculiar to St. Matthew, Pilate's wife's dream was not miraculous; and the earthquake and appearances of the dead at the time of the Crucifixion, if they occurred, were natural phenomena—the latter were perhaps visions. Against the truth of St. Peter's walking on the lake, Thompson appeals back to the Apostolic authority of the second Gospel (Matt. 14: 28f.)[5] The miracle of the coin in the fish's mouth is rejected as a late piece of Petrine tradition: it ascribes supernatural knowledge to Jesus and has an ecclesiastical interest (Matt. 17: 24). Of the miracles peculiar to St. Luke's Gospel, the draught of fishes, Luke 5: 1f., may be a variant on the tradition underlying John 21. The healing of Malchus' ear, Luke 22: 51, would have been unique—the restoration of a limb—for which adequate testimony could scarcely have been forthcoming at

[1] *op. cit.*, pp. 26-32.
[2] Thompson, *op. cit.*, pp. 32-40.
[3] *ibid.*, pp. 54-55.
[4] *ibid.*, pp. 64f., 83f.
[5] *ibid.*, p. 72.

such a moment of confusion. The raising of the dead man at Nain is a story of uncertain origin (Luke 7: 12).[1]

III

The miracles associated with Our Lord's person were the subject of protracted controversies especially in the first two decades of the present century, particularly with regard to their place in the Creed, and the question of the conformity of the clergy. Concerning the Virgin Birth, the modernist found himself unable to take as his starting-point the dogmatic arguments of catholic theology, so many of which appeared to turn upon docetic or biological errors.[2] The historical evidence was held to be altogether insufficient to establish the supposed fact; and the other considerations were only weighty enough to have an inhibitive force, forbidding denial and suggesting a state of suspended judgment.[3] The difficulty arising from the comparative study of mythology was especially grave in regard to this event. Every mythology had its stories of gods walking as men and of intercourse between divine and human beings.[4] The Virgin Birth, again, is but one amongst a number of explanations to be found in the New Testament of Christ's exalted position. We have, it is urged, a theory of adoption in the story of Christ's Baptism; a theory of adoption at the Resurrection, in the speeches in Acts; a theory of the "Heavenly man", in St. Paul; and of the Incarnation of the Logos, in the Fourth Gospel. The authors of the books in which these "theories" appear either did not know of the Virgin Birth tradition, or it would have been foreign to their thought.

The doctrine, then, could not have entered into the theology of St. Paul.[5] Had he known of it, he would probably have vigorously attacked it.[6] The traditional proof-texts

[1] Thompson, *op. cit.*, p. 92.

[2] Bethune-Baker, *Miracle of Christianity*, 1914, p. 9; Major, *English Modernism*, ch. X, sec. II. Cf. Gardner, *Historic View*, p. 170; Baird, *Christian Fundamentals*, 1926, pp. 73-74; J. Mackinnon, *Historic Jesus*, 1931, p. 1.

[3] Bethune-Baker, *Faith of the Apostles' Creed*, 1918, p. 68n. Cf. Gardner, *Historic View*, p. 162.

[4] Gardner, *Exploratio Evangelica*, pp. 234f. Glazebrook, *Faith of a Modern Churchman*, p. 70.

[5] Henson, *Creed in the Pulpit*, p. 19.

[6] Gardner, *Exploratio*, p. 240.

were either irrelevant or contradictory to it. Galatians 4: 4 merely emphasizes the human aspect of Christ's birth. Romans 1: 3-4 contrasts Christ's human birth with His Divine rebirth at the Resurrection. 1 Corinthians 15: 47 refers to the Resurrection. Romans 5: 12-21 and 1 Corinthians 15: 21 again merely illustrate the Second Aadm doctrine.[1]

In St. Mark, we have a theory of Jesus' adoption at His Baptism. The conduct of His mother and relatives (Mk. 3: 21, 31-35) is inexplicable on the view that they knew of His supernatural origin.[2] Thompson makes heavy weather with the words "Son of Mary" in Mark 6: 3; and indeed it is fair to point out, as R. A. Knox did at the time, that had these words been found in SS. Matthew or Luke, with the words "Son of Joseph" in St. Mark, no modernist could have resisted the temptation to use the fact as evidence against the Virgin Birth. Mark 12: 35 assumes Jesus' genuine Davidic descent: which Thompson takes to imply natural descent through Joseph.[3]

With regard to the material attributed to "Q", it is argued that the citation from Psalm 2: 7 in connection with Jesus' Baptism (Matt. 3: 17=Luke 3: 22), excludes the ideas of pre-existence and miraculous birth; whilst the Baptist's message (Matt. 11: 2=Lk. 7: 18) would be difficult to reconcile with the stories of Luke 1 and 2.[4] Similarly, on St. Peter's speech (Acts 2: 25) Thompson writes—"It would be impossible to use plainer language of the physical descent of Christ."[5] In the Gospel of St. Luke there is nothing to suggest the Virgin Birth, not even in the first two chapters apart from the passage 1: 34-35. This passage, moreover, contains two questionable points. First, the earlier words of the angel about the throne of David would lose their point if the child were not to be Joseph's son, and secondly, Mary's question and surprise would seem strange if she were already betrothed. Either the note of the betrothal is premature (1: 27), in which case the miraculous birth disappears, or, more easily, the words, "epei andra ou gignosko" are an interpolation.[6] St. Matthew presents the same

[1] Thompson, *op. cit.*, p. 135. Bethune-Baker, *Faith of the Apostles' Creed*, pp. 68, 71, 106-10n.
[2] Thompson, *op. cit.*, p. 137. [3] *op. cit.*, p. 138.
[4] *ibid.*, p. 140. [5] *ibid.*, p. 141. [6] *ibid.*, p. 148.

appearance as St. Luke: apart from its opening section, the Virgin Birth is ignored or contradicted. The second chapter contains a series of glaring contradictions to the narrative of Luke 1 and 2, whilst the first chapter represents an advanced stage of dogmatic, rather than personal, interest in the narrative. The genealogies provided by the first and third Gospels were each intended to give the pedigree of Joseph.[1]

IV

In the case of the Virgin Birth, the modernist historical investigation led to a serious doubt of the fact. In the case of the Resurrection, however, it was claimed that it was not the fact, but only its interpretation, which was in question. Belief in the Resurrection had been the pivot of Apostolic faith, and the only adequate cause of the church's existence.[2] Earlier rationalistic explanations of the belief are given short shrift: Christianity could not have grown out of fraud, fiction or frenzy.[3] The New Testament writings afforded adequate testimony to the Apostolic experience of Our Lord's living personality after His death, but was their testimony adequate to the assertion of His bodily rising?

The modernists deliberately abandoned the traditional exegesis of trying to harmonize the narratives and sought to elucidate both the origins and the development of the Resurrection tradition. There was a good deal of disagreement as to the precise form which the reconstruction of the tradition must take. Some writers held to the priority of the Jerusalem tradition of Christ's appearances, whilst others favoured the Galilean. The latter hypothesis had two particular things in its favour: first, the original conviction that Christ lived was dissociated from the story of the empty tomb, and secondly, the Jerusalem appearances with their suggestions of corporeality could be dismissed as late accretions. If we assume the literary dependence of the Matthean and Lucan narratives upon Mark 15: 42–16: 8, all the additions and deviations can be

[1] *op. cit.*, p. 155.
[2] Glazebrook, *op. cit.*, p. 23. Gardner-Smith, *Narratives of the Resurrection*, p. 10.
[3] Henson, *Creed in the Pulpit*, p. 196.

accounted for as inferences from the Marcan story.[1] These additions, indeed, serve to make the story more confused: for instance, in St. Matthew, because the sepulchre is sealed, the women have no motive for their visit except to "see the sepulchre" (Matt. 28: 1). But the Marcan narrative itself is patient of other explanations. Kirsopp Lake and Gardner-Smith suggest that the women went to the wrong sepulchre. The western reading of Mark 16: 6, without the word "egerthe", would be "ouk estin hode, idete *ekei* topon autou": i.e. a young man was directing the women to the right sepulchre. This alone, it is urged, accounts for the silence of the women, Mark 16: 8, because they had nothing to tell, until the return of the disciples from Galilee with news of Jesus' appearance.[2] Alternatively, the young man (perhaps St. Mark himself) may already have seen the empty tomb and become convinced that the Lord had risen.[3] The evidence of the women is in any case of uncertain value; Percy Gardner tells us that St. Mary Magdalen was "subject to nervous derangements".[4]

It was held that there was convincing testimony to the reality of Christ's appearance to the Apostles after His Passion, but that this conviction did not extend to the details which implied a bodily presence.[5] In support of the Galilean tradition, we have the inference that St. Mark originally contained a Galilean appearance, together with the testimonies of Matt. 28 and John 21. In the apocryphal Gospel of St. Peter, furthermore, the Apostles return to Galilee after the Passion uncheered by news of the Resurrection. The Galilean stories contain no suggestions of a corporeal appearance.[6] In so far as they are historical, the Jerusalem appearances may be regarded as transferred, antedated, Galilean appearances.[7] They contain specific notices regarding the character of the Lord's Resurrection body—which may be touched, and which is capable of assimilating food; which at the same time can appear and

[1] Lake, *Historical Evidence*, p. 47; Thompson, *op. cit.*, p. 180; Gardner-Smith, *op. cit.*, p. 26.
[2] Lake, *op. cit.*, pp. 61f. and 251f. Gardner-Smith, *op. cit.*, pp. 134f.
[3] Thompson, *op. cit.*, pp. 175-76.
[4] *Exploratio*, p. 256.
[5] Gardner-Smith, *op. cit.*, pp. 115-18, 171-72.
[6] Gardner-Smith, *ibid.*, pp. 72, 119, 94, 143. Thompson, *op. cit.*, pp. 193, 199.
[7] Gardner-Smith, *op. cit.*, pp. 123, 153, 168. Thompson, *op. cit.*, p. 197.

disappear at will, can pass through locked doors and is hard to recognize. It is suggested that we have here two different theories—of a corporeal Resurrection body and an ethereal—unconvincingly blended. The story of the bodily Ascension in Acts is yet another corollary of the later corporeal theory.[1]

The attempt was also made to enlist the support of St. Paul on the side of the modernist reconstruction. In his statement regarding the Resurrection, 1 Cor. 15: 3-8, there is no reference, explicit or implicit, to the empty tomb.[2] It is argued, again, that St. Paul in classing his own vision of Christ with the rest "allows us to conclude that in all the appearances there was nothing of the nature of a resuscitated body."[3]

In St. Paul's theology, R. H. Charles, Glazebrook and Thompson think of him as progressively shaking off the shackles of the Jewish conception of a bodily resurrection. Thompson holds that the analogy of the seed, in 1 Cor. 15: 36, implies the real death of the earthly body and not its growth into something else. It was thought at the time that seeds really did die.[4] The passage, 1 Cor. 15: 42-44, refers explicitly to those who are now dead: it is these people whose natural body has rotted away, and who are to be given a newly created body at the parousia, vv. 35-49, who constitute the true analogy to the Resurrection of Christ. The following verses, 50-52, deal only with those who will be alive at the parousia. This, Thompson claims, is supported by 2 Cor. 5: 1f., where the earthly tent must be dissolved.[5]

To some writers, the disentangling of Christ's "spiritual" Resurrection from its corporeal associations appeared to shed fresh light upon the resurrection of the faithful. R. H. Charles, in his *Resurrection of Man*, 1929, and B. H. Streeter, in his

[1] Gardner-Smith, *op. cit.*, pp. 21, 75, 79, 86, 155. Thompson, *op. cit.*, pp. 196-200. Some critics, however, strongly supported the priority of the Jerusalem tradition of appearances; e.g. Burkitt, *Christian Beginnings*, p. 85; *Jesus Christ*, pp. 57-58. Kirsopp Lake came subsequently to doubt his own Galilean theory; cf. *Beginnings of Christianity*, vol. V, pp. 8, 14.

[2] Thompson, *op. cit.*, pp. 164f.; Gardner-Smith, *op. cit.*, pp. 4f. Lake on the other hand argues that St. Paul did know the story, and that the empty tomb was necessary to his theology; *op. cit.*, pp. 36, 202-3, 28, 190.

[3] Henson, *Value of the Bible*, p. 204. Cf. Thompson, *op. cit.*, p. 204.

[4] *op. cit.*, pp. 168f.

[5] Cf. Glazebrook, *op. cit.*, pp. 25-27.

Immortality, 1917, build up a most helpful exposition, from Scripture and Christian doctrine, of the idea of a "spiritual body"—a new organ of personal experience bestowed upon man in the future life. V. F. Storr, in his *Christianity and Immortality*, 1918, and A. H. McNeile, *The Problem of the Future Life*, 1925, expound the same theme, though they ascribe to the empty tomb of Christ the significance of a miracle, wrought for the sake of the disciples.

The idea of the bodily Resurrection, it appeared, was an almost inevitable development in the church's faith, at a time when the human personality was not thought to be complete without the body.[1] But in the modern world, this development repelled the man of science and offended the spiritual.[2] Everything seemed to point to a view of the Resurrection which, though objective, was independent of the miraculous elements of the empty tomb, the materialized appearances and the bodily Ascension. Characteristic of such a reconstruction is the appendix which Streeter added to his contribution to *Foundations*, on the occasion of the controversy arising from Thompson's *Miracles in the New Testament*. No one who believed in a God like the Father of Our Lord Jesus Christ could believe that Jesus' life ended on the Cross. Here, if ever, was the place for God to lift the veil: we weakly demand a sign in this test-case, but there shall be no sign given.[3] Streeter here shows real insight into the nature of revelation: that we are given no point of sheer physical fact where faith can shed its nature and become sight. But Streeter holds that a sign was given to the Apostles, but of such a kind that it cannot by itself serve as a sign to us. The discovery of the empty tomb, which rests upon adequate historical evidence, does not determine the decision in favour of the traditional theory. "With a little ingenuity," he says, "it is not difficult to imagine more than one set of circumstances which might account on purely natural grounds for the tomb being found empty."[4] On the other hand,

> only if the possibility of personal immortality be dogmatically denied can there be any real difficulty in supposing that the

[1] Glazebrook, *op. cit.*, p. 27.
[2] Gardner, *Exploratio*, p. 261.
[3] *Foundations*, p. 129.
[4] *ibid.*, p. 134.

> Master would have been able to convince His disciples of His victory over death by some adequate manifestation;—possibly by showing Himself to them in some form such as might be covered by St. Paul's phrase, "a spiritual body"; possibly some psychological channel similar to that which explains the mysterious means of communication between persons commonly known as telepathy . . .[1]

This treatment of the Resurrection brings us to a further examination of the modernist theological presuppositions, for it is an excellent object-lesson in the attempted discrimination between miraculous and non-miraculous.

V

The movement which attempted to discard the category of miracle from the Christian credenda is admirably illustrated in the theoretical realm as in the exegetical by the writings of Sanday. In his *Position of Liberal Theology*, 1920, he has described the Odyssey of his beliefs; and in his successive writings from 1907, we can see his viewpoint developing as he wrestled with one of the gravest crises that ever confronted Christian theology. The problem of miracles, as he saw it, was one of definition. Conceived as a breach or suspension of natural law, miracle had come into grave doubt; but such a definition was neither necessary nor right.[2] The problem was to make both ends meet: the scientific presupposition of the order of nature, and the Christian assumption that there is such a thing as an answer to prayer.[3] On the basis of the Augustinian dictum, that a miracle is "*contra quam est nota natura*", Sanday thought that miracles might be divided into two categories: those which, though beyond the normal range of experience, do not violate the order of nature—"*supra naturam*"; and those which do involve such a breach—"*contra naturam*". The great mass of miracles in the Bible fall within the *supra naturam* class, and they are still truly miracles, exhibiting the Divine act, not less so because they are fundamentally in accordance with law.[4] Three miracles alone

[1] *Foundations*, p. 136.
[2] "*Miracles*", in *Guardian Papers*; cf. *Position of Liberal Theology*, p. 17.
[3] *Life of Christ in Recent Research*, pp. 203f.
[4] *ibid.*, pp. 213-23.

fall within the *contra naturam* category: the Virgin Birth, the Resurrection and the Ascension. The Gospel testimony was weakest at these very points. We were indeed prepared for extraordinary forces in the universe showing themselves in extraordinary phenomena, and such would be fitting signs or effects of Christ's Divine presence. But this was far different from admitting breaches in nature's regularity: indeed, Sanday found the evidence for this regularity so overwhelming that he could not help regarding it as an expression of the character of God Himself.[1]

Liberalism, says Sanday, stands fundamentally for the unification of thought. It means that the universe is all of a piece. It means that life from the beginning has been in essence just what we see it around us today. The only question is, whether we are to make a single large exception in the interests of religion. Are we, in that one case, to mark off a solitary land of Goshen in the history of the past? Sanday holds that we can still retain the conception of miracle if we are prepared to regard it as no longer involving a breach or suspension of natural law. He believed that on these terms it was possible to rewrite the history of religion in such a way as to bring it into line with every other branch or form of history. That, he conceived, would put the final crown on the unification of thought and life.[2]

The rewriting of the history of religion which Sanday called for had, of course, largely been carried out already. The whole panorama of human life and thought, including the history of Judaism and Christianity, had come to be visualized as a genetic pattern without break or cataclysm. Somewhat varied answers might have been given to the question, What is evolving?—but the broad stream of 19th-century historical studies bore witness to the belief that man's ethical and religious life had been a process whose episodes might be described in terms of causal relations. Hegel had provided what might be called the classical form for this idea on the speculative level; but the historical sciences themselves were far more influential in creating the habits of thought which characterize the period.

The religious doctrine believed to correspond with the genetic

[1] *Form and Content*, pp. 99-101.
[2] *Position of Liberal Theology*, pp. 31f.

view of history was Divine immanence. The idea itself was not new: the novelty of its modern use lay in its being used as a solvent and principle of reinterpretation for the whole history of God's dealings with men. The treatment of the Biblical history as but one chapter of the whole human story, with Divine immanence as its illumination, had certain obvious advantages. It is difficult, even at so short a remove, to realize what a gap was torn in men's religious thinking by the breakdown of the literalist view of Biblical inspiration. That God had revealed Himself through the gradually awakening spiritual insight of religious men seemed the only practical alternative to the discarded view of the Bible, and this seemed to be borne out by the development of Hebrew religion as laid bare by higher criticism. Other gains appeared to be no less striking. In contrast to the idea of God's ruling the world from without by imposed laws, and intervening at certain crises, the immanental view was thought to bring God closer to man.[1]

In our own generation, the belief in God's transcendence has again become a dominant theological interest. When we appraise the modernist movement we must be careful to remember that much of the standard theology that was read in the 19th century was Deistical in temper, and the thought of God's intimate relation to the life of the universe seemed like a breath of fresh air. It was urged that, in the older view, the supernatural had become almost equated with the Divine, and nature degraded to the level of a machine. The immanentalists saw God at work everywhere, and they rejected the distinction between natural and supernatural which seemed to impute partial or sporadic activity to God.[2] The scandal of particular revelation and the difficult distinction between natural and revealed religion appeared likewise to be removed: God was leading all men according to their spiritual capacity.[3]

One of the most striking aspects of immanental theology has

[1] Raven, *What Think Ye of Christ?*, 1916, p. 19; C. J. Wright, *Miracle*, p. 38; J. M. Wilson in *Cambridge Theological Essays*, pp. 223f.; J. Caird, *Fundamental Ideas*, 1899, I, pp. 129, 136.

[2] Raven, *op. cit.*, pp. 20-24.

[3] Wilson, *Camb. Theol. Essays*, pp. 227f. His language is almost reminiscent of Tindal.

been the working out of what may be called a non-miraculous supernaturalism. All we have or know of God, it is said, is mediated through the natural order, without, as it were, ruffling the surface of its mechanical uniformities.[1] This view covers not merely the events of Christ's life but the whole of man's spiritual relations with God. The essence of the supernatural is to be found, not in material abnormalities, but in the spiritual and moral life lived by the human individual. The Aristotelian idea of secondary causation is useful in certain contexts as it safeguards the relative independence of created agents. But the creation is not merely the raw material with which man grapples and expresses his spiritual life, it is also the veil through which God communicates Himself to us. Readers of de Caussade are familiar with the idea of the things and situations which make up the outward world mediating to men the will of God.

The study of the supernatural character of man's spiritual life has been very fruitful, and we shall return to it in a later chapter. Meanwhile, however, the English modernists were preoccupied with the elimination of miracle in the traditional sense. The spiritual realm, though it is a higher order in meaning and power, acts upon the order of nature only within a closely defined area. In the world outside ourselves, the action of God is to be seen by interpreting events in the natural order. This view was thought to provide an eirenicon between scientific historiography and religious insight. All is well, says Thompson, provided that faith does not dispute the dictates of reason that such and such were the historical facts.[2] Modernists contended that human free will gave us no expectation of miracles: for it is not in itself miraculous, but represents merely the conversion of existing energy, and is exercised within a rigid framework of natural law.

The position is illustrated by the attempt to see in the New Testament nothing that goes beyond the bounds of the non-miraculous supernatural. It was conceived that the post-Resurrection appearances of Christ would not have been miraculous in the strict sense, whilst the raising of His body from the tomb would have been. It is difficult to see how such a

[1] Major, *Modern Churchman*, vol. XI, p. 196; C. J. Wright, *op. cit.*, p. 122.
[2] *op. cit.*, p. 212.

sharp distinction can be justified in theory. Surely the most that could be said is that THIS and not THAT is the way in which we have been led to believe that God will act, in the light of all His dealings with the creation. Streeter tried to describe the personal activity of God in the mechanically-conditioned universe along the lines of the Divine guidance of nature. He thought that miracles were to some extent contingent, acting as a corrective to the havoc wrought by the vagaries of the human will. In which case, he says, it would seem as though the Divine personality had an analogy to human personality in that its freedom operates by combining, arranging and directing, rather than in adding to or subtracting from, the system of forces which make up the normal working of nature.[1] Indeed, the denials and distinctions made by modernists were often combined with assertions of the wide powers of spirit within nature; and this aspect of their thought forms a link with the more conservative theology of the present century. The Pauline miracles, writes J. M. Wilson, being such exceptional action of mind over body, are evidential of the spiritual conditions producing them. From St. Paul's consciousness of absolute subordination to Christ, we could infer that Christ possessed far more astonishing gifts than himself. Our knowledge is altogether inadequate to define the limits of Christ's powers: we are ignorant of the relation of will to organization, of mind to matter, and of our spirits to God.[2]

VI

It was as inevitable as anything can be in the history of human thought that the immanental view of religion should come to be applied to Christ, not simply to His deeds but to His person. It is impossible to deal with the question of miracles at this epoch without considering the Christological situation. The older orthodoxy had envisaged the Saviour in a manner not altogether dissimilar from that in which the Hebrew writer

[1] *Foundations*, pp. 137-39.

[2] *Essays and Addresses*, pp. 210-22. Cf. similar statements in Raven, *op. cit.*, pp. 45-47; E. W. Barnes, *Rise of Christianity*, p. 66; Major, *English Modernism*, p. 130; J. Mackinnon, *The Historic Jesus*, p. 349; and E. F. Scott, *New Testament Idea of Revelation*, p. 3.

had pictured Yahweh as walking and talking with our first parents. Jesus was thought of as acting in virtue of the Divine omnipotency, and as thinking and speaking with the Divine omniscience and authority. The evidence for these powers, moreover, had formed the core of the apologetics for Christ's Divinity. But there had now been a century of effort by theologians in Germany and elsewhere to seek for the historical, as opposed to the dogmatic, truth about Jesus. This meant, trying to understand Christ's personality and life on the assumption that He possessed none but human attributes. Personality, conceived after the Kantian tradition as essentially self-consciousness, appeared to make the dual-nature formula of Chalcedon totally unmeaning.[1]

The moorings to the traditional position were cut, even for most English high churchmen, in the eighteen-nineties, by the admission that Christ possessed a truly human consciousness with a limited human knowledge. The gap was bridged, however, for these theologians by the kenotic theory. To the more liberal thinkers, the gap continued to widen, to such an extent that the traditional framework of doctrine no longer formed a consistent rationale of the Incarnation.[2] The task for English modernists, therefore, was the creation of such an apologetic as would reach upwards from the historical Jesus (without His transcendental attributes) to the church's faith in Him as Divine Redeemer. This endeavour was not by any means the sole preserve of modernists: their work is taken here as typical since it was they who had to face the problem in its most acute form. An apologetic based upon other evidences than Christ's miraculous powers had long been in existence under various forms: we have seen it developing in such writers as Wesley, Coleridge and Maurice. By the close of the 19th century, attention had come to be focused not so much upon the power of Christ over the believer as upon the mind in Christ—the unique quality of His consciousness of Messiahship and sonship. The Ritschlian idea of value-judgment gave, as it were, a philosophical analysis of this apologetic. This edifice still deserves close attention, for it was the first

[1] e.g. T. H. Green, *Works*, III, p. 175.
[2] Cf. the author's *Conflict in Christology*, 1948.

systematic attempt to rebuild theology in the era of Biblical criticism.

If the value-judgment was the means by which Christ was recognized as Divine Saviour, the theology of immanence was the means by which Christ's Divinity was defined. Since man was the crown of evolution, made in the image of God, was it not legitimate to infer that Jesus, simply in virtue of His perfect manhood, was thereby the most complete possible revelation and Incarnation of God? "Perfect humanity is Deity under human conditions", says Major.[1] Since, then, the Incarnation was grounded in the nature of things, it required no miracle, such as the Virgin Birth, to bring it about; nor did it involve Christ's possession of miraculous powers.[2] Miracles might even be looked upon as out of keeping with the Incarnation. Henson writes, "What the physical sciences did for the Christian belief in Divine creation, that Biblical science seems to be doing for the Christian belief in recreation . . . in the one case disallowing the notion of special creations, . . . in the other case, disallowing the belief in an Incarnation effected by miracles and illustrated by prodigies."[3] Inge urged that the whole point of the Incarnation was, not that Jesus broke natural laws and had no human father, but that Divine life could be lived under human conditions.[4]

The modernist theological scheme, however, was not without its special problems. English modernism, like Ritschlianism, had put most of its eggs into the basket of the "liberal" picture of the life of Jesus—the view that after stripping off the layers of catholic dogma, supernatural myth and Jewish apocalyptic, the ethic and spiritual glory of the perfect man, Jesus, was revealed. The "eschatological" view of the life of Christ administered a serious challenge to the former view, the consequences of which were only slowly realized.[5] The optimism of some of the Girton fathers of 1921 regarding their simple immanental Christology contrasts strangely with the undercurrents of uneasiness in some speakers at the Conference regarding the historical basis of the scheme. The first volume of Foakes-Jackson and Lake's *Beginnings of Christianity* and

[1] *Modern Churchman*, vol. XI, p. 196.
[2] Rashdall, *God and Man*, pp. 68f.
[3] *Creed in the Pulpit*, p. xxiv.
[4] *Contentio Veritatis*, p. 88.
[5] *Foundations*, p. 76.

the former's *Landmarks in the History of Early Christianity* had recently appeared. Foakes-Jackson was invited to explain his position at this Modern Churchman's Conference, and pronounced the doom of the liberal Christology in no uncertain terms.[1] C. W. Emmet made a bold attempt at the Conference to delineate the unique power of Jesus' personality, despite the embarrassment of eschatology,[2] and followed this up with a large work written in collaboration with Lily Dougall, entitled *The Lord of Thought*.

Catholic modernism had appropriated the thoroughgoing eschatological interpretation of the Gospels. The Jesus of eschatology appeared to be a more appropriate forerunner of the catholic church than the Jesus of liberal protestantism. The essence of Christianity was deemed to lie in the dogmatic truths of catholicism, which were pre-eminently represented in the story of Jesus' life by the picture of His miraculous Incarnation and exaltation.[3]

In a perplexing situation, English modernists have tried to combine elements from both liberal protestantism and catholic modernism. First, they have continued to maintain that Christianity was created and is sustained by the unique ethical and spiritual quality of the historic Jesus. Secondly, the stony road of historical reconstruction has caused many to turn wistful eyes towards those who hold that the spiritual truths revealed by Christianity now shine by their own light, independently of the historicity of past events.[4] Thirdly, we find repeated emphasis of the idea that the Virgin Birth, the Resurrection and the Ascension are vehicles of peculiarly significant truths, despite the discounting of the evidence for their physical occurrence. This indeed was one of the grounds on which modernists claimed that they recited the Creeds with sincerity.

The treatment of miracles as the vehicles of spiritual truths, irrespective of the physical nature of the events described, is not to be dismissed merely as a desperate remedy in an ecclesiastical crisis. Men of various schools had accustomed themselves to think of miracles primarily as "signs"; and it is in this light that

[1] *Modern Churchman*, vol. XI, p. 231. [2] *op. cit.*, pp. 215-17.
[3] e.g. Tyrrell, *Christianity at the Crossroads*, chs. VII-IX., esp. pp. 39-41.
[4] e.g. Gardner-Smith, *Narratives of the Resurrection*, p. xxiv.

we should see those who bid us recognize that it is precisely in the religious interpretation of certain events that revelation finds its habitat. To some minds, says Inge, dogma is an impure mixture of thoughts, sensible images and legends. But this criticism assumes that philosophy and allegorical myth are the only two ways of representing the highest intuitions.[1] But "the normal FORM of religious faith is an event, or series of events, which is conceived as having actually taken place, and which is valued as the symbol or sacrament of an eternal and spiritual truth."[2] So long as men are convinced that a spiritual revelation must have as its inseparable concomitant certain events in the visible order, they are justified in stating positively that those events actually occurred. They usually appeal to external historical evidence in support of their belief; but it is quite certain that this is not the ground of their conviction. The evidence for miracles, for example, if treated in the manner of Paley and the evidential school, is almost worthless, because, on the hypothesis of its being false, we could say with confidence that it or something like it would have been invented. But the connection of ideas, proved by the value set upon the historical narrative, and the vitality of belief in the supernatural are hard facts, says Inge, which those who impugn the truth of history often forget that they have to account for. "The real basis of our belief in the resurrection of Christ is a great psychological fact—a spiritual experience. We know that Christ is risen, because, as St. Paul says, we are risen with Him. If this basis is forgotten, the event becomes an isolated occurrence in past history, which from its very uniqueness is unimportant, and also impossible to establish."[3]

It is unfortunate that Inge did not go on to develop a wider view of symbolism, in which the outward event is conceived as the creative agent in the spiritual life of man. The Cross and the Resurrection do not merely reveal, they redeem. Inge's picture of the relation of faith to history, though helpful, is incomplete, and leads to a reversal of the causal relation that faith perceives; it is not simply that we recognize the truth conveyed by certain events, but that "while we were yet sinners, Christ died for us."

[1] *Contentio Veritatis*, p. 83. [2] *op. cit.*, p. 84. [3] *ibid.*, p. 87.

No better illustration could be found of the varied influences working upon English modernism than the writings of Bethune-Baker. He produced a skilful combination of elements drawn both from Ritschlianism and catholic modernism. He welded together a Christology based upon an evaluation of the human experience of Jesus with a pragmatic reinterpretation of the Creeds. The Creeds, he tells us, had been built up as a coherent presentation of belief, which took for granted the pre-scientific view of the universe, with the world at its centre, and God intervening miraculously from the heaven above. The piecemeal reinterpretation of the Creed had simply destroyed the coherence of the whole: a complete reinterpretation was therefore called for.[1] There was no question of denying the Incarnation or the Resurrection as such; but it was right for the church, by virtue of the Spirit's presence, to rethink its beliefs in the light of the changing intellectual background. The true miracle of Christianity was belief in the living God, the living Christ and the indwelling Spirit—a faith attested by Christian experience down the ages.[2]

Bethune-Baker describes with approval the account of dogma given by Le Roy, that its primary object is to be a rule of action, not a piece of information. But he takes this principle from the catholic modernists, not as a solvent for all positive religious affirmations, but as a way of justifying the view that the articles of the Creed are the practical, living value-judgments of believers upon the unique experiences of Jesus and His disciples.[3] In dealing with the life of Jesus, the facts and their valuation by Jesus and His followers had to be taken together. For instance, in the incident recorded in John 12: 28, some said it thundered; to Jesus it was the voice of God. Here, as in the story of the Temptations, the fact for us is the experience which Jesus underwent and His valuation of it.[4] Since our faith is thus founded, it is dependent upon the historic truth of His life—that He lived, died and rose again.[5]

He found himself unable to make use of the traditional beliefs in either Jesus' miraculous birth or His personal

[1] *Faith of the Apostles' Creed*, pp. 33-39. [2] *Miracle of Christianity*, p. 9.
[3] *Way of Modernism*, pp. 6f. [4] *op. cit.*, pp. 41-47.
[5] *ibid.*, p. 49; *Faith of the Apostles' Creed*, pp. 13, 42, 57.

pre-existence.[1] The latter was an almost inevitable inference from the belief in His Godhead in the primitive Christian religiosity, "with its background of angels and daemons . . ."[2] His own understanding of this doctrine is that Jesus is the crowning manifestation of the power, love and purpose of God, in whom God's ideal in the creation of man is actualized, and who is therefore the perfect expression in time of the personality of God.[3] The Virgin Birth is inappropriate to the Incarnation, and altogether inadequately attested.[4] The Resurrection taken together with the Ascension is "the one central proof of the Divine mission, and therefore of the Divine authority of Jesus of Nazareth."[5] The truth of this came to the disciples only as they were able to receive it, in terms of their mental and spiritual constitution.[6] The resuscitation of Christ's body, implied by the narratives, "stands for the conviction that it was the whole man, the whole personality, all that has gone to make Him what He was in this life" that was raised.[7] The Ascension and Session means that Christ "attained to the highest place in the sphere of the things of the spirit."[8]

The masterful style of Bethune-Baker tends to veil some of the problems which inhere in the positions which he represents. The question has to be raised, Where is the reinterpretation to stop? Shall it proceed to dissolve all the historical credenda and all the positive statements about the nature of God, after the manner of catholic modernism? Today we have the same problem under the name of "demythologization". Amongst English modernists there were a few, like Kirsopp Lake, who loudly preached the funeral oration of traditional Christianity. The Creed, with its three Divine hypostases, the second of which came down from heaven, was derived exclusively from the pre-critical interpretation of the Bible.[9] The modernist was acutely conscious of the revolution brought about by Biblical criticism, and the problem in what sense he could remain faithful to the traditional Creed was a very real one.[10]

1 *Way of Modernism*, p. 94. 2 *op. cit.*, p. 106. 3 *ibid.*, p. 109.
4 *Miracle of Christianity*, p. 11; *Faith of the Apostles' Creed*, pp. 68-69, 78, 91-92, 95.
5 *Faith of the Apostles' Creed*, p. 23.
6 *op. cit.*, pp. 24-25. 7 *ibid.*, pp. 131-32. 8 *ibid.*, p. 134.
9 Lake, *Religion of Yesterday and To-morrow*, 1925, esp. pp. 77-80.
10 A. L. Lilley, *Religion and Revelation*, pp. 1-7.

Discussing the case of Voysey, C. W. Emmet contended that it was possible to draw a line between legitimate reinterpretation and the construction of a scheme of belief not essentially Christian. There was a real difference between a critic, however advanced, who could "feel a real continuity between his own position and that of the Christianity of the past, and one who is really cutting himself loose from it."[1] The irony of this position is that every heretic believes himself to be the true interpreter of the past. But the unsympathetic treatment that modernists received from bodies of ecclesiastics (whose beliefs really differed little from their own) made it extremely difficult for them to think clearly at all about the church's commission to teach and guard the truth. Every step taken by authority was simply ultramontanism to them. To put a ring-fence round the Virgin Birth and the Resurrection, says Henson, is the same kind of policy as that adopted by the Vatican.[2]

The importance attached to the historical beliefs of Christianity turns largely upon what the Gospel is believed to be. Broadly speaking, the modernists thought of revelation as consisting in truths about the nature of God and His attitude towards man. The person of Jesus is central in their thinking, but particular Divine acts hitherto associated with the Incarnation are regarded as no more than figurative representations of truths belonging to the spiritual order. Thus, Sanday thought that the discarding of the miracles in favour of abstract truths was not unlike the changes that have taken place in the metaphorical understanding of the atonement.[3] To the traditionalist, on the other hand, even so general a doctrine as that "God is love" depends for its surety upon the historic acts of redemption, cf. 1 John 3: 16; 4: 9-10. It could be argued further that modernism tends to lose something of what had been gained in the 19th- over against the 18th-century theology: it tends towards a Gospel of "truths", rather than of saving acts. The truth that Wellington defeated Napoleon is entirely dependent upon the historical occurrence in the "correspondence" meaning of truth. The more a truth has reference to a personal being, the more will it be found to depend upon belief in

[1] *Conscience, Creeds and Critics*, p. 50.
[2] *Creed in the Pulpit*, p. xvii.
[3] *Form and Content*, p. 4.

actual occurrences; in the "correspondence" rather than the "symbolic" sense of truth. This is easily comprehended of human affairs: the question is, does it apply to revelation? The pivot of both Old and New Testament thinking is that God reveals Himself in history, not merely in nature.

Chapter Twelve

CONSERVATIVE APOLOGETICS AND HISTORICAL CRITICISM

I

For those who strove to defend the integrity of the New Testament tradition in the ripening years of Biblical criticism there were many urgent tasks. A more adequate philosophy of the supernatural had to be created, which would cut the ground from beneath the anti-miraculous presuppositions (ch. 14). Detailed answers had to be found for the negative criticisms; but perhaps above all, the New Testament picture of Christ had to be presented in its wholeness. As Professor Dodd pointed out in his review of Dr. Barnes' *Rise of Christianity*, in every piece of evidence, taken by itself, it is possible to find dubious or questionable elements, and one by one they may be set aside. But the nature of the evidence rather demands that the early Christian tradition be envisaged as an organic whole, so that as the pieces of a jig-saw puzzle assume their meaning only when fitted together, so "our aim is the reconstitution of the tradition out of our various materials, and the reassessment of those materials, in turn, in the light of their place in the whole."[1] One of the highroads to the dissection and disposal of the supernatural tradition had been the treatment of the contents of the Gospels as a conglomeration of traditions, rather than as part of the testimony of responsible witnesses like St. Peter and St. Luke. "In proportion as we approximate to the idea of an aggregate of anonymous fragments, joined together more or less loosely," says T. B. Strong, "the easier it is to give conjectural explanations of difficult incidents."[2]

[1] *Christian Beginnings*, 1947.

[2] *Miraculous in Gospels and Creeds*, 1914, p. 18.—A powerful pamphlet in reply to Sanday's *Bishop Gore's Challenge*.

From the beginning of the present century we find the rapid assimilation into conservative apologetics of the "assured results" of New Testament criticism, especially the two-document hypothesis. This appeared to carry the authentic written Gospel tradition well back into the first century: an achievement denied to earlier apologists.[1] A collection of papers contributed to *The Guardian* in reply to J. M. Thompson, subsequently published together under the title *Miracles*, may be taken as an epitome of the arguments suggested by the "assured results". Exception is taken to the assumption made by Thompson that the tradition of Our Lord's miracles rests solely upon St. Mark. We know little of the source "Q", and hence conclusions drawn from its supposed contents are perilous. But in fact the material attributed to "Q" does contain both miracle and passages which assume other miracles. For in addition to the cure of the centurion's servant, Matt. 8: 5f.; Lk. 7: 1f., we have the story of the temptations, the reply to the Baptist's messengers, the upbraiding of the cities, and the Beelzebub controversy.[2] It was not true that SS. Matthew and Luke merely represented a more highly coloured version of the Marcan narrative. Their variations might well be accounted for by additional information: they give a more complete view of the life of Our Lord, whilst making no substantial changes either in the narrative or in the presentation of His person. The miracle stories could not be excised from the Gospel tradition, not merely because they were inseparably linked with certain sayings of Christ, but because the written Gospels presuppose an oral tradition, and to cast doubt upon the church's memory of the facts of Our Lord's life was to cast even greater doubt upon the memory of His words.[3]

The moral and spiritual characteristics of Christ's miracles continued to receive stress.[4] Even more striking is the way in which the miraculous element is presented in the Gospels. Yet, points out Scott Holland, this side of the matter is wholly overlooked by Thompson. The amazing thing is the limitation

[1] Temple, *Faith and Modern Thought*, 1910, pp. 75f.; Gore, *Belief in God*, 1921, pp. 184f.

[2] *Miracles*, 1911, W. Lock, pp. 29f; Headlam, pp. 39f. Cf. Gore, *Belief in God*, p. 255.

[3] Gore, *op. cit.*, p. 225.

[4] *Miracles*, Headlam, p. 47. Chase, in *Camb. Theol. Essays*, p. 204. H. S. Holland, *Creeds and Critics*, 1918, p. 139.

(not the presence) of the Christological element. That these writers managed to leave out of account so much of what they believed, and to transport themselves back to those early days—there is no parallel in literature to this capacity.[1] Again, the Gospels represent Jesus as having taken up a definite attitude towards His works of power. He worked them under certain recognized conditions; distrusted their general effect; and withdrew from the crowds and from the healing ministry in order to accomplish His higher baptism.[2]

In view of the great pressure of rationalism it is not surprising to find accommodations regarding particular miracles, which bear no apparent relation to a writer's principles. To cite an example which caused much comment at the time: George Salmon, in his last work, *The Human Element in the Gospels*, 1907, whilst accepting the miracles of the raising of Jairus' daughter and the feeding of the multitude, suggested that Jesus was not walking upon the sea, but that He walked out to the disciples through the surf.[3] It was generally recognized, however, that the ultimate question was far wider than the acceptance of any one particular miracle. In England, Gore urged, there was the odd spectacle of men who rejected miracles yet accepted the miracle of the Incarnation, in the naïve belief that the former could go and the latter remain.[4] The only alternative to the church's view of Jesus, says Rawlinson, is not the "liberal" Jesus, but historical scepticism.[5]

II

A sustained and concentrated effort was made to vindicate the New Testament tradition of the Resurrection in its wholeness: though, as we shall see, there were some remarkable doctrinal developments. Apologists contended that what was at stake was an actual happening on the physical level. It is erroneous, says Westcott, to imagine that in the case of the Resurrection there is some mean between truth and falsehood.

[1] *Miracles*, p. 61.

[2] *ibid.*, pp. 66-70; cf. Holland's *Creeds and Critics*, pp. 133f. Cf. Strong, *op. cit.*, p. 18; Peake, *Christianity*, p. 175.

[3] *op. cit.*, p. 324. Cf. A. F. Smethurst, *Modern Science and Christian Beliefs*, 1955, p. 205.

[4] *Belief in God*, p. 223.

[5] *Christ in the Gospels*, 1944, p. 9.

For as a matter of history, it is obvious that the power of the event which changed the character of the disciples was that it was independent of them and unexpected by them.[1] It was fully recognized that even if the phenomenal occurrence could be established by the rules of evidence, its significance must depend upon moral and spiritual valuations. This did not mean trying to split apart history and interpretation, but laying bare the strength of the evidence in its various aspects.

"I know of no fact in the history of mankind which is proved by better and fuller evidence of every sort," said Thomas Arnold of the Resurrection.[2] But in 1908, two eminent Scottish divines have a slightly different story. Only twenty years ago, says James Orr, books were still being written to deal with the hypotheses of "fraud" and "swoon": now the whole vast Protean resources of critical technique are available for the dissolving of the miraculous element in any narrative.[3] It is now not so much that the veracity of the Apostolic testimony is called in question, writes James Denney, but its meaning and value.[4] Nevertheless, the trustworthiness of the Apostolic witness rests upon a moral udgment, which takes into consideration the whole context of the proclamation of the Gospel.[5]

Despite the general assimilation of the two-document hypothesis, many writers continued to maintain that the several narratives of the Resurrection each contain fresh, independent, reliable testimony. The differences between the narratives are so great that the theory of development from St. Mark is far-fetched, and would reduce the later Gospels almost to complete fiction.[6] It is maintained that in the Second Gospel we have the witness of St. Peter; in the Fourth, the witness of St. John; and in the Third, the careful researches of St. Luke.[7] H. Latham's *The Risen Master* is the most striking example of the attempt to vindicate the verisimilitude of the Gospel record, in the case of St. John.[8]

[1] *Gospel of the Resurrection*, 1874 ed., pp. 5-7, 51.
[2] *Sermon on the Sign of Jonah*. [3] *The Resurrection of Jesus*, pp. 10-29.
[4] *Jesus and the Gospel*, p. 119.
[5] Selwyn, *New Commentary*, III, p. 303. Rogers, *Case for Miracle*, p. 43.
[6] Orr, *op. cit.*, pp. 64, 74, 95.
[7] *ibid.*, p. 85. Chase, *Camb. Theol. Essays*, p. 393.
[8] Cf. Gore, *Belief in God*, p. 269; Milligan, *Resurrection of Our Lord*, 1881, 1884 ed., p. 46; Sparrow Simpson, *Our Lord's Resurrection*, 1909 ed., pp. 1-40; Orr, *op. cit.*, p. 73; Selwyn, *op. cit.*, III, p. 306.

It was a long step, however, from the pre-critical position that conservative writers were now prepared to admit the fact of real discrepancies as a concomitant of independent witness. The minor disagreements are signs of veracity rather than of weakness in the tradition; and they contrast sharply with the agreement of the different documents on the main facts.[1] The building of negative theories upon the discrepancies is as inadequate a mode of historical criticism as the old "fraud" theory.[2]

Evidentialist writers had never failed to adduce the fact of the Apostles' sufferings and achievements as evidence for their veracity. Now, however, with the question of the documents in the melting pot, the historic achievement of the Apostolic church assumed an even greater importance. The Resurrection was preached as no isolated marvel, but as the crowning act of a revelation and redemption; it is in this concrete reality alone that it exists or has interest for the primitive witnesses.[3] The Resurrection alone could have rescued the disciples from their plight, made them see a Divine significance in the Cross, and given that mighty impetus for their mission. Only an event commensurate with the Crucifixion in its objectivity and certainty could have achieved this.[4] The Resurrection was preached in Jerusalem, and believed long before any of the New Testament documents were written: the Resurrection and the church alone explain the existence of the New Testament, and powerfully reinforce the witness of the documents.[5]

The Gospel tradition must be accepted or rejected as it stands, with its combination of stress both upon the empty tomb and the appearances. Despite the attacks of unbelievers and modernists, conservative writers resisted the temptation to lay undue stress upon the empty tomb.[6] But they, nevertheless,

[1] Milligan, *op. cit.*, p. 56; Liddon, *Easter in St. Paul's*, I, pp. 74-75; Swete, *Appearances of Our Lord*, p. xv; Orr, *op. cit.*, pp. 89, 116, 145.

[2] Marcus Dods, *Supernatural in Christianity*, p. 98.

[3] Denney, *Jesus and the Gospel*, p. 121. Cf. Orr, *op. cit.*, p. 206; Chase, *op. cit.*, p. 401.

[4] Selwyn, *New Commentary*, III, p. 301.

[5] Milligan, *op. cit.*, p. 67; Orr, *op. cit.*, p. 111; Denney, *op. cit.*, p. 111; Chase, *op. cit.*, p. 377; Temple, *Faith and Modern Thought*, pp. 77-79; W. L. Robbins, *Christian Apologetic*, p. 102; Headlam, *The Miracles of the New Testament*, pp. 244-45; Ramsey, *Resurrection of Christ*, p. 40.

[6] Denney, *op. cit.*, p. 144; C. H. Robinson, *Studies in the Resurrection*, p. 69.

had to go on performing the apologist's thankless task of refuting the stream of rationalistic theories advanced in explanation of the super-normal elements in Our Lord's life. Much of this work naturally centres upon the Resurrection. Replies to the opponents who seek a "natural" explanation of the empty tomb largely comprise arguments designed to show the improbability of the body of Jesus having been removed by any of the known parties—Joseph of Arimathea, Pilate, the Sanhedrin or the disciples. It is indeed difficult to see what motive could have led anyone to have removed the body—particularly any Jew—and still more difficult to imagine silence being afterwards maintained in view of the proclamation of the Resurrection; though the complacency with which the universal negative is assumed to have been demonstrated leaves one a little uneasy.[1] The hypothesis that the women went to the wrong tomb is rejected as a travesty of historical method. The identity of the tomb could have been settled at once—and certainly must have been by the interested parties.[2] Other elements in the tradition support the belief that the empty tomb was germane to the Apostolic belief in the Resurrection. The story of the guard at the tomb, Matt. 27: 62; 28: 11, bears witness to the acceptance at an early date (even by enemies) of the empty tomb tradition.[3] Indeed, six weeks after the event, we find the Resurrection being proclaimed in its literal sense in Jerusalem—from the reference to Ps. 16: 10 (Acts 2: 22f.; cf. 13: 35f.).[4] The expression "the Third Day" appears not only in the Resurrection narratives but in Christ's predictions, and in the institution of the first day of the week as a holy day (Acts 20: 7; 1 Cor. 16: 2; Rev. 1: 10). In the passage 1 Cor. 15: 3-8, the Apostle says Christ was "raised", not "seen", the third day.[5]

Turning to the appearances of Christ, we find that the first concern of apologists in modern times has been to establish the objective character of the Apostolic experiences. Belief and

[1] Milligan, *op. cit.*, p. 71; Orr, *op. cit.*, pp. 127-29; Simpson, *Our Lord's Resurrection*, p. 100, *Resurrection and Modern Thought*, p. 42; W. K. L. Clarke, *New Testament Problems*, pp. 106-7; and F. Morison, *Who Moved the Stone?*

[2] Simpson, *Resurrection and Modern Thought*, p. 17; Orr, *op. cit.*, p. 78; W. K. L. Clarke, *op. cit.*, pp. 105-6.

[3] Simpson, *Resurrection and Modern Thought*, p. 41; Headlam, *op. cit.*, p. 255.

[4] Simpson, *op. cit.*, p. 32.

[5] Denney, *op. cit.*, p. 112; Clarke, *op. cit.*, p. 103.

expectation, it is argued, are the essential pre-requisites for visions; yet both were lacking to the disciples. There seems to have been no Jewish belief in individual resurrections before the last day: and Jesus' predictions were unheeded—His body was anointed at burial. Nor were appearances multiplied at random: at first, in fact, the disciples did think that they saw a phantom.[1] There is no evidence that a myth pattern concerning the death and resurrection of a Divine being had ever been associated with the expectations of Messiah; and the myth hypothesis totally ignores such positive historical connections, as that St. Paul knew James, the Lord's brother.[2]

We find considerable divergence amongst our apologists in the critical treatment of the narratives of the appearances—ranging from the attempt to construct a harmony, to the treatment of them simply as typical encounters of the Lord with His disciples. The passage 1 Cor. 15: 3-8 is of primary importance. It is instructive that the two persons mentioned by name, St. Peter and St. James, are the very Apostles whom St. Paul had first met in Jerusalem.[3] Two points are generally stressed. First, the argument from the silence of different evangelists is of little weight, since the Gospels are strictly selective in their material; and secondly, there was ample time and opportunity for all the recorded appearances to have taken place, especially if such obvious parallels as Luke 24: 36 and John 20: 19 be taken as versions of the same event.

Some of the critical problems melt away for those who accept Swete's assumption that the Lord held sustained personal intercourse with the Apostles after the Resurrection. His harmonization follows the traditional pattern, with the Galilean appearances between the two sets of Jerusalem ones. Only by attempting to build up a consecutive reconstruction, he says, is it possible to see the greatness of the event.[4] Sparrow Simpson was one who attempted to vindicate the Jerusalem tradition. St. Mark's narrative implies that the disciples were

[1] Milligan, *op. cit.*, pp. 93-106; Orr, *op. cit.*, pp. 224-25; Peake, *op. cit.*, p. 201; Dods, *op. cit.*, p. 100; Rogers, *op. cit.*, p. 92.

[2] Orr, *op. cit.*, pp. 235f.

[3] Denney, *op. cit.*, pp. 113-15; Chase, *op. cit.*, pp. 392f.; Headlam, *op. cit.*, pp. 248-49; Simpson, *Our Lord's Resurrection*, pp. 106, 135; *Resurrection and Modern Thought*, pp. 123f.; Peake, *op. cit.*, p. 199; Robinson, *op. cit.*, pp. 50-52.

[4] *Appearances of Our Lord*, pp. xiiif. and 51.

still in Jerusalem on the third day, and St. Matthew and St. John equally testify to a Jerusalem—as to a Galilee—tradition. The church, moreover, was born in Jerusalem, not Galilee.[1] Dean Selwyn adopts a quite different course, and takes the Lucan narrative as the basis of his reconstruction.[2] A different treatment still is to be found in Denney. The Gospels, he says, were not conceived by their authors to be exhaustive statements of the evidence; they were written to bring out the permanent significance of the Resurrection for the church. Hence they condense the evidence into a representative scene, which in each case brings out those elements most appropriate to the Evangelist's purposes.[3] We have here an example of a not uncommon occurrence in modern times, viz. an exegetical suggestion being subsequently used to solve a problem in historical criticism. Milligan had worked out many years previously the relation of each appearance narrative to the Gospel in which it stands: in St. Matthew, for instance, we have the Galilean ministry with the bestowal of the new law and the true righteousness, and in St. John the manifestation of Christ's glory and the triumph of belief over unbelief. In each case these emphases are reflected in the Resurrection narratives.[4] C. H. Dodd adds yet another step to this development when, from the angle of form criticism, he shows a number of definite points which each and every version of the tradition brings out.[5]

III

To one who began his study of the theology of the Resurrection, say, at 1880, the issue would appear simply as a discussion of the value of the tradition of the empty tomb. When seen against a wider canvas, however, it becomes apparent that the conservative, no less than the liberal, view is the product of a striking restatement which had come about during the 19th century. The literal, corporeal understanding of the Resurrection of Christ and of the faithful, which had become standard

[1] *Resurrection and Modern Thought*, pp. 64f.; cf. Chase, *op. cit.*, pp. 398f.
[2] *New Commentary*, III, pp. 303, 305, 309.
[3] *op. cit.*, p. 140. [4] *op. cit.*, p. 60.
[5] *The Appearances of the Risen Christ*, in "Studies in the Gospels", ed. D. E. Nineham.

in western theology, is represented in Anglican thought by the Fourth Article of Religion and the writings of Pearson, Stillingfleet and Hody. The article reads: "Christ did truly rise again from death, and took again his body, with flesh, bones, and all things appertaining to the perfection of Man's nature . . ." But with Locke, who thought of the persistence of personality as a continuity of consciousness rather than of substance, there began a movement towards the Origenist idea of a "spiritual resurrection". Isolated representatives of this view appeared, such as Burnet, *De Statu Mortuorum*, 1715; but in the middle of the 19th century there come three writers whose work hails the demise of the literalist view. The point to be noticed about these writers is that their view was shaped wholly by theological considerations, not by difficulties in the historical evidence or by prejudice against the miraculous.

Goulburn, seeking confirmation from the Resurrection of Christ for his view of the spiritual nature of our own resurrection, argues that although the Gospels seem to show an "animal" resurrection it was in fact an adaptation of revelation to human mental conditions.[1] By a miracle, the spiritual Resurrection body of Christ was rendered cognizable to human senses.[2] The more forthright Bush maintains that a corporeal Resurrection is not incontestably taught in Scripture, and a spiritual interpretation brings the Resurrection of Christ and that of the saints into a perfect analogy.[3] We either have to say that Christ's material body became spiritualized so as to pass through doors, or we have to posit a miraculous adaptation of His spiritualized body to the disciples' senses: the latter seems to fit the facts more adequately.[4] The fact to be established was that Christ lived, and for this purpose, the raising of His physical body was unnecessary: but in order to prevent misunderstanding, His corpse was miraculously dissolved in the tomb.[5] The idea of Christ's possessing a risen body essentially spiritual in nature was popularized by Westcott, and most conservative and modernist writers are indebted to him.[6]

[1] *Bampton Lectures*, 1850, pp. 149f.

[2] *op. cit.*, p. 161. This view is nearer to Keim's theory of "objective visions" than to the IVth Article.

[3] *Anastasis*, 1845, p. 152. [4] *op. cit.*, p. 154. [5] *ibid.*, pp. 164-66.

[6] For a fuller account of this development see W. J. Sparrow Simpson, *The Resurrection and Modern Thought*, ch. XXVII.

According to Westcott, the Resurrection body of Christ is essentially ethereal; but in order to accomplish the victory over death, the redemption of the whole of human nature, and to provide adequate evidence of the fact, it was the body which hung on the Cross which was thus transformed. So that, though "true personality lies in the preservation of the individual formula or law which rules the organization in each case, and not in the actual but ever-changing organization which may exist at any moment", resumption of the crucified body conveyed to ordinary minds a conception which could not otherwise easily be gained, and brought the fact of the Resurrection within the reach (as far as could be) of continuous observation.[1]

It will now be easier to understand the apparent tension which characterizes the writings of conservative apologists in the present century. They have sought to hold together both the belief in the spiritualized conception of the Resurrection and also the historic tradition of the empty tomb. But this is no makeshift; its fine balance is precisely that of the Gospel tradition itself, in which Jesus "took bread", and "vanished out of their sight". The material aspects of the Resurrection have continued to be justified by arguments of two kinds; first, the historical plea that only such a resurrection could have appealed to the disciples; and secondly, the theological thesis of the redemption of the whole of human nature and the carrying through of the act of Incarnation into and beyond the grave. The combination of ethereal and corporeal qualities attributed in the narratives to Christ's risen body was occasioned by the originality of the conception, the unique evidential purpose to be fulfilled and that there might be both continuity with the past and a revelation of the new life.[2]

[1] *Gospel of the Resurrection*, pp. 111-12, 144.

[2] Simpson, *Resurrection and Modern Thought*, pp. 89-90; Milligan, *op. cit.*, pp. 7-11, 14, 29, 31; Denney, *op. cit.*, pp. 113, 143, 146; Bruce, *Apologetics*, pp. 392-93; Illingworth, *Divine Immanence*, p. 99; Headlam, *Miracles of the New Testament*, pp. 259-60, 249.

IV

The historical evidence for the Resurrection, strong though it was, gained its ultimate power to convince through its association with the total fact of Christ. Whereas such a report would be discredited at once of anyone else, says Denney, when asserted of Jesus—in whom men had recognized power and goodness beyond that of common humanity—it was accepted by His followers as being in keeping with all they had known, hoped and believed of Him.[1]

For this juxtapositing of the historical and religious considerations, conservative writers have been assailed from more than one quarter. On the one hand, it has been urged by some of the Ritschlians and Barthians that this position, like catholic theology in general, abandons the true meaning of faith by confusing it with the intellectual apprehension of historical facts on evidence. On the other side, it has been said that the historical enquiry has been sold, by the introduction of the *deus ex machina* of the moral argument. But what was happening to our apologists was this. The rigours of historical study plus the awakening of religious insights were making them see that if the Resurrection is anything at all, it is, along with the Cross, the supreme revealing and redeeming act of God. This is the reinterpretation applied to the great miracle, which we have seen already being applied to the deeds of Christ (ch. 10). On such a view, meaning must go with fact, and personal faith with reasonable historical evidence—like grace with sacrament and soul with body.

Westcott, who had so much to say about the deeds of Christ, also pointed the way to the fuller understanding of the place of the Resurrection. In discussing it as a fact, he says, it is impossible not to take into consideration its moral significance. No external evidence alone could ever establish more than an otiose belief in the occurrence of an isolated miracle in a distant age, "while a combination of external and internal evidence is capable of producing a measure of conviction which is only less certain than an immediate intuition."[2] The Resurrection is not an accessory, but the sum of the Apostolic Gospel, and the fact

[1] *op. cit.*, p. 125. Cf. Temple, *Faith and Modern Thought*, p. 76.
[2] *Gospel of the Resurrection*, 1874 ed., pp. 12-13.

on which hangs the question whether all hope, impulse, knowledge and life are bounded by the world of sense.[1] Consider what a development is implied in this thesis, put forward so long ago as 1865. First, belief in Christ is an act of the whole man: a difficult operation for the post-renaissance man with his mind split into intellect and feeling. For this act of receiving revelation, neither the evidentialist nor the Ritschlian theologies can provide an adequate diagram. Secondly, consider the implicit development in the idea of revelation, alluded to over and over again by Westcott as though it were self-evident. Revelation is held to consist in the Incarnation, and not least in the cycle of miraculous occurrences relating to Christ's person. These miracles thus assume a more profound significance than ever they had in the evidentialist scheme.[2]

In view of the great changes that had come about in regard to the character of revelation and its epistemology, it was necessary for theologians to be very clear about the arguments which they were using. The clarification of two points was essential. First, no rationalistic scheme of belief could furnish an intellectual framework for the apprehension of revelation as it was now envisaged. Secondly, the idea of an intuitive or Divinely infused perception of revelation had to be guarded both against the tendency to use it as a short-circuit of historical problems, and against the assertion that the reception of the strictly historical credenda is no real part of Christian believing. The exclusive concentration upon the "historical Jesus" was no more an adequate account of the Christian affirmations than the older evidentialism. "That the Word has been 'made flesh', and made flesh in just the specific person whom the Christian calls Lord, is a proposition which admits of no establishment by the empirical appeal to established fact." A. E. Taylor thought that this needed to be recognized more unreservedly by apologists.[3] But the pendulum swung far the other way, and in some minds the moral arguments came to

[1] *op. cit.*, pp. 18, 53.

[2] Other presentations of the moral considerations for the Resurrection will be found in Macpherson, *The Resurrection of Jesus Christ*, 1867, pp. 99-117; Milligan, *op. cit.*, pp. 35f., 117ff.; Robinson, *op. cit.*, p. 27; E. L. Strong, *Incarnation of God*, p. 110; H. S. Holland, in *Miracles*, pp. 118f.

[3] *Faith of a Moralist*, II, pp. 126-27.

stand as a kind of make-weight for the apparent lack of historical certitude. Then there were those who made it a matter of principle to distinguish the act of faith from the belief in the historical credenda. Sparrow Simpson strenuously maintained that the reception of the historical data was not out of harmony with the New Testament conception of faith. The idea that faith can only be in a person, and hence that the bodily Resurrection can only be a matter of intellectual assent, is falsely premised. For personal faith itself, he says, cannot be destitute of an intellectual element, or religion would be reduced to mere illusion. Hence, he concludes, "Faith in Jesus Christ is indeed faith in a person. But it is faith in Him as what? If it be answered as Incarnate, as Mediator, these answers represent historic facts. Faith in His Person, in the Christian sense, cannot be separated from faith in His Incarnation and His death and His Resurrection."[1]

V

At this point we must turn to consider the Virgin Birth, which like the Resurrection became a subject of heated controversy amongst professing Christians with the coming of higher criticism.

To the English modernists, the Virgin Birth was but one of several early Christian interpretations of the Incarnation. Opinion has differed somewhat among traditionalist theologians as to the value of some of the familiar arguments in support of the congruity or necessity of the Virgin Birth; but they agree that, without this belief, the idea of the Incarnation would be definitely altered. There is a considerable difference of status between the miracle of the Virgin Birth and that of the Resurrection from the standpoint of apologetics. The former was never pressed as a proof of the claims of Christ in the same way as the latter even by the evidentialists. Further, it is supposed by most modern theologians that during the lifetime of the Blessed Virgin the manner of Our Lord's birth was at most known only to a small number of His followers. The

[1] *Resurrection and Modern Thought*, pp. 443f., 451f., 457. A trenchant discussion of the anti-intellectualist tendencies in Ritschlianism was given by J. K. Mozley, *Ritschlianism*, esp. pp. 243-50.

majority of the first Christians embraced the Faith, not only unpersuaded by the Virgin Birth, but in ignorance of it. It is arguable, however, that the situation in Apostolic times was necessarily abnormal: that once the Virgin Birth had been proclaimed and its significance understood, belief in it became a necessary part of the deposit of faith. We must distinguish between what may be necessary to the faith of any particular individual and what may be necessary to the truth of Christianity as a whole.[1] This would appear to be experimentally true, for the modern era has furnished many examples of men and women of outstanding Christian faith who have not accepted the tradition of the Virgin Birth. But the place which this doctrine should hold in the church's teaching must be guided by the consideration of its relevance to the Incarnation.

A great deal of the critical work carried out by conservative apologists has of necessity been negative in character. The apparent silence of the New Testament writings, apart from the birth narratives, is a problem that has come into view with the modern approach to the documents as separate sources. Bishop F. H. Chase was one of the very few conservative scholars before 1914 to admit the almost complete extent of this silence.[2] Many writers, however, have continued to see a number of allusions to the Virgin Birth, and have suggested various reasons for the absence of direct discussion of the subject. Such discussion in public writings would not have been natural during the lifetime of the Blessed Virgin.[3] Silence was appropriate during the ministry of Christ, as He would have wished men to recognize Him as Son of God before they thought of Him as a prodigy.[4] The birth and infancy did not enter into the plan of the Gospels of St. Mark and St. John, which significantly begin in each case with statements regarding Christ's person.[5] It is considered probable that the author of the Fourth Gospel knew the First and Third Gospels and the tradition represented by St. Ignatius. The text of John 1: 13, even as it

[1] Hodgson, *And Was Made Man*, p. 129; Orr, *Virgin Birth*, pp. 24-26.

[2] *Camb. Theol. Essays*, pp. 406-7. Cf. V. Taylor, *The Historical Evidence for the Virgin Birth*, 1920, ch. I.

[3] Orr, *op. cit.*, p. 96. [4] R. M. Benson, *The Virgin Birth*, 1904, p. 9.

[5] Gore, *Dissertations*, p. 6; Orr, *op. cit.*, pp. 106-8; J. Armitage Robinson, *Thoughts on the Incarnation*, p. 39; Swete, *Apostles' Creed*, pp. 48-49; Rogers, *Case for Miracle*, p. 100; V. Taylor, *op. cit.*, p. 8.

stands, is thought by some to imply a conscious parallel between Jesus' supernatural birth and the spiritual rebirth of believers.[1] The Prologue as a whole, far from being in opposition to the Virgin Birth tradition, may well be a deliberate discussion of the principle underlying it.[2] The question of Jesus' parentage and birth-place is alluded to a number of times in the Fourth Gospel: 1: 45-46; 6: 42; 7: 27, 41-52; and the most natural way to understand these passages is to suppose that the Evangelist and his readers know the stories of Bethlehem and the Virgin Birth.[3]

Of St. Paul's writings, James Orr says that there is hardly an allusion to Christ's entrance into our humanity which is not marked by some significant peculiarity of expression to which the Virgin Birth would be the key, assuming that the Apostle knew of it.[4] Gore writes that, "Considering how strongly St. Paul expresses the idea of the solidarity of man by natural descent, and the consequent implication of the whole human race in Adam's fall, his belief in the sinless second Adam seems to me to postulate the fact of the Virgin Birth."[5] Other writers are less sanguine, and criticism appears to have hardened against the conservative interpretation of the Pauline passages supposed to refer to the tradition.[6]

With regard to the birth narratives, two charges had to be met:—first, that they are mutually contradictory on matters of history, and secondly, that each shows traces of a tradition contrary to that of the Virgin Birth. Discrepancies merely point to independent witness; and in fact the narratives undesignedly supplement one another.[7] The genealogies are only inconsistent with the Virgin Birth in the form in which the critics suppose them originally to have existed: the Evangelists see no contradiction in them.[8] Others point out the midrashic character of the Matthaean genealogy, with its inclusion of three women (Matt. 1: 3, 5, 6) which itself presupposes the Virgin Birth

[1] Orr, *op. cit.*, pp. 108, 112.
[2] Gore, *op. cit.*, pp. 7-9; F. R. M. Hitchcock, *Christ and His Critics*, pp. 38-40.
[3] Orr, *op. cit.*, p. 113; V. Taylor, *op. cit.*, pp. 15-19.
[4] *op. cit.*, p. 117. [5] *Dissertations*, p. 11.
[6] Swete, *Apostles' Creed*, p. 55; Headlam, *The Miracles of the New Testament*, p. 281; V. Taylor, *op. cit.*, p. 6.
[7] Chase, *Camb. Theol. Essays*, p. 408; J. A. Robinson, *op. cit.*, pp. 32-35; Benson, *op. cit.*, p. 7; Gore, *op. cit.*, p. 36.
[8] Orr, *op. cit.*, pp. 101-3; Benson, *op. cit.*, p. 28; Chase, *op. cit.*, p. 411; Rogers, *op. cit.*, p. 111; Gore, *op. cit.*, p. 37.

tradition.[1] Box thinks that the Lucan genealogy is intended to suggest that, like the first Adam, Jesus owed His human existence to a direct creative act of God.[2] Box and Chase point out that a contrast, not a parallel, is drawn in the Lucan narrative between the births of Jesus and the Baptist.[3] The Davidic descent and the description of St. Joseph and the Blessed Virgin as "parents" cannot legitimately be cited against the Virgin Birth tradition. There is not the slightest evidence to suggest that Luke 1: 34-35 is an interpolation, and vv. 36-37 would be pointless if something miraculous were not to happen.[4]

The origin of the tradition in a heathen myth is impossible. The parallels adduced are far-fetched and contain debased ideas of the Deity which would have been repugnant to Jews. The narratives in St. Matthew and St. Luke, moreover, are completely Jewish in thought and expression. A Jewish myth as the original is out of the question on account of the complete absence of such an idea from other Jewish literature. Jewish ideas of God would have virtually precluded such an expectation. Finally, Armitage Robinson has called attention to the emphasis laid upon "truth" in the primitive church; such an atmosphere would be uncongenial to the existence of such dark corners of legend.[5]

On the more positive side, it is generally contended that the narratives in St. Matthew and St. Luke represent independent testimony. Swete believes that the style of the first two chapters of St. Luke points back to a Judaeo-Christian source earlier than the fall of Jerusalem. St. James and the church of Jerusalem would have been a natural repository for such a document.[6] Vincent Taylor points out that the tradition belonged to the influential circles from which our First and Third Gospels came. Each narrative implies, rather than reproduces, what may be thought to have been a single, earlier tradition.[7] The narratives lay the emphasis, not on the element of prodigy

[1] G. H. Box, *The Virgin Birth*, pp. 10-11; Headlam, *op. cit.*, p. 272.

[2] *op. cit.*, p. 39. [3] Box, *op. cit.*, p. 40; *Camb. Theol. Essays*, p. 413.

[4] Headlam, *op. cit.*, p. 275.

[5] Box, *op. cit.*, pp. 7-18; J. A. Robinson, *op. cit.*, p. 42; Orr, *op. cit.*, pp. 151f.; Chase, *op. cit.*, pp. 411-14; Gore, *op. cit.*, p. 35; Headlam, *op. cit.*, pp. 293-94; Rogers, *op. cit.*, pp. 108-17; V. Taylor, *op. cit.*, p. 124.

[6] *op. cit.*, pp. 49-50. [7] *op. cit.*, pp. 116-17.

in the Virgin Birth, but upon its evangelical significance.[1] Assuming the tradition to be true, could the historical evidence which we possess have been stronger?[2]

On the doctrinal considerations, our apologists may be roughly divided into those who have maintained the traditional arguments and those who, whatever their private convictions, have confined themselves to a much shorter front. To R. M. Benson, the Virgin Birth is the connecting link between Jesus' essential Godhead and the acts which He does for us in our human nature thus assumed. The Son of God could not lay aside His eternal personality, so as to become a finite agent, deriving His activity from a finite source.[3] A similar argument had been used in the previous decade to show that Our Lord could not have possessed a human mind with limited knowledge. Nevertheless (as Gore argues) granted the Eternal Son did at a certain moment of time take flesh by a real Incarnation, and was born as a man without change of personality, or addition of another personality, but simply by the addition of a new nature, can we conceive it to have taken place by the ordinary process of generation?[4] Then there is the belief in Christ as the sinless second Adam. When we consider the real moral gulf that exists between Christ and all other men, can we think of this new moral creation involving anything less than a new physical creative act?[5]

There have been conservative writers who were dubious indeed as to the value of the *a priori* arguments for the Virgin Birth: the very uniqueness of the Incarnation precludes our expectation as to the manner in which it would be accomplished.[6] But it seemed significant that denial of the Virgin Birth had generally been one step towards what Sanday called a "reduced Christology".[7] Dean Armitage Robinson lectured on the subject at a time when the Anglican hierarchy was being pressed to insist upon conformity to the belief in the Virgin Birth on the part of the clergy. It was a belief, he contended, which might be appropriated in the light of full Christian faith in the Incarnation, but should not be imposed by authority.

[1] Rawlinson, *Christ in the Gospels*, pp. 23-24.
[2] Chase, *op. cit.*, p. 115; C. Harris, *Creeds and Modern Thought*, p. 52.
[3] *op. cit.*, pp. 1-4. [4] *Dissertations*, p. 64.
[5] Gore, *op. cit.*, pp. 65-66. Cf. Illingworth, *Divine Immanence*, p. 95.
[6] Chase, *op. cit.*, p. 414. [7] Orr, *op. cit.*, pp. 9f; V. Taylor, *op. cit.*, p. 130.

If "a wholly new departure in human history was being made, is it unreasonable to suppose that this departure might be marked by a signal miracle?"[1] Very similar are the conclusions of Dean Matthews. He adds that, "though we may still believe in the Incarnation without the Virgin Birth, it will not be precisely the same kind of Incarnation, and the conception of God's act of redemption in Christ will be subtly but definitely changed."[2] Dr. Rawlinson has also entered a strong caveat against a facile immanentalism in respect of the act of Incarnation. The coming into the world of a Person in whom history itself is transcended is an event which (if it occurred at all) is by its very nature not explicable in terms of the normal sequences of human generation, conception and birth.[3] As a historical question, concludes Vincent Taylor, the Virgin Birth is "not proven" and must ultimately be decided on doctrinal grounds. He looks forward to the day when we shall have the unfettered mind of the whole church on the meaning of Christ, and hence on the truth of the Virgin Birth.[4]

VI

The writers considered above have maintained the thesis that the miracles associated with the person of Christ may only properly be received as integral parts of the total apprehension of Him by the believing church. English Modernists, on the other hand, had been preoccupied with the task of building a new structure of apologetic beneath the Creed, and they could not see their way to undergirding those parts which took the form of assertions about physical miracles. For nearly forty years the Church of England was especially agitated by repeated controversies regarding the legitimacy of its officers' reciting the Creeds whilst declining to accept the literal sense of the miraculous clauses. Modernists considered that the Virgin Birth and the bodily Resurrection could be disbelieved and treated symbolically without compromise to the essential Christian revelation. But here was the real point at issue: What is the Christian revelation? Conservative theologians continued to

[1] *Some Thoughts on the Incarnation*, 1903, p. 27.
[2] *Essays in Construction*, 1933, pp. 128-29.
[3] *Christ in the Gospels*, p. 22. [4] *op. cit.*, pp. 128-31.

urge that it is primarily a series of acts of God in history—all of them unique; some of them miraculous, in the traditional sense of the word.

Dr. Gore found himself repeatedly at the centre of the controversy.[1] He acknowledges the legitimacy of symbolic interpretation in two categories of religious thought: first, in all our statements regarding the being and attributes of God, and secondly, in the case of a whole group of subjects which lie outside present human experience. It was, however, the distinctive boast of Christianity that, by a personal Incarnation, God had in quite a new way passed inside the region of human experience; that God had revealed Himself, distinctly, in words and acts, some of them miraculous. Symbolic interpretation, contended Bishop F. H. Chase, was a euphemism: first, for the denial of the truth in question, and secondly, for the substitution of something else—putting a spiritual truth in place of the event. The same principle of interpretation could be applied to the Incarnation itself.[2] Modernists were accustomed to argue that, since the idea of the three-tier universe had been abandoned, and the Descent, Ascent and Session of Christ were received in a figurative sense, it was only carrying the same principle further to accept the Virgin Birth and Resurrection in a symbolic manner. But, replied Chase, the idea that all these articles were once taken literally was quite erroneous. The early church never believed that God had a body, so that the session of Christ must always have been taken symbolically; and the descent and ascent of Christ were certainly interpreted symbolically in the Fourth Gospel—so there was no question of modern knowledge rendering the literal belief in these statements impossible.[3] Nor was it true, as was often urged, that the narratives of the Virgin Birth and Resurrection were the best way of expressing the underlying truths, if the events did not literally take place.[4]

Sanday and others had distinguished between the "content" of the Creed, its permanent meaning, and its "form", which

[1] Cf. G. L. Prestige, *Charles Gore*, pp. 81, 191, 243-47, 342f. Gore, *Basis of Anglican Fellowship*, 1914, pp. 8-20; "The Place of Symbolism in Religion", *Constructive Quarterly*, March, 1914; *Belief in God*, 1921, pp. 172-81; *New Commentary*, III, p. 313.

[2] *Belief and Creed*, pp. 159f., 170-81.

[3] *op. cit.*, pp. 41, 46f.; *Creed and the New Testament*, pp. 11, 15f., 26.

[4] Gore, *Belief in God*, p. 181.

must change with the intellectual outlook of the day. Many traditionalists had come to question the permanent value of the "form" in the matter of the Patristic Christology, but they contended that to treat the miracles of Christ as a transitory form was to misunderstand the character of the Christian affirmations, and to sanction an erroneous view of the development of doctrine. Christ had either crowned His outward Incarnate acts by rising from the dead, or He had not: content and form were here identical. The distinction between content and form was inapplicable to historical statements. So argues N. P. Williams in his correspondence with Sanday.[1] It was natural also that the modernist plan to reinterpret the Faith should be challenged from the standpoint of the belief in a definite deposit of faith once delivered to the church. Theology is a progressive science, says Charles Harris: it grows through the logical consequences of its first principles and appropriates the best thought of subsequent ages; but it is erroneous to suppose that because doctrines develop, all doctrines change—belief in a historic fact is incapable of change.[2]

The man who seeks a middle course in theology is always vulnerable to the charges of eclecticism and compromise. Yet in the matter of the relation of Christian faith to its historical foundations, the two extreme positions which have been proposed as substitutes for the traditional way are surely dead ends. On the one hand, the historical vehicle was deemed to be inessential to the further progress of the religious truth brought by Christianity. But thinkers so far removed from one another as Tyrrell and Kirsopp Lake confessed that whatever survived on such a view would be something very different from the traditional faith of the church. On the other hand, the essence of Christianity was held to lie in the evaluation of a piece of history, thought to be laid bare by stripping off the layers of dogmatism and supernaturalism, in which it had been parcelled up for its preservation. This view fails to recognize that the history as we have it is bound to come to us through the medium of the Apostolic faith, and that what has been accepted after the stripping is bereft of those transcendental experiences

[1] *Form and Content in the Christian Tradition*, 1916, pp. 84-87. Cf. T. B. Strong, *Miraculous in Gospels and Creeds*, 1914, pp. 10-14.

[2] *Creeds and Modern Thought*, 1919, pp. 16, 24, 32f., 46-48. Cf. N. P. Williams, *Form and Content*, pp. 22f.

which played so vital a part in creating that Apostolic faith. The element of value and interpretation is already present in the selection and isolation of historical facts which are preserved, writes Dr. Rawlinson.[1] Liberals wanted a positive and scientific account of the life of Jesus, not in order to discard all interpretation, but to substitute another interpretation for the old one; to arrive at what significance Jesus may have as a purely human phenomenon.[2] Catholic modernists, holding that dogmas were practical conceptions, believed that the Christian experience was capable of maintaining itself independently of the truth of historical facts.[3] But such an agnostic position could make little missionary appeal, and is an entirely different thing from the Christian faith. Christianity begins from the assumption of the living personal God—a dynamic, as opposed to the Greek static view; and likewise the Gospel is proclaimed as a fact, rather than as a metaphysical theory.[4] Christianity, therefore, in so far as it is doctrinal, is not an abstract doctrine, but "an apprehension of the inner significance of certain events past and present in which God is pre-eminently operative and active". To distinguish, then, as modernists do, between fact and interpretation is to Hellenize the Gospel.[5]

In the fourth decade of our century, two Gifford lecturers have, from very objective standpoints, emphasized the connection between Christianity and its historic foundations. If it be admitted, argues Professor A. E. Taylor, that truths relating to the supra-temporal order may be revealed in history, there is the further complication that the credenda of the great positive religions include in every case some propositions which are themselves statements about events of the historical order.[6] This is most pronounced in the Christian Creed; and here, and not in the mere concept of revelation, lies the real crux for a philosophy of religion. The historical religions regularly treat the whole of their credenda as "saving truth"; but how is it possible for the philosophical mind to attach this kind of value to any statement of historical fact?[7] The function of religion in human life Professor Taylor defines as the transformation of personality by the substitution of the abiding and

[1] *Dogma, Fact and Experience,* 1915, pp. 24-25. [2] *op. cit.*, pp. 29f.
[3] *ibid.*, pp. 31f. [4] *ibid.*, pp. 39-44. [5] *ibid.*, pp. 45-46.
[6] *Faith of a Moralist,* II, pp. 109-10. [7] *op. cit.*, p. 111.

eternal for the merely temporary and transient as the centre of man's interest. It should be expected that in proportion as a religion succeeds in effecting this transformation, it will show a keener sense of the reality of both terms of the opposition. It might therefore be foreseen that the religion which grapples most successfully with the practical task of reorganizing life with an eternal good as its centre will be the religion which brings its God down most intimately into contact with the temporal, historical process, and consequently that it will find its historical connecting link between God and man in a personality standing in a much closer relationship to God than that of the prophet, the mere bearer of a message from the other side. We should therefore expect, he concludes—what we actually find in Christianity—that its historical revelation of God consists primarily, neither in a body of propositions about God nor in a code of precepts from God, but in the whole of a concrete Divine personality and life; that the revealer is the content of his own revelation.[1] If this were so, the historical credenda would be evidence of strength rather than of weakness.[2]

A further problem is created by the fact that so many of the events included in the credenda are of a kind unparalleled in the ordinary course of nature. A miracle creates a very real difficulty for a mind in earnest with the conviction on which all philosophy is based, that the world is an intelligible unity.[3] Professor Taylor, however, holds that

> it is clear, in fact, that the first believers were led to their belief neither by inference from the observed moral perfection of their Master, nor by reflection on the excellence of His moral precepts. What weighed with them, as we see clearly enough from the synoptic story and the Acts of the Apostles, was, first and foremost, the direct and immediate impression made by His whole personality of the presence in Him of something "numinous", not to be understood in terms of the categories of ordinary human life, and next, the confirmation of this impression by the transcendent events of the Resurrection on the third day and the wonderful manifestations of the day of Pentecost.[4]

But though Christianity is thus dependent upon its historical

[1] *op. cit.*, p. 121. [2] *ibid.*, p. 123. [3] *ibid.*, p. 112. [4] *ibid.*, p. 129.

credenda, "it does not follow that it is ever possible to say with finality just how much of what has been handed down as historical fact in the tradition of the community really has this character."[1]

Dr. Edwyn Bevan in his lectures makes two important preliminary points. First, he claims to deal simply with the kind of symbol which purports to give us knowledge of another order which in some sense it resembles; only since Plato had it been thought that there was a world in which our concepts of this world did not apply.[2] Secondly, "Not to get rid of anthropomorphism, which is impossible if man is going to have any idea of God at all, but to make the division between right and wrong anthropomorphism where it ought to be made—that is the main problem for all philosophy of religion."[3] Religious symbols, he says, fall into two classes: those behind which we can see, and those behind which we cannot see. The latter class may be typified by many of those representing the life of God, though there are many degrees in this category. Traditionalists believe that the Resurrection is also of this second class, a truth that cannot be better expressed than by the historical statement. But the question is wider even than this; for modernists put forward symbolism as the right interpretation of ALL religious beliefs.[4]

As a suggested criterion for distinguishing those symbols which take their value from being facts, Bevan begins with the principle that value always has reference to the activities of persons. From the point of view of history and religion, as opposed to that of Greek philosophy and natural science, a fact gets its value, not from exemplifying a general type or law, but on account of the unique quality of each person or set of persons or events.[5] We may not be able to see how an historical event can have supreme value for religion, if we look at it simply in isolation; but if we consider its place in the whole process, it is possible to draw the line in principle between symbolic and historical doctrines. If our communication with other personal spirits here and now would not be essentially different, even if certain figures or events in the religious tradition never actually existed or occurred, then we should

[1] *ibid.*, p. 138. Cf. pp. 113f.
[2] *Symbolism and Belief*, pp. 11-17.
[3] *op. cit.*, p. 26.
[4] *ibid.*, pp. 257-63.
[5] *ibid.*, p. 265.

not mind regarding them as mythical symbols.[1] Christians believe themselves to be in communion with the living Christ today. If Jesus is only symbolic, the symbol must cover a quite different idea from that which Christians have hitherto embraced.[2]

The context of Christ and His saving acts is of paramount importance. Religion, C. C. J. Webb shows, takes its rise in the action and tradition of a community; and this is pre-eminently true of the community which received the Biblical revelation.[3] The Biblical revelation through the community culminated in the Incarnation, in the death and Resurrection of Christ, which become not merely exemplifications of timeless realities, but the individual Christian's ground of hope for forgiveness and eternal life. Webb traces the influence of Cartesianism in the modern attempt to dismiss the idea of historical revelation, and he portrays the church as the community created by, and witnessing to, the Resurrection.

These candid examinations, and others like them, by students of the philosophy of religion provide some of the best apologetic work for the church's belief about itself that have been produced in the present century. They have set the stage on the level of philosophy for the new Biblical theology: the turning away from the abstract and the subjective study of Christian truths to the examination of the life and faith of the actual community created by Christ.

[1] *op. cit.*, p. 266. [2] *ibid.*, p. 274.
[3] *Historical Element in Religion*, 1935, p. 40.

Chapter Thirteen

EXEGESIS AND THE IDEA OF REVELATION

I

THE intense activity in the realm of New Testament criticism, and the sustained effort to discover the relevance for Christian faith of the events described in the New Testament, has borne fruit in yet other fields than those already described.

As early as 1909, the English high-churchman, Percy Dearmer, published his volume on faith-healing, in which he developed the thesis already enunciated by Westcott that the Gospel miracles are to be viewed, not as the arbitrary acts of omnipotence, but as the responses of God to faith; the perfect human faith of Jesus, and the faith of those who accepted His mediation—a power whose present operation is limited only by our own lack of faith.[1]

Better known is the volume by the Scottish divine, Principal Cairns, *The Faith that Rebels* (1928), in which the thesis is carried further. The Synoptic Gospels, he argues, present a consistent view regarding the conditions under which Our Lord's miracles were wrought; even the Fourth Gospel is in general agreement with this view, despite some traces of evidentialist motive. He works through the first half of St. Matthew's Gospel, showing that, in every instance, faith is posited (explicitly or implicitly) as the condition both of the works of healing and of power. The miracles, therefore, are not portents, but manifestations of the Kingdom of God.[2] Hence, "According to these Gospels, and their presentation of the teaching of Jesus, both the realm within the soul and the realm without, both the sin within man and the tragic element in human life, are regarded

[1] *Body and Soul*, pp. 154f. [2] *op. cit.*, pp. 66-70.

as alike spheres for conquest by the victorious energy of faith."[1] Modern theology had tended to deny the power of faith over the physical world. But take the crucial case of disease—"Jesus never seems to have hesitated in treating it as something alien to the Kingdom of Heaven. . . ." There is not one single instance recorded in which He refused the appeal of a sick man on the ground that it was God's will that he should continue to suffer. The belief of Jesus and His disciples that disease could best be attacked from within, by reinforcing the powers of spirit, was being increasingly corroborated by modern psychotherapeutics.[2]

Moreover, Cairns contends, in the Gospels, faith is not merely the subjective condition of those able to receive Jesus' ministry; it is the *modus operandi* of the sacred humanity of Christ Himself. Christ is thus a prototype of what the believer can himself achieve: for in Him the Kingdom has already come both actually and potentially. The "signs" are manifestations of the Kingdom, wrought by the Spirit of God through the ideal faith of the founder and in response to the faith of those who, through Him, enter into the Kingdom. The signs are "anticipations and proleptic manifestations of the Kingdom in its perfection."[3] It follows that Jesus' teaching about prayer, as in Luke 11, presupposes the kind of faith by which He wrought His own mighty works. Jesus here disclosed the secret of His own miracle-working power: prayer sustained by unique faith, hope and love.[4]

If Principal Cairns be asked whether he believes that the Kingdom as at present should be characterized by the Messianic signs, he replies that it depends on what is meant by a miracle. The difference between Christ's achievements and those of His followers is the measure of the difference between His personality and theirs. All spiritual phenomena are miraculous; there are answers to prayer every day; whilst in the mission field, away from the spiritual deadness of our time, very surprising things occur.[5]

It will at once be apparent that the reconstruction offered by D. S. Cairns is a direct continuation of the work of those scholars considered in our tenth chapter, who sought to relate

[1] *op. cit.*, p. 72. [2] *ibid.*, pp. 76-78. [3] *ibid.*, p. 67.
[4] *ibid.*, pp. 83-84. [5] *ibid.*, pp. 153-55.

the miracles of Christ more directly to the act of revelation, to the faith of believers, and to the Incarnate life of Christ. Here our attention is drawn chiefly to the miracles as bearing witness to the essentially supernatural character of the Christian life of faith, ideally realized in the perfect humanity of the Saviour. The approach to the Gospel miracles is thus brought directly into line with the Christology which has steadily become predominant in Britain since the time of *Lux Mundi*—that the revelation of God in Christ is to be seen, not in the direct manifestations of the Divine metaphysical attributes, but in the subsuming and transforming of humanity itself.[1]

Some writers have tried to relate the miracle stories to the modern critical approach to the Gospels even more closely than did Cairns. For instance, A. G. Hogg took as his basis for the examination of the miracles what we have come to call "realized eschatology". Our historical sense demanded, he argued, a recognition of continuity on the spiritual as well as on the material plane. The New Testament experience either had to be levelled down, or our estimate of the present possibilities of faith had to be levelled up.[2] Too narrow a view of redemption had often prevailed, in which it was conceived merely as a moral redemption within man; whereas to the first Christians redemption was "from the many-sided tyranny of an evil world-order, of which guilt and moral impotence were only factors."[3] Christianity, as opposed to Jewish apocalyptic, held that God was ready NOW to intervene to aid miraculously those who surrendered to His plan for the world. To Jesus, the Kingdom was knocking at the door, and His miracles were "powers of the age to come" (Heb. 6: 5). The miracles were not part of the essential nature of the Kingdom, but were "peculiarly associated with the momentous crisis of that cosmic struggle by which the old age was to be expelled."[4]

Unfortunately this writer gives no real answer to the question: in what way did Christ overcome the powers of evil by His physical miracles which was not brought about *ipso facto* by His moral perfection? It rather looks as though pressing the function of the miracles too literally is a blind alley, such as

[1] Cf. the author's *Conflict in Christology*, and D. M. Baillie, *God was in Christ*, p. 14.
[2] *Redemption from This World*, 1922, pp. vii-ix.
[3] *op. cit.*, p. 13. [4] *ibid.*, pp. 29-40.

when the Fathers began to ask, to whom was the atoning ransom paid? And in spite of his bold language about levelling up our expectations to the New Testament experience, Hogg's final word to us is simply to trust more in God's providence; which is rather an anticlimax. But Cairns and Hogg have recalled attention to a fact that should have been obvious all along to students of the New Testament—that in the thought-world of the early church, dominated (like the Old Testament) by the vivid picture language of type and fulfilment, the miracles of Christ had a profound significance, such that their experience of His person and work cannot fully be understood without grasping this significance.

II

In the light of all the recent penetration into the thought-world of the primitive church, it has become natural for the attempt to be made to discover the place which the miracle stories held in the first preaching of the new faith. The most thorough of such approaches is Dr. Alan Richardson's *The Miracle Stories of the Gospels*, 1941. One of his first tasks is to criticize the view of the Gospel miracle stories advanced by some of the leading exponents of form-criticism. These critics had sharply distinguished the miracle stories from the stories designed to present some special point of Christ's teaching, the paradigms, and had designated them "tales", which, it was held, had been disseminated by a class of story-tellers with the object of exhibiting the superiority of Jesus as a wonder-worker. The miracles were thus not part of the proclamation of the Gospel as such.[1]

Richardson discounts this view on a number of points. First, miracles in the first century, apart from some special significance in their character, would not have been a particularly compelling proof of Christ's powers.[2] Secondly, the apparent likeness of the Gospel stories to heathen tales is quite inconclusive; for it is difficult to see what other form a miracle story could have than a description of the patient, followed by an

[1] He cites Bultmann, *Form-criticism*, E.T. 1934, pp. 36f.; Dibelius, *From Tradition to Gospel*, E.T. 1934, pp. 79f.; V. Taylor, *Formation of the Gospel Tradition*, p. 119.
[2] *op. cit.*, p. 22.

account of the act of healing, and a statement of the patient's subsequent condition.[1] Of more weight are two further contentions. The form-critics find it quite impossible in practice to keep up their sharp distinction between the paradigms and the miracle stories. For instance, the cure of the withered hand, Mark 3: 1f., and the dropsical man, Luke 14: 1f., they call paradigms; whilst they disagree as to whether the exorcism, Mark 1: 23f., the palsied man, Mark 2: 1f., and the Syro-Phoenician woman's daughter, Mark 7: 24f., are paradigms or tales.[2] Again, the view of the form-critics utterly ignores the theological context and presuppositions of the Gospel writers. Other modern reconstructions—that the miracle stories were instances of faith-healing in the modern sense, or that they illustrated Jesus' compassion—were also open to the latter objection, for they obliged us to postulate a different reason for the telling of the miracle stories from the rest of the narrative.[3]

A great deal of modern study, in fact, of historical evidence and philosophical presuppositions has left out of account the question as to what the first makers of the Gospels believed about the miracles. If we begin with the Biblical theology, says Richardson, the question whether the miracles happened will be found to have answered itself—though it will still not convince those who do not understand the Gospel.[4] He shows how the Old Testament designation of God as "power", the living God, manifested in nature and history, is continued in the New Testament, where Christ is repeatedly represented as acting, especially in the miracles, by virtue of God's *dunamis*, *exousia* and *pneuma*, in the inception of the *basileia*—which, like the foregoing terms, indicates the acting, saving power of God. The miracles of Christ are thus in Biblical thought a revelation of the power and saving purpose of God.[5] The miracle stories were therefore told with the object of deepening the understanding of WHO JESUS IS. They were thus integral to the proclamation of the Kingdom of God; they were the powers of the Kingdom manifested in its Lord.[6] Healing and preaching are coupled together both in the missions of the disciples, Mark 6: 7-13, Matt. 9: 35; 10: 1f., Luke 9: 1-6; 10: 1-20,

[1] *ibid.*, p. 28. [2] *ibid.*, p. 27. [3] *ibid.*, pp. 29-33.
[4] *ibid.*, pp. 34-36. [5] *ibid.*, p. 17. [6] *ibid.*, p. 38.

and in the message to the Baptist, Matt. 11: 4f., Luke 7: 22.

Richardson thinks that the words, "He could there do no mighty work", Mark 6: 5, probably meant that people without faith in Him as Messiah were not vouchsafed the signs of the Kingdom: it would not have occurred to St. Mark that Jesus' power was limited by the subjective belief of the onlookers—a purely modern view. Jesus in fact refused signs to those who would not understand Him, and the sin of Bethsaida and Chorazin was, not that they did not wonder at His miracles, but that they did not repent.[1] In the passage, Mark 8: 14-21, the miracles of feeding are represented as signs; and the words, "having eyes, see ye not?", v. 18, indicate that these signs are a veiling of the *dunamis*, parallel to the way in which the parables work; Mark 4: 11.[2] Richardson adds little to the great 19th-century expositions of the meaning of the miracle stories in relation to the work of Christ. But he does draw attention to the great difference between the saving, personal faith in the Gospel stories and the modern idea of psycho-therapeutics. The leper, for instance, unclean in the religious sense, is enabled through faith in Christ to offer the things commanded by God; a perfect parable of the Pauline teaching[3] (Mark 1: 40-45).

Faith in Christ also supplies the key to the Old Testament Scriptures, and the miracles are seen to fulfil prophetic types. We have healings of the deaf and blind, prophesied as signs of the Messianic age, Isa. 29: 18; 32: 3f.; 35: 5; 42: 7; 61: 1 and Ezek. 24: 27; whilst the feedings of the multitudes recall the miracles wrought through Moses and Elisha.[4] The dilemma for the modern exegete is that if he does not find such thought-patterns, the Gospel stories become isolated marvels; whilst if he does, it is possible for others to argue that the stories have been invented or modified so as to conform to Old Testament types. Richardson and many others of our day seem prepared to sail close to the wind on the latter alternative. But he urges that in the Gospel of St. Mark we have not simply the reminiscences of St. Peter, but stories already in use in the church's teaching: we have, in other words, the authority of the church in Rome a generation after the Crucifixion of the Lord.[5] He

[1] *op. cit.*, p. 45. [2] *ibid.*, pp. 47-48. [3] *ibid.*, p. 61.
[4] *ibid.*, pp. 85f. [5] *ibid.*, p. 101.

admits that we cannot tell how much the writer of the Second Gospel modified the oral tradition; and of St. Luke he writes: "It is hard to escape the conclusion, especially if we have regard to some of the miracle-stories of Acts, that St. Luke did not hesitate to construct such stories, in harmony alike with the main purpose and general content of the church's tradition."[1] In selecting and interpreting the facts, the Gospels were exactly fulfilling the proper task of the historian. The only alternative to receiving this history from believers is complete scepticism.[2] Everyone who approaches the Gospels is already either a believer or an unbeliever; so that the answer to the question, Did the miracles happen?, must be a personal one. But since our faith includes our reason, we must make an intelligible assessment of the evidence.

The work of discovering the meaning which the miracle stories had for the early church, though it has put to flight some of the older scholastic and rationalistic assumptions, has led many writers to an attitude towards the Gospels which cannot be regarded with equanimity by those whose beliefs are built upon the complete New Testament picture of the acts of God in Christ. Since the first world war, the Gospels have to an ever-increasing extent been expounded as documents most carefully constructed to portray the early church's beliefs about Christ. It has thus not been difficult to discover typological and theological interests in almost every jot and tittle of the narrative; and this work has sometimes been carried on with a cheerful agnosticism regarding the historicity of the material. Sir Edwyn Hoskyns, for example, tells us that "there is no event or utterance recorded of Him which does not wholly proceed from a conception of the Messiahship smelted and sublimated from the ore of the Old Testament Scriptures; and that this complete Christological control is not imposed awkwardly upon the material, but underlies and penetrates every fragment of it."[3] The connection of the incidents and the grouping of the logia also belong largely to the literary structure of the Gospels or to the parenetic and hortatory character of primitive Christian instruction: a fact which opens new insight into the way in which the healing miracles and the

[1] *ibid.*, pp. 104-11. [2] *ibid.*, pp. 123f.
[3] *Mysterium Christi*, ed. Bell and Deissmann, 1930, p. 70.

teaching are related to one another.[1] Hoskyns' essay is in line with the attitude of several of the foreign contributors to the same volume. Sasse distinguishes the Resurrection narratives from faith in the event itself.[2] Gerhard Kittel avers that a mere historian can perceive no more in the life of Jesus than the crowds which saw Him; faith alone gives the key to the Jesus of History.[3]

We have already glanced at certain criticisms of this attitude to Christian origins in the foregoing chapter. Certain theologians have first made up their minds as to what is to be understood by Christian faith—that it denotes no less and no more than surrender to a person, the living Christ. Therefore, they say, it is of an entirely different order of apprehension from the intellectual act by which we accept the evidence for historical events. This ready-made view of faith is then brought to the historical Gospel. It cannot be denied that Christian faith has as its object a historical person, the record of whose life has to be dealt with by rational methods of study. But these writers do all they can to keep the two processes, of faith and historic recognition, separate. They say that historical criticism must be autonomous; that in any case we are not looking straight at history in the Gospels but at history through the theological lens of Apostolic faith; and they say that revelation does not lie sheer upon the plane of history—that even the supernatural accompaniments of the life of Christ do not of themselves suggest the unique activity of God. We seem here to be witnessing an inability to hold together the two poles of the unique character of Christianity: the personal, moral character of faith, as the subjective counterpart of the concrete, unique acts of revelation in history. It is surprising that so astute a thinker as John Baillie should have found it difficult to understand, as he says, how Aquinas could hold together the two ideas of proofs of revelation, in miracle and prophecy, with the notion of faith as a supernatural virtue.[4]

It appears indeed that Christian thinkers have never found it easy to hold together in due proportion the two poles of objective and subjective as regards revelation. The age of the Fathers and the orthodox theology of the Illumination stressed

[1] *op. cit.*, p. 71. [2] *ibid.*, p. 104. [3] *ibid.*, pp. 44f.
[4] *Our Knowledge of God*, 1939, pp. 113-14.

the objective aspect, but the subjective side was largely understood in terms of believing orthodox dogma or accepting rational inferences. The 19th and 20th centuries have witnessed, on the other hand, a tardiness in apprehending the relevance of the objective historical element. This is strikingly manifest if we examine an English representative of the Barthian school —a school which takes great pride in its rediscovery of what it holds to be the basic elements of the Biblical view of revelation.

F. W. Camfield draws a sharp distinction between the modern liberal view, in which religion is treated as one aspect of man's attempt to discover the meaning of the universe, and the attitude which demands a categorical answer to the question whether revelation has been given or not.[1] This once-for-all happening is fully articulated only in the New Testament, and it brings with it the principle and categories for its own interpretation. Reason can deal only with knowledge of an object; revelation, however, is knowledge of being known by a subject. Revelation can never, therefore, be proved, for that would be to step down to the subject-object relation; revelation can only be heard.[2]

Few elements in this scheme of thought appear further from traditional ways of thinking than its attitude towards Jesus' earthly life, in which, as has been said, God has veiled Himself so completely that only faith can pierce the veil. Camfield tells us that in Christ's earthly life, His Christhood had to remain a secret: He had to die in order that His glory might appear.[3] Nowhere in the New Testament is the unity between the human Jesus and the transcendent Christ placed in anything that is rationally discernible and discoverable in the former. And it is Jesus under His transcendent aspect, not the historical Jesus, which is declared to be revelation.[4] The Gospel, Camfield says, is not that God is like Jesus. One wonders what Maurice or the *Lux Mundi* men would have said about this denial of the manifestation of God through the perfect humanity of Christ! Camfield goes on to urge that the demand to explain Jesus psychologically, rationally and historically, is virtually the denial of revelation.[5] Hence the Divinity of Jesus was not a historical judgment, or an inference from His influence on

[1] *Revelation and the Holy Spirit*, 1933, pp. 12-20. [2] *op. cit.*, pp. 31-32. [3] *ibid.*, p. 49. [4] *ibid.*, pp. 52-53. [5] *ibid.*, p. 63.

men: it came in virtue of what to human reason is sheer miracle—the endowment of the Holy Spirit. Historical criticism cannot imperil revelation; it can do good, in showing that revelation does not lie in anything sheer on the historical level.[1]

There is some valuable truth in the foregoing appreciation of the work of Christ, which makes it regrettable that it should have been combined with the exclusion of other valuable truths. Camfield also has much to say that is helpful about the mission of the Spirit in illuminating men's faith.[2] But this leads him to pillory the traditional scheme of historical evidences. In orthodoxy, he says, faith must first go through endless apologetic reasoning to prove the historical elements in the life, death and Resurrection of Jesus, before religious values can be attached and faith can be had in the dogmas thus revealed.[3] He rightly points out that the fact can never be attested in such a way as to eliminate all doubts; but he draws the conclusion that faith, in the traditional view, is just a prolongation of reason. This would only be true of the most naïve form of evidentialism. If the historical element is essential, does he imagine that faith is a substitute for historical enquiry? Our approach to the historical Gospel, even to the determination of its factual side, can only fully be achieved by the light of the Holy Spirit, as Camfield urges.[4] He says that it had not been perceived by orthodoxy that revelation by its very nature precluded such a proof as that from miracle or prophecy—"For to prove revelation presupposes that it can be regarded from the point of view of pure objectivity, that it is a datum which can be approached from the outside, and validated on merely rational and historical grounds."[5] One would largely agree with this, but it is misleading to think of the whole non-Barthian Christian world as being in the same class as 18th-century evidentialism.

On miracles, Camfield observes that the very thing which revelation shows is the dualism between natural and supernatural.[6] There are plenty of miracles in the world, but they are not capable of being isolated, and rationally discovered, let alone capable of objective proof and demonstration.[7] The

[1] *op. cit.*, p. 65. [2] *ibid.*, pp. 99f. [3] *ibid.*, p. 108. [4] *ibid.*, pp. 110-16.
[5] *ibid.*, p. 128. [6] *ibid.*, p. 129. [7] *ibid.*, p. 158.

Christian himself undergoes a miracle of death and resurrection—that of faith. To this inward miracle corresponds the Resurrection of Christ in the outward world; this is the absolute miracle, he says, the abrogation of the law-conditioned order. The appearances to the disciples were a transitory thing, nor was it necessarily true that their faith would have collapsed if they had been confronted with the Lord's body: "What corresponds to faith is not a crude realistic event, but the Resurrection as the critical event, the subversion and overcoming of the actual, empirical, world, and the beginning of the new order. . . ."[1] It is not difficult to see the difference between this scheme of thought and traditional Christianity, in which it is held that the paradox consists in that Very God is manifested, not veiled, in a unique cycle of "crude, realistic" events.

Although the Barthians have grasped both the unique character of revelation and the necessity for its apprehension by a personal act informed by grace, their description of the way in which revelation is related to the historic mission of Jesus is unconvincing. They side-step the assertion that the cycle of events constituting the Incarnation may be recognized as miraculous in the physical as well as the interpretative sense of the word. The would-be believer ought to know whether it is possible to be reasonably sure (by a combination of historical evidence and spiritual recognition) that the unique power and personality of Jesus and His Resurrection were historical realities.

In these matters, William Temple is one of the most helpful guides. He is as emphatic as the Barthians in his rejection of the attitude which supposes that God never does anything in particular in any other sense than that in which He does everything in general.[2] Christianity is committed to the convictions, first, that God has a definite purpose for the world which He is partly accomplishing in the arena of human history, and secondly, that He has not only revealed His character but taken personal action in Jesus, who is Himself the decisive fact in history.[3] Just as the character of a human person is not fully known in his normal activity but only in his

[1] *ibid.*, pp. 151-56. [2] *Christus Veritas*, Preface.
[3] *Revelation*, a symposium, pp. 85-86.

significant actions in moments of crisis, so if God is to be known as person or will, this must mean that He too acts normally in ways adapted to the fulfilment of His purpose in general, but acts in special, and therefore specially revealing, ways when emergency makes this fitting; and He is only known fully to those who know Him in these specially revealing acts. To suppose that He can be known by a general inference from observed nature or history is to deny His personality and to treat Him as a thing.[1] The possibility of our being able to recognize the special revelation of God in specific acts of His is grounded in the nature of all things to reveal God in general. Revelation, moreover, must conform to the nature of all human experience, that is, it must be both objective and subjective; and in the Bible we find that revelation consists in the Divinely-controlled events of history which are interpreted by the Divinely-inspired prophets.[2] The truly objective view of revelation finds its completest illustration in the Incarnation. Against all suggestion that the fact is indifferent, that the human nature of Christ may have been a mere phantasm, St. John urgently insists on the central importance of the fact that "Jesus Christ is come in the flesh." The revelation is a life actually lived, culminating in actual death and actual Resurrection, upon the plane of history.[3]

Thus the consideration of various types of exegesis has led us back to the study of the Christian philosophy of the relation of God to His creation, and this we must pursue in the following chapter.

[1] *Revelation,* a symposium, pp. 93-95. [2] *ibid.*, pp. 95f. [3] *ibid.*, p. 104.

Chapter Fourteen

PHILOSOPHY, SCIENCE AND HISTORY

I

We have seen that conservative apologists have continued to claim that the evidence for the New Testament miracles is adequate, assuming those events to be intrinsically credible on other grounds. This intrinsic credibility is afforded by the whole context of the life and work of Christ which crowns the religious view of the universe: that it is not a self-contained machine but a creation designed to fulfil spiritual ends, and plastic in the hands of God. The development of a Christian philosophy of the universe must therefore go hand in hand with the exegesis of Scripture and the clarification of the early Christian evidences.

In the hands of the *Lux Mundi* school we see the traditional doctrines regarding the relation of God to the physical order beginning to assume their familiar modern shape. The most noteworthy achievement of this school was the conjoining of the ideas of organic evolution, Biblical criticism and Divine immanence on behalf of traditional orthodoxy. Gore sets out to show in his Bampton Lectures that the supernatural activity of God in Christ was the natural climax to the process of evolution. His arguments are in form virtually those of Butler; and his picture of the universe similar to that of Bushnell, except that evolution is substituted for the static tiers in nature's categories. He attempts to present a convincing analogy between the miraculous works of Christ and the appearance in nature of higher forms of activity. Many other important classes of facts, he argues, as well as the miracles of Christ, fall outside nature, if nature be regarded simply as a mechanism. But nature is, first, an order, and secondly, it shows on the whole an advance from the inorganic up to human personality.[1] This process is itself a progressive revelation of God, of which the climax is the revelation in Christ, in whom the previous revelation is confirmed and transcended. Nature without Christ is incomplete, for He alone fully reveals God's love and righteousness.[2] Christ represents a new level in creation, a new relation of the Creator Spirit to matter: hence to Christ, miracles are "natural".[3]

Gore has to deal with the rejoinder (which he does not put in so many words)—Is not this final stage of evolution adequately represented by the character of Christ's moral and spiritual life, irrespective of His miracles? He points to the disturbing fact of sin: Christ comes, therefore, not simply to consummate an order but to redeem it. Like Trench, he sees in the miracles the manifestation of God's vindicating and restoring the true meaning of nature. The Crucifixion of Christ took place according to the natural law, but it does not manifest the true order of the world. The Resurrection was an intervention, but it shows and vindicates the fundamental law of the creation.[4] Unfortunately, Gore throws little fresh light upon the relation of the miracles of Christ to His redemptive work. If anything, his writings show up the kind of problem which was to beset apologists in the present century.

In Illingworth's writings, we begin to meet some of the practical implications of regarding nature as a living expression of the creative activity of God. Our increased knowledge of nature's powers, he thinks, makes it preferable to think of the "unity" rather than of the "uniformity" of nature. Unity is a mental, spiritual concept, which we find within ourselves, and read into the manifold varieties of the world outside.[5] This unity in nature must be due to the action of a spiritual power: thus the more science impresses on us the unity of nature, the more does it by implication assert that nature is rooted and grounded in spirit.[6] Spirit claims as a right to govern, never to subserve, nature. When we see men slaves to their physical inclinations, for example, we recognize that they are contradicting their essential nature.

[1] *Bampton Lectures*, p. 31.
[2] *op. cit.*, pp. 32-34.
[3] *Belief in God*, pp. 234-41.
[4] *Bampton Lectures*, pp. 36-46.
[5] *Divine Immanence*, p. 103.
[6] *op. cit.*, p. 105.

From these premises, Illingworth believed that the antecedent probability of miracles was greatly increased. For instance, the older objections to miracles implied that we had a complete knowledge of the processes of nature; but the more we recognize that nature always has a spiritual coefficient, the less confident does this assurance become. Since Hume's time, it had come to be recognized that physical causes were only antecedents or conditions that transmit causation which they cannot originate. The idea of causation was itself derived from human consciousness of free will, and it is inferred that nature must originate in a will which is its own law and therefore its own explanation.[1] We never know all the pre-conditions of any event, he contends, and among those conditions is the presence of the spiritual power on which their existence and operation depends.[2] The Incarnation throws light upon the meaning and place of the universe: "for on the one hand, against mere idealism, it emphasizes the value and importance of matter, as being the agent through which God's spiritual purpose is effected: and on the other hand, against mere materialism, it interprets this value and importance, as consisting in the capability to subserve that purpose."[3]

But materialism has insinuated itself into modern thinking in a subtle way, by the idea that the higher and more complex forms of existence can be explained in terms of the lower. Theologians have to some extent been joined by workers in other branches of study. Biology, psychology and historiography have each been obliged to struggle for the independence of their own peculiar categories.[4] Apologists urged that nature was to be thought of as a living unity, whose higher elements were constantly moulding the lower to new issues, and in which forms of existence different in kind from the lower had successively appeared.[5] The idea of miracle, says Charles Harris, is implicit in the concept of "emergent evolution". The process of evolution contains new, and therefore discontinuous, qualities and values, whose miraculousness is

[1] *ibid.*, pp. 106-7. [2] *ibid.*, p. 114.

[3] *ibid.*, p. 116. Bishop C. F. D'Arcy pushed the argument still further, and contended that in the different modes of Divine activity in the world we can distinguish the operation of the members of the Blessed Trinity. *Idealism and Theology*, 1899, esp. pp. 41, 148ff.

[4] A. E. Taylor, *Faith of a Moralist*, II, p. 166. [5] Lock, in *Miracles*, p. 26.

veiled by the vast time over which the process is spread.[1]

If we take this view of the universe seriously, and regard the Incarnation as the miracle of miracles, is it not quite erroneous (some writers urge) to try to rule out miracles which may be *contra naturam* as Sanday does? His distinction, they say, is valid neither scientifically nor philosophically, and would only have a semblance of truth on a strictly mechanistic view of the universe, with God's relation to the world conceived on the Deist pattern. The distinction simply has reference to what the science of a particular decade finds credible—as if at a certain date a man had admitted that one might be able to communicate by telegraph across the Thames but not across the Channel.[2]

This is perfectly true as far as it goes. The impartial study of psychical phenomena—in the broadest sense—fragmentary though it still is, makes many of the older rationalistic objections to the miracles of Scripture appear quite childish. But this is not enough; it is not enough even to conclude that the material universe is completely pliable in God's hands. What we actually have to deal with are stories of miracles of a very diverse kind. It is most significant that all modern conservative apologists end by adopting canons of discrimination from the realm of value. The only possible *a priori* against miracle, N. P. Williams tells us, would be that on other grounds we knew it to be out of keeping with the character of God: like the story of the parrot, pursued by a hawk, which cried "*Sancte Thoma, ora pro nobis.*"[3] In actual fact, the only road left open—the genuine road—for apprehending the importance of the Biblical miracles is their analogy with the revealed character and purposes of God and with the spiritual powers conferred on man in His Kingdom. The phenomena of the day of Pentecost, for example, can all be paralleled in the history of mysticism and spiritualism: what gives the story its value is its setting in the Divine plan, the fulfilment of Christ's promises and the dynamic of the new era which was thus initiated.

[1] *Creeds or No Creeds*, 1922, pp. 151-52, 178-83.

[2] Harris, *Creeds or No Creeds*, pp. 171f.; T. B. Strong, *Miraculous in Gospels and Creeds*, pp. 23f.; H. S. Holland, *Christ or Ecclesiastes*, pp. 38-39, 45; *Creeds and Critics*, pp. 141-43; T. J. Hardy, *The Religious Instinct*, pp. 125-28; A. C. Headlam, in *Miracles*, pp. 44f.; D. S. Cairns, *The Faith that Rebels*, p. 4.

[3] *Form and Content*, pp. 137-38.

II

The conservative plea that modernists admitted the principle of the miraculous by their acceptance of emergent evolution, the direct action of God upon the soul, and the Incarnation, was a justifiable *tu quoque*; but it did nothing to answer the problem which the modernist compromise had been designed to meet, viz. the difficulties created for religion by the axiom of science that the objects making up the physical universe fall exclusively into a pattern of mechanical relationships. Christian thinkers had long cherished the belief that it was possible to mark off a definite area within the universe where the mechanical formula did not apply. But by the close of the 19th century this idea was already redundant.[1] The problem of induction was seen to be wider than science; it involved man's expectation of his own continuance and that of everything round him.[2] Science had something valid to say about all experience.[3] The mechanical pattern had now come to be traced within the area of human activity—in the physico-chemical movements of the brain, and in the "laws" of human behaviour. Here was a problem for secular philosophy no less than for theology. An absolute dualism between a human spiritual consciousness and a totality of mechanical patterns—a ghost driving a machine—was no rational account of the human situation. Approaching the question from the physical side, theories of parallelism have been advanced to show that mental and physical activity are virtually the same thing. But such theories are open to the objections to all deterministic theories: they are, for instance, self-invalidating, since the mind that conceives them is incapable of free thinking.

A door was opened, however, by the investigation of the structure of scientific thought itself. The idea that scientific knowledge was but a description of the relationships of phenomena had been familiar since the time of Hume.[4] It now came to be realized that all the categories with which the natural scientist deals are a system of abstract concepts designed to aid man in the conquest of his physical environment. Nature,

[1] Cairns, *The Faith that Rebels*, pp. 95-96.
[2] M. B. Hesse, *Science and the Human Imagination*, p. 152. [3] *op. cit.*, p. 155.
[4] Cf. the application of this in K. Pearson, *The Grammar of Science*.

say thinkers like Bergson and Whitehead, is more adequately thought of, not as a collection of static things, but as a process whose units, events, are of infinite variety in kind and context.

From the standpoint of the philosophy of religion it has been found possible to draw two kinds of conclusion from this analysis. First, since science deals with ideal experiments and with the isolated threads of causation, it is not possible for it ever to give a complete account of any particular situation in life, even on its physical plane. Hence the ultimate explanation and significance of events in the physical world lies outside its ken. Secondly, the understanding of the true nature of natural science provides a real justification for challenging the pretensions of positivists that the scientific method is the key to all reality.

One of the first theologians to exploit this position was J. Wendland, in a work which appeared in an English translation in 1911 under the title *Miracles of Christianity*. Belief in miracles, he says, is synonymous with belief in the living God, whose intra-mundane action—if He transcends the world—must wear the aspect of miracle. Miracle cannot be experienced apart from faith; and it is of the nature of faith to be indemonstrable. But the subjective view is not sufficient: recognition must also be given to the perception of Divine activity in the element of inexplicability in nature. Every event in nature has an aspect in which it is inexplicable; for science is concerned merely with charting causes on a superficial level and over restricted areas, and is therefore not competent to declare upon whether there is a transcendent factor manifesting itself in the world. Science is unable to give any fundamental account of factors such as "force", "causality", or the human spirit. The determinism in which everything is thought to be completely explained by its physical antecedents arises from an erroneous hypostatization of the purely mental idea of causality. Science grapples with particular aspects of things and particular causal connections, but all conceptions derived from the empirical sphere lose their significance when applied to the cosmos.[1] The idea of impersonal cosmic laws determining everything is no more demonstrable than Divine providence.[2]

[1] *op. cit.*, pp. 252-55. [2] *ibid.*, p. 260.

Faith holds that God can open up a new future at any moment; for every new effect is in a sense a new creation of God out of an infinity of possibilities.[1] Wendland claimed that this was not building religion upon gaps in our knowledge, but drawing attention to the ubiquity of the gaps—an inscrutability which stretched from the life of the individual to the widest causal sequences we knew.

The most important English contribution to this line of thought is Professor H. H. Farmer's *The World and God*, 1935. Farmer thinks that one of the pitfalls which beset the early enthusiasts in the field was that, in viewing the world as the continuous creative expression of God, sufficient room was not left for the relative independence of the created order: the condition necessary for man's moral life. He believes that this tendency is apparent in Wendland, and in Hogg's *Redemption from This World*. He therefore contends for a view of reality in which the basic factor is the personal encounter of God with men, the Divine demand and succour being mediated to man through the situations in which he finds himself in the visible creation.

The action of God in answering prayer, argues Farmer, does not violate the causal principle, and is assumed to be regulated by a consistency of wisdom: the only question is, whether this kind of causation is absolutely contradictory to that which is presupposed by science.[2]

> Doubtless [he says] from the angle of Theistic faith and philosophy there is a sense in which the character of the universe in general, and in particular the regularities without which it would neither have character nor be a universe, must derive from the will of God, but such a highly general truth obviously gives us no warrant for believing that any regularity we may have observed by our science belongs without qualification to one of the ultimate and unchangeable constancies.[3]

Some principles, like the conservation of energy, seem to be more like a jump of intuition than empirical laws; but it is possible that such laws derive their accent of necessity from the

[1] *ibid.*, pp. 246, 271-73. [2] *op. cit.*, p. 145. [3] *ibid.*, p. 148.

fact that they are, or include, disguised mathematical identities or truisms.[1]

Nevertheless, says Farmer, whereas nothing in science warrants us in setting limits to what is possible, science is bound to believe that generalizations are always possible. Would this scientific belief be impugned if it were admitted that events were initiated by God?[2] First, he urges, science can make no claim to give an exhaustive account of the reality with which it deals, nor even of any single event. Science is a continuous process of abstraction, whereby the richness and particularity of the real world is deliberately set on one side in favour of a scheme of conceptual symbols and their relations with one another. The correspondence between such a scheme and the real world can never be exhausted, for science has to accept any group of phenomena as a going concern: it can sort out the individual strands of causation, but it is unable to say why those particular causal series should have coincided to produce just that situation.

Secondly, he finds a key to the apparent contradiction between will and the seeming solidity of nature in the time-perspective of the human onlooker. From the standpoint of one's own conscious life, one believes the future to be indeterminate, and that one has in a measure the power to mould it. But if one looks out on events as a mere spectator, it is not difficult to imagine that they are unfolding according to some cast-iron necessity.[3] The present creates the past; the past does not create the present or the future, but provides the conditions for it. The relation of the fixity of the order of nature, which science observes, to the ultimate creativeness of will, which religion intuits, may be one form of the relation of the fixity of the past to our own present creativeness in our personal experience. The impression of unalterableness in nature would simply be the result of the fact that we are always observing what has happened already; always looking at what Bergson called "filled time".[4] Reality is a ceaseless upspringing of something new; and as, in the case of our past actions, we can easily find antecedents of which they might in a sense be the

[1] *op. cit.*, p. 151. Cf. Eddington's imaginary bursar, who thought that all the activities of the college could be expressed and explained by the equation of his profit and loss account. *Nature of the Physical World*, p. 237.

[2] *op. cit.*, p. 152. [3] *ibid.*, p. 164. [4] *ibid.*, pp. 165-67.

mechanical resultants, yet an action involving our whole person could not have been foreseen, even though its antecedents explain it when once it has happened.[1] Science will still give its own account of any specific intervention of God once accomplished: religious insight can alone determine that such and such was an answer to prayer. [*ibid.*, p. 177. This is a much more satisfactory version of Rothe's theory. The original form of the theory—that Divine activity is fed into the stream of natural causation—continues to attract some writers; cf. C. S. Lewis, *Miracles*, p. 72; F. Sherwood Taylor, *The Fourfold Vision*, 1945. How the above view of the world, as the scene of ever-creative activity by God and men, can be expanded into a Christian philosophy of history may be seen in R. Bultmann's Gifford Lectures, *History and Eschatology*, 1957. The most powerful refutation of the "bogey of mechanism" as applied to human action to be furnished in recent years is to be found in Gilbert Ryle's *The Concept of Mind*, 1949. Whatever may be thought of the rest of the book, this task is performed magnificently. If we watched a game of chess, not seeing the players actually moving the pieces, we could deduce the precise laws which governed the movements of each piece—but the game is still not wholly explained mechanistically, for in fact it is played by freely acting persons. In billiards, the laws of physics do not force the player's hand.[2]]

III

On the assumption that the scientific picture of the universe was but an outline in black and white of something infinitely more rich and colourful, was it not possible for some fresh light to be shed upon the old distinction between miracle and providence? At first sight the distinction might seem to be unmeaning, if nature was an organic expression of Divine creativity. But Christian thinkers were pledged both to the belief in the relative independence of the creation and to faith in the unique action of God in the Incarnation. During the past quarter of a century, it has been possible for theologians to discuss this question with far less dogmatic prejudice than heretofore. It was not long since Illingworth had taken it as a corollary of the belief that miracles were part of the furniture of revelation that such acts were confined to Biblical times, as opposed to God's normal succour through providence.[3]

[1] *ibid.*, pp. 167-69. [2] pp. 75f. [3] *Divine Immanence*, pp. 121f.

On the other side, modernists were bent on establishing a certain view of providence as the exclusive mode of Divine activity in the world. It is a great gain that this subject has come to be approached from a more philosophical angle.

As it appeared to A. E. Taylor, we had a choice between two ways of conceiving the pervasion of the sensible by the supra-sensible order. We could think of the dominance of the supra-sensible as always pervasive, but never obtrusive, like a craftsman working upon a material that is thoroughly pliable to his purpose.[1] But "it is equally possible to think of the sensible order, with its system of 'customary experiences' articulated in the process of adapting ourselves to our immediate bodily environment, as being always something of a 'misfit' for a reality so much richer than this extract which has been shaped from it under the pressure of urgent physical need." Hence the possibility might arise of occasions when the misfit would make itself specially apparent: "There will be something catastrophic, violently irruptive, at moments of critical importance in the relation between the transcendent reality and its sensible temporal disguise, and at such times anticipations based on 'customary experiences' will be liable to be suddenly and startlingly shattered."[2]

Farmer believed that there was a peculiar danger in some of the current tendencies towards an all-inclusive monism; and he therefore leaned towards a pluralistic view of the universe, seeing it as a play of a vast number of lower created agents.[3] In this order of things, human personalities stand as created creators, set in the dimension of personal relationship with the eternal personal. There may be other relatively independent created entities, both lower and higher than man. Nature may thus be the depositum of the activity of these agents, the relatively settled outline on which future creativity must rest, but by which it is never completely determined. God's problem would thus be to achieve His own purpose in a way that does not negate this system. His activity would be at two levels: first, perhaps by direct rapport with sub-personal entities, using the routines of their activity in relation to a given situation, and secondly, where the level of personality is reached,

[1] *Faith of a Moralist*, II, p. 162. [2] *op. cit.*, II, p. 163.
[3] *The World and God*, pp. 173-74.

by a direction which takes account of will in the full personal sense of that term.[1] The first method may still be used of man, so that when he refuses to be God's agent, he may still be taken up into His purpose as an unwitting instrument.

Two types of Divine intervention are also envisaged by Dr. Hodgson. Viewing the purpose of human life as a movement from the mechanical world up to perfect freedom, it is necessary for God to exercise towards us, in our imperfect state, an influence both of external conditioning as well as of interior grace.[2] Such conditioning does not constrict our freedom, but directs the development of our character. "If this be true," he continues, "then there is no more mistaken approach to the problem of the miraculous than that which regards God as reserving to Himself a right to interfere in human life which He has renounced in respect of the 'laws' of the physical world."[3] It is more reasonable to regard the physical order as the passive instrument of God's will, aiming at the creation of free beings: it can be controlled as they can not, and there would be no irrationality in accepting adequate evidence that it had sometimes deviated from its observed uniform manner of behaviour if that deviation could be thought of as fulfilling the aim of the whole process. "It is not without significance that He whom we believe to have been God Incarnate thought of the power over storms and bread and mountains as lying in His hands, but of men as those into whose hands He was to give the power over Himself."[4]

IV

The miracles of Scripture are very diverse in kind; and another fruitful aspect of the newer freedom has been the recognition, even by conservative writers, that many of them may have been brought about through the agency of natural causes. In 1884, Frederick Temple had urged that theology must take seriously the position that a miracle could no longer be established as such in the traditional sense on the phenomenal level of scientific investigation, and that the New Testament miracles might have some connection with the

[1] *op. cit.*, p. 176.
[2] *Towards a Christian Philosophy*, pp. 94, 116.
[3] *op. cit.*, p. 117.
[4] *ibid.*, p. 117.

order of nature.[1] This factor came gradually to enter the purview of apologetics, and was counterbalanced by the growing stress laid upon the spiritual significance of the miracles and the revelation through Our Lord's perfect humanity. At the same time, the desire on the philosophical level to see some rational connection between the events called miracles and the rest of the creation was gaining ground. Apologists had often taken their stand against the adversaries of the miraculous on a radical empiricism. But to save the miraculous at the expense of a belief in rational order was a hazardous procedure, argued Dr. H. H. Williams in his contribution to the replies to J. M. Thompson. An absolute contradiction of the uniformity of nature would be literally unthinkable, a denial that anything in the world possessed a determinate nature or that science could discover universal laws. Nothing could be called miraculous when anything could happen. None the less, continued Dr. Williams, scientists were becoming increasingly chary of regarding their descriptive principles as universal laws; free will was no longer treated as inherently absurd; whilst the way in which mind controlled matter was in a certain sense not known at all.[2] Jesus' mighty works, though greater than the power that humanity has elsewhere known, might not necessarily differ in kind from the power possessed by human wills; nor do we know what additions to human capacity in controlling nature might be brought by an advance to perfect goodness.[3]

As a retort to J. M. Thompson's method of excising from the Gospel narrative whatever appeared to him to be unnatural, Dr. Williams' thesis is unanswerable. But less cautious apologists were to tread too far in the direction of imagining that the powers of nature are almost boundlessly elastic; and this tends to evacuate the miraculous of its significance in the same way that Mozley's empiricism did. It is doubtless desirable to disseminate the results of the recent critique of scientific knowledge and method; for men at large are to a considerable extent still dominated by the popular scientific cosmology of the 19th century. But it is difficult to see what can be gained by the effort to discern some of the seeming parallels in nature to the

[1] *Relations between Religion and Science*, p. 31. [2] *Miracles*, 1911, pp. 103ff.
[3] *op. cit.*, pp. 107-8. Cf. Chase in *Camb. Theol. Essays*, p. 405; cf. also the optimistic prognostications about the N.T. miracles in T. H. Wright, *Hastings' Dictionary of Christ and the Gospels*, II, pp. 186f., and Headlam in *Miracles*, p. 44.

Christian miracles. We are told of the strange powers of cosmic rays and of hypnotism; whilst parthenogenesis in dandelions and frogs is said to offer a suggestion as to the "naturalness" of Our Lord's birth.[1] [On the other hand, some apologists have continued to make everything turn upon the inexplicability of miracles; e.g. E. O. Davies, *The Miracles of Jesus*, pp. 18, 66, 76-78, 155. Roman catholic apologists expound the view that the essence of a miracle lies in its inexplicability by natural causes, and their church's claim to declare this in certain cases; e.g. B. C. A. Windle, *The Catholic Church and its Reactions with Science*, pp. 142f. Arnold Lunn believes that every advance of science has reinforced, if indirectly, the case for miracles by defining the powers of nature. *The Third Day*, pp. 3-4, 6, 14.]

V

Miracles might now appear less irrational, but there were still the grave problems of historical evidence and historical significance. The principles of historical criticism received their form and ethos in an atmosphere dominated by the positivist conception of knowledge—the description of phenomena and the search for uniformities. At certain levels, the technique has been as fruitful as the methods of science in the physical sphere; but the plotting out of causal patterns has tended to reduce to a minimum the really significant aspect of history, that it is created by the action of self-conscious individual agents. Taken at its face value, the scientific conception of historiography presents the same kind of stone wall barrier as did the mechanistic view of the physical universe against the recognition of the unique action of man, and *a fortiori* of God.

Secular historians like Collingwood have come largely to recognize the limitations of the so-called scientific method, but Christian scholars had already become convinced that there was some fundamental fallacy behind it which not only foreclosed the question of miracles, but made nonsense of the Christian assertions that God has made Himself known in specific historic occurrences.[2] Only if the study of history is concerned primarily with understanding the lives and circumstances of

[1] e.g. W. Osborne Greenwood, *Christianity and the Mechanists*, p. 245; J. H. Best, *The Miracles of Christ*, p. 129; J. O. Bevan, *The Scientific Basis of Religion*, ch. VIII.
[2] Cairns, *The Faith that Rebels*, pp. 116-19.

particular conscious beings, and embraces man's aesthetic, moral and religious approaches to reality, can the Biblical idea of particular revelation even seem possible. Nor was the liberal compromise satisfactory—that of allowing scientific historiography to elicit the facts before faith passes its judgment upon them. For the selection of data, and the weight to be attached to particular evidence, is profoundly influenced by the principles which govern the investigation.

Thus, Gore pointed out that it was no accident that thinkers differing so widely as liberals and eschatologists should agree in rejecting such large portions of the Gospel narrative.[1] He quotes a trenchant passage from Creighton:

> Historical criticism is not a science: it is only an investigation of the value of evidence. It rests on presuppositions which are derived from experience. I am disposed to believe what is analogous to my experience: my criticism is awakened by what is not analogous. The destructive criticism of the New Testament rests on the presupposition that miracles do not happen. . . . The miracles connected with the person of Jesus are analogous to the spiritual experience of the believing Christian. Therefore he is not moved by the presupposition that they are contrary to nature. The real question in dispute is the conception of nature. Biblical criticism will not solve that question.[2]

Bishop Frank Weston was regarded by many of his contemporaries as an enemy of free enquiry, but looking back on his protests against the liberalism of his day, we can see that he appreciated one important aspect of the position which they did not. Experiments with modern thought, he says, are justifiable so long as the scholar is conscious of "a God-given power of faith in the strength of which he can see things as no mere modern thinker as such can see them." But some are adopting the fatal attitude of wanting to stand side by side with the modern thinker, to throw away faith, to start fair, so to speak.[3] A further third of a century of critical study has borne out Weston's contention. Writing of the breakdown of the

[1] *Belief in God*, pp. 215f.

[2] Cited from *Life of M. Creighton*, pp. 330-31; cf. Illingworth, *Divine Immanence*, pp. 110f; W. Lock in *Miracles*, p. 26; J. N. Figgis, *Gospel and Human Needs*, pp. 36, 56f.

[3] *Ecclesia Anglicana*, p. 12. Cf. the Barthian position.

purely historical method of approach to the Gospels, Dr. Hodgson says that when we review the results of the removal of these events, especially the miracles, out of the sphere of philosophical or theological discussion, and the attempt to discover whether they took place by the ordinary rules of historical evidence, we see that it has been found impossible as a matter of pure history either to establish them as certain facts or to deny that they ever happened.[1]

Dr. Quick analyses this position still further. The flaw in the critical approach is the assumption that the historian must treat the life of Jesus like that of any other man. Scientific methods of historical criticism assume that, in all events which have ever happened, human and physical nature conform to a certain order. Scientific criticism will therefore tend to dismiss as untrue any alleged event demanding supernatural causation; and if it finds no satisfactory alternative to the alleged facts it will content itself with saying that no certain conclusion can be reached. The Christian believer, on the other hand, having reached his faith by the acceptance of religious teaching verified in his own moral and spiritual experience, will approach the primitive records with a quite opposite presupposition. He will have no antecedent objection to the hypothesis that certain things happened which were only possible because Jesus was the unique person whom he has always believed Him to be.[2] Again, the Christian position, points out Quick, is already surrendered by an approach to the historical evidence in a spirit of complete impartiality as to the truth of the Christian faith; for Christian faith is faith in the living Lord who died and rose again.

> According to Christianity therefore the life of Jesus stands in a unique relation to history as a whole, and the truth of that relation is of the essence of its faith. Therefore to suppose either that the main facts alleged by Christianity concerning Jesus are not historical facts at all, or that they are simply historical facts to be judged like any others, is necessarily to judge that the Christian faith is false, or at any rate that its truth is something essentially different from what the main tradition of Christianity has supposed it to be.[3]

[1] *And Was Made Man*, pp. 112-14.
[2] *Doctrines of the Creed*, pp. 146f. [3] *op. cit.*, pp. 151-52.

It was indeed imperative for apologists to preserve and foster a view of history which sees in it, not merely a web of material forces, but the related activity of spiritual agents. Only thus does man's spiritual experience have meaning; only thus can it be intelligible to consider the revelation of God in situations in which He confronts man; only so can the understanding be adequately applied to the evidences about Christ.[1]

[1] Cf. T. B. Strong's excellent little book, *Religion, Philosophy and History*, 1923.

Chapter Fifteen

CONCLUSION

We must now sum up the profit-and-loss account for the Christian faith in the debate of the past two and a half centuries. Theological schemes have crumbled into decay and cherished beliefs have been abandoned or left in doubt, but there is not one of the principal terms in the discussion that has not been deeply enriched in its meaning.

We may first consider the order of nature. Peculiar coincidences of phenomena may produce sudden and unexpected calamities or blessings, but there are certain relatively stable things and events in the world which enable us to eat our food and build bridges. Indeed, much of the insecurity in life arises, not from the unsettlement of the natural order, but from our ignorance and mismanagement of it. Life within this order is made possible by a combination of our prevenient instinct of trustfulness together with its confirmation in experience. The man of science regards the seamless garment of nature as a necessary complement to his reason and sanity. The Hebrew and the Christian believe that they see the meaning of the pattern of nature to be the creation of the all-wise, loving and purposeful God, as a stage upon which the moral and spiritual life of man may be lived. God's will for man, and man's response to it, are alike expressed in the language of material situations. The visible creation as a whole—in addition to things within it that are thought specially to manifest the Divine purpose—must be a revelation of God's character and mode of action. The believer in the living God cannot therefore be indifferent to the fact of the order of nature nor to the advance in human knowledge about it through scientific and historical study. Indeed, he is committed to the idea of order at an even deeper level than the man of science. He believes that nature manifests the consistent purpose of God, which will triumph despite the empirical facts which seem to point the other way, such as human sinfulness, disease and natural calamity.

To those who have grasped the idea of general revelation informed by modern knowledge, the conviction has been borne that God may be expected to do nothing which is not in a real sense harmonious with the general constitution of nature. Modern Christians therefore find that the faith is strengthened and purified by the rejection of whole classes of recorded miracles which once excited the wonder of mankind. Some types of reported miracles are intrinsically credible because they fall within the possible domain of nature, and in so far as they served spiritual ends they may be said to reveal the ultimate character of the natural order. Miracle stories which approximate to reasonable answers to prayer may never be categorically rejected by believers in God. The evidentialists were justified in drawing a line of distinction between the welter of heathen and ecclesiastical tales and the miracles which were held to form part of the saving acts of God. The 18th-century theologians used language of the miracles of Scripture which suggested the sporadic interference of God with the world. But their defective view of nature is seen chiefly, not in the way they postulated specific personal activity of God, but in their limiting of this recognition to those few events which it was thought were wholly beyond the power of nature to have produced. As William Temple pointed out, the possibility of recognizing God's action in specific events is dependent upon the capacity of the natural order as a whole to mediate a general revelation of God.

In a sense, the men of the Illumination took their natural theology very seriously indeed, but they had little grasp of nature as a sign-language through which God speaks. Had they, for example, realized the full significance of the spiritual phenomena of the Evangelical revival—of the psychology of conversion and its remarkable by-products—the profound change in the theological treatment of nature would have been anticipated by more than a century. Today, when a theologian looks at nature, he sees not merely a system of uniformities but an intelligible process of becoming, *natura*, which has begotten man himself with his spiritual and moral potentialities. He sees this nature as a reality in which mind and matter coexist so intimately that in certain respects they appear as two aspects of the same process. The material world provides the medium for the I-thou relationship of man with man; and under favouring circumstances the power of mind over body produces effects far beyond our common experience.

Scarcely less striking is the change that has come about in the connotation of the term "supernatural". In the older theology, the supernatural generally indicated the action upon the world of God and of angels and demons. Miracles were the result of such interposition in the normal course of nature. Prophecy was a particular kind of miracle. Grace was supernatural too; but the theologians of the Illumination were busy stressing the freedom of man's will, as opposed to Calvinism, and the doctrine of grace was never really integrated into their system. But the mind of the Evangelicals, of the Tractarians, and of individuals like Coleridge and Maurice was very different. To them, Divine revelation and its miraculous accompaniments had their complement in the life of the believer and the church. This life was lived in virtue of the ever-present, recreative activity of God within the individual soul and the community; it was indeed supernatural, and its fruits in their own way were just as marvellous as the miracles of Christ had been, for like them they broke the chain of evil causation. The life of the Christian's communion with God is supernatural in its essence and in its fruits; and its power to convince is no less than the works of the Incarnate Christ to those who have eyes to see.

The philosophy of religion, as it has been developed in these islands in the past half century, has been a faithful handmaid to the revivified religious tradition. A new Christian philosophy had indeed been urgently needed. It had to be inductive, to replace the scholasticism which most people regarded as effete; and it must preserve all the personal elements in the Divine-human encounter, which idealism had failed adequately to do. A new edifice was therefore built by many hands. Balfour, Tennant, Ward, Oman, Webb, Temple, Sorley, Taylor, Farmer and others created no neat logical scheme: what they did was to interrogate and articulate human experience at every level, from the barest glimmerings of self-consciousness to the most refined ethical, aesthetic and mystical perceptions. They weighed the value of every separate element, and they assessed the cumulative significance of man's spiritual experience. All has gone to the making of what we may fairly call a "philosophy of the supernatural"—which sees man's transcendence over mechanism not merely in the bare fact of his free will but in every activity which is truly human. Some of the finest work in this field has been carried out by men who had little direct interest in the traditional questions about miracles; Oman's monumental work *The Natural and the Supernatural* contains no discussion of miracles at all. But all has gone to provide the apologist with a substructure of the utmost importance. Not always has preoccupation with the supernatural produced such fruits. Iamblicus in Patristic times and Henry More the Cambridge Platonist were prepared to accept even ghost stories and witch tales as evidence of the proximity of the supernatural. But Oman, Temple and the rest had their feet firmly planted on the ground: the evidences which they bring together can be verified—at least in some degree—by any human being.

There is a lesson here for apologists. The physical phenomena of mysticism, the annals of psychical research and the records of faith cures obviously all have something to tell us about the character of the supernatural; but the most convincing proofs today of the spiritual dignity of man are those which show the triumph of his ethical personality. Few people could name one celebrated faith cure of our time, yet everyone knows of Helen Keller. The profound appeal of human triumph over physical handicap is proved by the ever-increasing biographical literature on the subject.

This broadening of the concept of the supernatural has also woven a much closer analogy between special and general revelation. It is now possible for an orthodox theology to be built up in which the specifically revealing acts of God form the apex of man's whole awareness of the supernatural. The 18th-century divines contended that the miracles of Scripture carried their own intrinsic marks of Divine authorship. It was argued that these acts bore an analogy to the rational, purposeful structure of creation. But it cannot be denied that a deep gulf separated the miracles from the rest of human experience; and the plea that this fact added strength to the evidences for revelation has lost much of its appeal. Many theologians of the 19th century came to believe that God's revealing acts themselves—the whole drama of the Old Testament and the total fact of Christ—shone with their own light as Divinely originated. To those rooted in the older ways of thinking, this seemed a very tenuous affair in comparison with the massive logical structure of the previous age. It remained for the philosophy of religion to create a spiritual environment in which this revivified theology could grow. There is a very real analogy between such personal apprehensions of the supernatural as the moral imperative and the awareness of being faced with Divine demand, and the idea of Divine revelation through specific events which carry with them direct intuitive certainty.

There is one aspect of the life of man's spirit which constitutes in a very significant manner an analogy to special revelation in history. It was seen above that one of the most notable things about the material order is its capacity to act as a medium for the spiritual life of man. Man, to use Sir Thomas Browne's expression, is the great amphibian; but his spiritual and material lives are not lived in entirely separate compartments. The whole of the life of his spirit, with the possible exception of some mystical states, is lived through the medium of the physical world. Man's learning, thinking and self-expression work in this way. His moral life is realized wholly through his body and the external creatures with which he comes into contact; and so is his life of personal intercourse with other human beings. If one man strikes another, it is assumed (unless the assailant be insane) that the blow is not merely caused by one part of his physical mechanism, but is a personal act. Similarly, we do not find it difficult to dismiss the dualism by which it was argued that the purity of the soul is not necessarily affected by bodily licentiousness. The body may be accidental to the life of the spirit, but as long as we are in the body we are organically united to it, and not simply clamped in it like a Jack-in-a-box.

Nature, be it the subject's body or the things outside himself which he uses, thus comes to be invested with the character of symbolism. Now symbols differ very greatly in their acquired power in proportion as they are directly related to the personal life of an individual. Take for instance, the sign of the Cross. In one sense this is a piece of most perfect shorthand; never did so simple a sign mean so much. But also, to make or to catch sight of this sign in time of temptation or danger may produce incalculable results. Again, a gesture of affection is a material process; it may foster the feelings both of the subject and the object. The more an action is wrought by the whole of a man's personality, so much the more does it reveal him; and if it be of spiritual significance, so much the more will it have the power to influence, for good or ill, other personal beings.

The question necessarily follows: To what extent does the mediation of the material world enter in when the relationship is betwixt man and God? At first sight it might appear, as some of the devotees of the inner light have contended, that the material creation enters in little. But on the other hand, man has in every culture sought to express his thoughts towards God in outward forms, and the multitude of stories of theophanies witnesses to man's natural expectation that God will meet him through that nature and environment in which he finds himself. Again, the modern study of the history of religion shows us that it has been through reaction with his material environment, through contact with peculiar circumstances and places, that man has gradually become aware of his own spiritual nature and has been led to form ideas about the unseen world.

In the Bible, we have the record of human experiences in which men perceived the special revelation of God manifested within the created world through a unique cycle of events and persons. Not only does the creation in general bear witness to God—especially that aspect of it which constitutes the conscious life of men—but particular things and circumstances, many of which are more than usually inexplicable, are peculiarly signs of God's character and purpose. These events are the Divine counterpart of those significant symbolic actions of human behaviour. Man's significant actions may be unusual; under stress of circumstances he may perform feats which one might have imagined to be far beyond his capacity. They derive their interest for us from their revealing the subject's character; not simply what he can do in this one moment, but what he is really like and what are the deepest motives of his life. This is precisely what is claimed for the acts of God recorded in Scripture. Such a rationale presupposes a view of reality which takes within its ken every aspect of man's experience—and this will include the faith of those whose experience is recorded in the Bible and which created the Christian church. To those whose view of reality is constructed out of the positivist picture of nature, the acts of God, including the miracles, must appear irrational. As Edwyn Bevan points out, those who believe in the Resurrection of Christ mean that the pattern of the universe is more complicated than is imagined by those who think that a certain range of uniformities are sufficient to give a theory of the whole.[1] Human experience at its heights and depths, and not some artificially constructed dead world, must be the starting-point for the discussion of miracles. It is irrational, moreover, to neglect the simple religious truth that the whole of the creation is in the hands of God, transcendent as well as immanent, who can, to serve a proper end, produce outward results which it is impossible directly to relate to known patterns of causation. The only problem which has really exercised the church in modern times is the forms which may be admitted as revealing God in a special way.

There is a variety of ways in which it is possible to think of the specially revealing acts of God as having been brought about, none of which militate against human freedom—which to religious thought is a far more serious question than the disturbance of the flight of atoms. We may think of direct influences upon the minds of men, which, like all the actions of grace, do not coerce but free men to do acts which they would not otherwise have been able to do. We can conceive of additions made to the sum of created forces, or the direction from within of existing entities in nature. (What would Baden Powell have thought of the theory held by some physicists today that the universe is fed by the "creation" of "new" matter?) Finally, we can envisage the providential disposition of forces in the world. It is a remarkable development in Christian thinking that all these methods of Divine activity are recognized without prejudice as equally important ways of thinking about God's personal action in the world.

For our present purpose, let us take the miracles of the

[1] *Hellenism and Christianity*, pp. 228f.

Exodus and Sinai, the work of the canonical prophets, and the unique personality of Christ together with His Resurrection and works of healing. It has been thought plausible by some to argue that none of these events did in fact wear the aspect of complete discontinuity from nature traditionally associated with the idea of the miraculous. If this approach continues to lead some towards the acceptance of the Christian revelation, it cannot be regarded as illegitimate. Many continue to hold, however, that this approach tends to obscure some of the most significant aspects of revelation, and at the same time fails to answer some of the questions which it purports to resolve.

First, if an immanental explanation be offered for the Biblical miracles named above, Divine causation is not rendered one whit more demonstrable. Secondly, if the part played by faith is not lessened by the immanental view, neither are the facts themselves rendered more credible. To the mind dominated by the positivist ideals, the unique is neither credible nor interesting unless it opens the way to new generalizations. Thirdly, to argue that the Biblical miracles are non-miraculous operations of Divine immanence does not make them any more explicable in the scientific sense than did the Duke of Argyll's "higher laws". To discard elements of the tradition because they bear the character of legend, or because they seem to be incompatible with what we take to be the manner of God's operation as shown by revelation as a whole, is a different matter. Lastly, does it really help us in thinking about revelation to eliminate the category of the miraculous? The healing works of Jesus have analogies elsewhere, but they come to us as part of the tradition of a life which exhibits spiritual miracles even more startling than these; whilst Our Lord's personal manifestation of Himself after His death can only be represented as "non-miraculous" by a strange stretching of language. Conservative theology has surely been right in continuing to urge that the fundamental religious interest in these events is the personal intervention of God in the affairs of men, and that in fact the events with which we are concerned do wear an aspect of mysteriousness even on their external side.

There are new factors in the apologetic situation: the recognition of the limitations of scientific method, in itself and in historiography; and the realization that given miracles may have been brought about by the co-operation of natural causes. This has tended to exercise a liberating influence upon the discussion of the miraculous: it has become possible to approach it primarily as a religious category. Miracle, says Dr. Farmer, is a special form of that experience which finds expression in the idea of revelation, and like the latter, therefore, it lies very near the heart of religion. It is fatal to begin the discussion with the philosophical or scientific conception of natural law. A miracle is an event or situation which is so designed by God as to be recognized as a special revelation of His personal activity in the world, and which contributes in some recognizable way to the fulfilment of His purpose for mankind.[1] We thus find ourselves again faced with our postulate that in the activity of God in the world miracle holds the same kind of place as the most significant symbolic actions of a man do to the rest of a man; we not only distinguish its outward peculiarities by our intellect, we intuit its meaning by our capacity to know other personal beings. And so it will be with our apprehending of the Divine miracles; which, furthermore, we shall expect to be symbolic in the two senses—both revealing the purpose of God and actually carrying it into effect.

Our Lord's Incarnation is the miracle *par excellence.* Here is God's personal activity in the world exhibited and recognized in the way most perfectly adapted to human nature and apprehension. This life is different from all other human lives and yet is truly human; for otherwise it could not reveal God to us. Like the dynamic symbols of human action, moreover, this life actually accomplishes, as well as reveals, the purpose of God—the opening up of a new relationship between man and God and the creation of a new humanity. The apprehension of this revelation consists, not merely in perceiving that "God was in Christ, reconciling the world unto Himself", but in a personal surrender to Him.

Within the Incarnate life there are particular events which, despite the true humanity of Christ, possess that kind of singularity associated with the miraculous. Some modern Christians feel that there is a real theological difficulty in accepting certain aspects of these on the ground that they militate against the principle of the Incarnation, the revealing

[1] *The World and God,* pp. 108f.

of God in the moral and spiritual character of a human life. But it is difficult to envisage any really convincing reconstruction of the events relating to the origin of the church which does not take account of the empty tomb. Many thinkers continue to see in the Resurrection the climax to the Incarnate acts. In the theology of the New Testament, says Quick, the Resurrection of Christ is inseparable from His atoning death: the risen Christ is the first fruits of the eschatological drama in which God redeems and begins to renew His whole creation.[1] Since sub-Apostolic times, the belief in the Virgin Birth has been bound up in the most intimate manner with belief in the Incarnation; and the denial of the former has in fact usually been accompanied by a very definite change in the manner of regarding the latter. The miracles ascribed to Christ's ministry are not unconnected with the radical and realistic character of the redemption which the New Testament claims to have been wrought by Christ, and of which the "mighty works" are the signs. There are many intricate questions connected with the relation of the outward signs to the inward truth of revelation, but they do not relate merely to the miracles. There are analogous questions relating to the outward and inward in the sacraments, to the visible and the invisible church, to the letter and the inspiration of the Bible, and above all, to the humanity and the Deity of Christ. This tension is inherent in the approach of God to man through man's own contingent nature and environment.

Finally, we may note the great enrichment that has come about in the ideas of revelation and of faith. Far from being merely buffeted about by the changing intellectual winds from without, theology has repeatedly taken the initiative in rethinking its attitude towards the historical sources of Christianity. The popular idea that miracles were once a bulwark of the faith and then became an embarrassment to it thus requires to be drastically modified. Certain elements of the Biblical tradition have indeed become an embarrassment to religion, but the central facts of Christ's historic life remain the ground of Christian certitude. Miracle has actually moved from the circumference to the very centre of revelation. No longer are the signs of the supernatural thought of as mere

[1] *Gospel of the New World*, p. 53.

credentials, but as part of the very substance of what is revealed. The Resurrection and the mighty works are seen as an essential part of the drama by which God personally discloses Himself, and by which He achieves victory over evil and the creation of a new humanity.

But what a profound change does this show in the idea of revelation! That God should bestow upon mankind with unique certitude the laws of life, the pattern of human perfection, and the promise of immortality, was a theological conception which did justice to some of the central aspects of the work of Christ, but it did not go to the root of the New Testament Gospel. The Incarnation, by the very completeness of its disclosure of God, opens up the possibility of the most perfect communion between man and God. The hypostatic union, moreover, means that Christ is both Our Lord and our brother: and because of this fact the Incarnation is not a mere episode in history—the personal relationship thus opened up is made permanent. Christ is the Lord and the brother of all believers: His body is continually given for their life; and they are His body through which His life is continually lived in the world. If these beliefs are well understood today, it is partly as a result of the search that has gone on for the true understanding of the Christian miracles.

With this has gone a searching discussion of the nature of Christian assent, whose issues have often been sharpened by their having been debated in the context of the belief in miracles. The Cartesian philosophy had fostered the idea that man's apprehension of external reality could be expressed in terms of knowledge, doubt and ignorance.[1] In the 18th century, an attempt was made to meet this situation, by erecting an apologetic in which assent was described in terms of cognition and inference. But from the time of Wesley a new Christian epistemology was required, and its distinctness from scientific assent was elucidated; the Christian does not say he "knows", but he "believes", as Dean Wace puts it.[2] It has come to be realized that the acts of God in history can only be apprehended for what they are by the exercise of a human decision which

[1] Webb, *Historical Element in Religion*, p. 53; Quick, *Modern Philosophy and the Incarnation*, p. 81.
[2] *Christianity and Agnosticism*, p. 5.

includes all the intuitive aspects of personality, in the same way as these are called for in the most vital concerns between man and man.[1] But this does not mean that religious faith and sacred history are two separate domains, any more than our trust in a human friend can be dissociated from our knowledge of the things he has done for us. Against the liberal idea of the merely historic recognition of the origins of Christianity, and the catholic modernist plan for a faith divorced from a literal Incarnation, English conservative theology has contended masterfully that the wholeness and uniqueness of the Christian revelation consists in its sacramental mediation through history. Consequently, its right apprehension involves an act of the whole man: his intellect, his spiritual discernment and his will to surrender to God's Word.

[1] A. E. Taylor, *Does God Exist?*, pp. 129f.

BIBLIOGRAPHY

ABBOTT, E. A. *Through Nature to Christ*, 1877. *Oxford Sermons*, 1879. *The Kernel and the Husk*, 1886. *Philomythus*, 1891. *St. Thomas of Canterbury, his death and miracles*, 1898.

ADAMS, W. *Essay on Hume*, 1752.

ADDISON, J. *The Evidences of the Christian Religion*, 1730.

ANNET, P. *Judging for Ourselves*, 1739. *The Resurrection of Jesus considered*, 1744. *Supernaturals examined*, 1747.

ARGYLL, DUKE OF, *The Reign of Law*, 1866.

ARNOLD, M. *Literature and Dogma*, 1873.

ARTHUR, W. *On the difference between Physical and Moral Laws*, 1883.

ATTERBURY, F. *Sermons*, 1708 ed., esp. III and IV of 1694.

BABBAGE, C. *The Ninth Bridgewater Treatise*, 1837.

BAILLIE, J. *Our Knowledge of God*, 1939.

BAILLIE, J. and MARTIN, H., eds. *Revelation*, 1937.

BAIRD, A. C. *Christian Fundamentals*, 1926.

BAKER, A. E. *The Divine Christ*, 1937. *Science, Christianity and Truth*, 1943.

BALFOUR, A. J. *Theism and Humanism*, 1914.

BALLARD, F. *Supernatural Christianity*, 1890.

BARKWAY, L. *The Creed and its Credentials*, 1935.

BARNES, E. W. *The Rise of Christianity*, 1947.

BEEBY, C. E. "Doctrinal Significance of a Miraculous Birth", *Hibbert Journal*, October 1903.

BELCHER, T. W. *Our Lord's Miracles of Healing*, 1872.

BENSON, G. *The Reasonableness of the Christian Religion*, 1743.

BENSON, R. M. *The Virgin Birth of Our Lord and Saviour Jesus Christ*, 1904.

BENTLEY, R. *A Confutation of Atheism*, Boyle Lectures, 1692.

BERKELEY, G. *Alciphron or the Minute Philosopher*, 1732.

BERNARD, J. H. Art. "Miracle", *Hastings' Dictionary of the Bible*, 1898.

BEST, J. H. *The Miracles of Christ*, 1937.

BETHUNE-BAKER, J. F. *The Miracle of Christianity: a plea for the critical school, in regard to the use of the creeds*, 1914. *The Faith of the Apostles' Creed*, 1918. *The Way of Modernism*, 1927. *Unity and Truth in the Church of England*, 1934.

BEVAN, E. *Hellenism and Christianity*, 1921, esp. Reason and Dogma. *Symbolism and Belief*, 1938.

BINCHY, D. A. "The Modernist Movement", *Cambridge Journal*, January 1948.

Bishops and Modern Criticism: being the report of debates in the upper house of the Convocation of Canterbury and the upper house of the Convocation of York, May 1922.

BLACK, J. B. *The Art of History*, 1926.

BLACKALL, O. *The sufficiency of a standing revelation in general and of the Scripture Revelation in particular*, Boyle Lectures, 1700.

BLEWETT, G. J. *The Christian View of the World*, 1911.

BLOUNT, C. *The two first books of Philostratus concerning the life of Apollonius of Tyana*, 1680. *Miracles no violations of the laws of nature*, 1683. (A paraphrase of Spinoza's *Tractatus*.)

BONNEY, T. G. *Christian Doctrines and Modern Thought*, 1892. *The Present Relations of Science and Religion*, 1913.

BOWNE, B. P. *The Immanence of God*, 1905.

BOX, G. H. *The Virgin Birth of Jesus*, 1916.

BOX, H. S. *Miracles and Critics*, 1935.

BOYLE, R. Lectures founded by—*Natural and Revealed Religion*, 3 vols. 1739 ed.

BRADFORD, S. *The Credibility of the Christian Revelation from its Intrinsic Evidence*, Boyle Lectures, 1699.

BRADLEY, F. H. *The Presuppositions of Critical History*, 1874.

BRIGGS, C. A. *The Incarnation of Our Lord*, 1903.

BROWN, W. ADAMS. *God at Work*, 1934.

BRUCE, A. B. *The Miraculous Element in the Gospels*, 1886. *Apologetics or, Christianity defensively stated*, 1892. *The Chief End of Revelation*, 1881.

BRUNDRIT, D. F. *Is the Resurrection true?*, 1934.

BRUNNER, E. *Revelation and Reason*, E.T. 1947.

BURNET, T. *The Demonstration of True Religion*, Boyle Lectures, 1724–25. *De Statu Mortuorum et Resurgentium*, 1715.

BURTT, E. A. *The Metaphysical Foundations of Modern Physical Science*, 1925.

BURY, A. *The Naked Gospel*, 1691.

BURY, J. B. *Selected Essays*, ed. H. W. V. Temperley, 1930.

BUSH, G. *Anastasis: or the doctrine of the resurrection of the body rationally and Scripturally considered*, 1845.

BUSHNELL, H. *Nature and the Supernatural*, 1858.

BUTLER, J. *The Analogy of Religion*, 1736.

CADOUX, C. J. *The Historic Mission of Jesus*, 1941.

CAIRD, E. *The Evolution of Religion*, Gifford Lectures, 1890–92.

CAIRD, J. *Fundamental Ideas of Christianity*, Gifford Lectures, 1899.

CAIRNS, D. S. *The Faith that Rebels*, 1928.

Cambridge Theological Essays, ed. H. B. Swete, 1909; esp. J. M. Wilson, "The Idea of Revelation"; A. W. Robinson, "Prayer in relation to the idea of law"; and J. O. F. Murray, "The spiritual and historical evidence for miracles".

CAMFIELD, F. W. *Revelation and the Holy Spirit*, 1933.

CAMPBELL, G. A. *A Dissertation on Miracles containing an examination of the principle advanced by David Hume*, 1762.

CAMPBELL, J. MCLEOD, *Thoughts on Revelation*, 1862.

CANDLER, H. *Groundwork of Belief*, 1879.

CARLYLE, T. *Sartor Resartus*, 1838.

CARPENTER, J. E. *The First Three Gospels*, 1890. *The Bible in the XIXth century*, 1903.

CHALMERS, T. *On the Miraculous and Internal Evidences of the Christian Revelation and the Authority of its Records*, Works, 1836–42, vols. III and IV.

CHANDLER, E. *A Defence of Christianity from the Prophecies of the Old Testament*, 1725.

CHANDLER, S. *A Vindication of the Christian Religion*, 1725. *A Discourse of the Nature and Use of Miracles*, 1725. *The Witnesses of the Resurrection of Jesus Christ*, 1730.

CHARLES, R. H. *The Resurrection of Man*, sermons, 1929.

CHASE, F. H. *The Gospels in the Light of Historical Criticism*, 1914. *Belief and Creed*, 1918. *The Creed and the New Testament*, 1920. *The Supernatural Element in Our Lord's Earthly Life*, Paper, 1902.

CHERBURY, LORD HERBERT OF, *De Veritate*, 1633; E.T. Carré, 1937.

CHEYNE, T. K. *Bible Problems*, 1904.

CHUBB, T. *Discourse on Miracles*, 1741.

CLARKE, J. *An Enquiry into the cause and origin of evil*, Boyle Lectures, 1719.

CLARKE, S. *A Demonstration of the Being and Attributes of God*, Boyle Lectures, 1704. *A Discourse Concerning the Unchangeable Obligations of Natural Religion and the Truth and Certainty of the Christian Revelation*, Boyle Lectures, 1705.

CLARKE, W. K. L. *New Testament Problems*, 1929. *Divine Humanity*, 1936.

COLERIDGE, S. T. *The Friend*, 1818. *Aids to Reflection*, 1825. *Confessions of an Enquiring Spirit*, 1840.

COLLIER, W. B. *Lectures on Miracles*, 1812.

COLLINGWOOD, R. G. *The Idea of History*, 1946.

COLLINS, A. *A Discourse of Free Thinking*, 1713. *A Discourse of the Grounds and Reasons of the Christian Religion*, 1724. *Scheme of Literal Prophecy*, 1727.

Contentio Veritatis, Six Oxford Tutors, 1902.

CONYBEARE, F. C. *The Historical Christ*, 1914.

CONYBEARE, J. *A Defence of Revealed Religion against the exceptions of a late writer in his book entitled "Christianity as Old as the Creation"*, 1732.

CRAGG, G. R. *From Puritanism to the Age of Reason*, 1950.

CREED, J. M. *Divinity of Jesus Christ*, 1938.

CREED, J. M. and BOYS SMITH, J. S. *Religious Thought in the XVIIIth century*, 1934.

CREIGHTON, M. *University and other sermons*, 1903, esp. III and IV.

CURTEIS, G. H. *The Scientific Obstacles to Christian Belief*, Boyle Lectures, 1885.

DAKIN, A. H. *von Hügel and the Supernatural*, 1934.

DALE, R. W. *The Living Christ and the Four Gospels*, 1890.

D'ARCY, C. F. *Christianity and the Supernatural*, 1909. *God and Freedom in Human Experience*, 1915.

DAVIES, E. O. *The Miracles of Jesus*, 1913.

DEANE, W. *The Development of the Supernatural in Human Experience*, 1937.

DEARMER, P. *Body and Soul*, 1909.

DENNEY, J. *Jesus and the Gospel*, 1908.

DITTON, H. *A Discourse Concerning the Resurrection of Jesus Christ*, 1712.

Doctrine in the Church of England, report of the Doctrinal Commission, 1938.

DODWELL, H. *Christianity Not Founded on Argument*, 1743.

DOUGLAS, J. *The Criterion: or Miracles Examined*, 1754.

DRISCOLL, J. T. Art. "Miracle", *Catholic Encyclopaedia*, 1907.

DRUMMOND, H. *Natural Law in the Spiritual World*, 1883.

ECK, H. V. S. *The Incarnation*, 1901.

EDDINGTON, A. S. *The Nature of the Physical World*, Gifford Lectures, 1927.

EDGHILL, E. A. *Faith and Fact*, 1909. *The Revelation of the Son of God*, 1911.

ELLICOTT, C. J. *Historical Lectures on the Life of Our Lord Jesus Christ*, 1860.

ELLICOTT, C. J., ed. *Modern Scepticism*, 1871.

EMMET, C. W. *Conscience, Creeds and Critics*, 1918.

EMMET, C. W. and DOUGALL, L. *The Lord of Thought*, 1922.

ERSKINE, T. *Remarks on the Internal Evidence for the Truth of Revealed Religion*, 1820.

Essays and Reviews, 1860.

EVANS, A. W. *Warburton and the Warburtonians*, 1932.

EVERETT, C. C. *The Psychological Elements of Religious Faith*, 1902.

FAIRBAIRN, A. M. *The Miracles of Christ*, addresses.

FARMER, H. *Essay on Miracles*, 1771.

FARMER, H. H. *The World and God*, 1935.

FARRAR, A. S. *Critical History of Free Thought*, Bampton Lectures, 1862.

FARRAR, F. W. *Life of Christ*, 1874.

FAWKES, A. *Studies in Modernism*, 1913.

FELDER, H. *Christ and the Critics*, E.T. 1924.

FELLOWES, R. *The Religion of the Universe*, 1836.

FERRIES, G. *The Growth of Christian Faith*, 1905.

FIGGIS, J. N. *The Gospel and Human Needs*, 1909. *Civilization at the Crossroads*, 1912. *The Fellowship of the Mystery*, 1914.

FISHER, G. P. *The Grounds of Theistic and Christian Belief*, 1883.

FOSTER, J. *The Usefulness, Truth and Excellency of the Christian Revelation Defended: against the objections contained in a late book entitled "Christianity as Old as the Creation"*, 1731.

Foundations, ed. B. H. Streeter, 1912.

GARDNER, P. *Exploratio Evangelica*, 1899. *Historic View of the New Testament*, 1901. *Modernism in the English Church*, 1926.

GARDNER-SMITH, P. *The Narratives of the Resurrection*, 1926. *The Christ of the Gospels*, 1938.

GARVIE, A. E. *Revelation Through History and Experience*, 1935.

GASTRELL, F. *The Certainty and Necessity of Religion*, Boyle Lectures, 1696.

GIBBON, E. *Decline and Fall of the Roman Empire*, 1776–88. Ed. J. B. Bury, 1901.

GLAZEBROOK, M. G. *Faith of a Modern Churchman*, 1918.

GLOVER, T. R. *The Jesus of History*, 1917.

GOOCH, G. P. *History and Historians in the XIXth Century*, 1913.

GORE, C. Bampton Lectures, 1891. *Dissertations*, 1895. *The Basis of Anglican Fellowship in Faith and Organization*, 1914. *Belief in God*, 1921.

GOUDGE, H. L. Art. "Revelation", *Encyclopaedia of Religion and Ethics*.

GOULBURN, E. N. Bampton Lectures, 1850—Lec. V. on Christ's Resurrection.

GREEN, T. H. *Works*, 3 vols. 1885, 1886, 1887.

GREENWOOD, W. O. *Christianity and the Mechanists*, 1941.

GRENSTED, L. W. *The Person of Christ*, 1933.

GROTIUS, H. *Two Discourses: Of God and His Providence, Of Christ, His Miracles and Doctrine*, 1653, E.T.

GURDON, B. *The Pretended Difficulties in Natural or Revealed Religion no excuse for Infidelity*, Boyle Lectures, 1721–22.

GWATKIN, H. M. *The Knowledge of God*, 1906 (Gifford Lectures, 1904, 1905).

HANCOCK, J. *Arguments to Prove the Being of God with Objections against it Answered*, Boyle Lectures, 1706.

HANNA, W. *The Forty Days after Our Lord's Resurrection*, 1863.

HANSON, R. D. *The Jesus of History*, 1869.

HARDMAN, O. *The Resurrection of the Body*, 1934.

HARDY, T. J. *The Religious Instinct*, 1913.

HARRIS, C. *The Creeds and Modern Thought*, 1919. *Creeds or No Creeds*, 1922.

HEADLAM, A. C. *The Miracles of the New Testament*, 1914.

HENSON, H. H. *Sincerity and Subscription*, 1903. *The Value of the Bible*, 1904. *The Creed in the Pulpit*, 1912. *Notes on Spiritual Healing*, 1925.

HESSE, M. B. *Science and the Human Imagination*, 1954.

HEY, J. *Lectures on Divinity*, 1796–98.

HITCHCOCK, F. R. MONTGOMERY. *Christ and His Critics*, 1910.

HOBSON, E. W. *The Domain of Natural Science*, Gifford Lectures, 1921–22.

HODGSON, L. *The Place of Reason in Christian Apologetic*, 1925. *And Was Made Man*, 1928. *Towards a Christian Philosophy*, 1942.

HODY, H. *The Resurrection of the (same) Body Asserted*, 1694.

HOGG, A. G. *Redemption from This World*, 1922.

HOLLAND, H. S. *Christ or Ecclesiastes*, 1888. *Creeds and Critics*, 1918.

HORNE, T. H. *Deism Refuted, or plain reasons for becoming a Christian*, 1819. *A Compendious Introduction to the Study of the Bible*, 1862.

HORSLEY, S. *Nine Sermons*, 1815.

HORTON, R. F. *My Belief*, 1908.

HUME, D. *An Enquiry concerning Human Understanding*, 1748.

HUTTON, R. H. *Essays Theological and Literary*, 1871.

HUXLEY, T. H. *The Evidence of the Miracle of the Resurrection*, 1876. *David Hume*, 1879. *Science and Christian Tradition*, 1894, collected Essays, vol. V.

IBBOT, B. *The True Notion of the Exercises of Private Judgement or Free Thinking in matters of Religion*, Boyle Lectures, 1713–14.

ILLINGWORTH, J. R. *Personality Human and Divine*, 1894. *Divine Immanence*, 1898. *The Gospel Miracles*, 1915. *Reason and Revelation*, 1902.

INGE, W. R. *Faith and Knowledge*, 1904—sermon, *The Risen Christ*. Outspoken Essays, 1919.

JACKSON, H. L. *The Eschatology of Jesus*, 1913.

JACKSON, J. *Remarks on a book entitled "Christianity as old as the Creation"*, 1731. *Remarks on Dr. Middleton's "Free Inquiry"*, 1749.

JOSEPH, H. W. B. *Introduction to Logic*, 1906.

KEBLE, J. *Sermons for the Christian Year*, e.g. vol. VI, ser. 42.

KING, J. H. *The Supernatural: its origin, nature and evolution*, 1892.

KNOWLING, R. J. *Our Lord's Virgin Birth and the Criticism of Today*, 1903.

KNOX, R. A. *Some Loose Stones*, 1913.

LACEY, T. A. *Nature, Miracle and Sin*, 1916.

LAIDLAW, J. *The Miracles of Our Lord*, 1890.

LAKE, K. *The Historical Evidence for the Resurrection of Jesus Christ*, 1907. *The Religion of Yesterday and Tomorrow*, 1925.

LANG, C. G. *The Miracles of Jesus*, 1900.

LANGHORN, W. H. *Aids to Belief*, 1898.

LATHAM, H. *The Risen Master*, 1901.

LAW, W. *The Case of Reason or Natural Religion fairly and fully stated. An Answer to a book entitled "Christianity as old as the Creation"*, 1731.

LE BAS, C. W. *Considerations on Miracles*, 1828.

LECKY, W. E. H. *History of the Rise and Influence of the Spirit of Rationalism in Europe*, 1865.

LELAND, J. *An Answer to a late book entitled "Christianity as old as the Creation"*, 2 vols. 1733. *Remarks on a late pamphlet by Henry Dodwell the younger entitled "Christianity not founded on argument"*, 1744. *A View of the Principal Deistical Writers that have appeared in England in the last and present century*, 1754.

LENG, J. *Natural Obligations to Believe the Principles of Religion and Divine Revelation*, Boyle Lectures, 1717–18.

LESLIE, C. *A Short and Easy Method with the Deists*, 1701.

LESTER-GARLAND, L. V. *The Idea of the Supernatural*, 1934.

LEWIS, C. S. *Miracles*, 1947.

LIAS, J. J. *Are Miracles Credible?*, 1883.

LIDDON, H. P. *The Divinity of Our Lord and Saviour Jesus Christ*, Bampton Lectures, 1866. *Easter in St. Paul's*, 1885. *Life of E. B. Pusey*, 1897.

LIGHTFOOT, J. B. *Essays on the work entitled "Supernatural Religion"*, 1889.

LILLEY, A. L. *Modernism, a Record and Review*, 1908. *Religion and Revelation*, 1932. *Programme of Modernism*, 1908.

LOCKE, J. *The Reasonableness of Christianity as delivered in the Scriptures*, 1695. *A Discourse of Miracles.*

LOCKTON, W. *The Resurrection and other Gospel Narratives*, 1924.

LODGE, O. *Man and the Universe*, 1908.

LUNN, A. *The Third Day*, 1945.

LUNN, A. and JOAD, C. E. M. *Is Christianity True?*, 1933.

LUNN, A. and HALDANE, J. B. S. *Science and the Supernatural*, 1935.

LYALL, W. R. *Propaedeia Prophetica*, 1840.

LYTTELTON, A. T. *The Place of Miracles in Religion*, 1899.

MACCOLL, M. *Christianity in Relation to Science and Morals*, 1890.

MACCULLOCH, J. A. Art. "Miracle", *Encyclopaedia of Religion and Ethics*, 1908.

MACDONALD, G. *The Miracles of Our Lord*, 1884.

MACHEN, J. G. *The Virgin Birth of Christ*, 1930.

MACKINNON, J. *The Historic Jesus*, 1931.

MACKINTOSH, R. *Essays towards a New Theology*, 1889.

MACKNIGHT, J. *The Truth of the Gospel History*, 1763.

MACLEAN, A. J. Art. "Miracles", *Hastings' Dictionary of the Apostolic Church.*

MCNEILE, A. H. *The Problem of the Future Life*, 1925.

MACPHERSON, R. *The Resurrection of Jesus Christ*, 1867.

MACRAN, F. W. *English Apologetic Theology*, 1905.

MAIR, A. *Studies in the Christian Evidences*, 1883.

MAJOR, H. D. A. *English Modernism*, 1927.

MANSEL, H. L. *The Limits of Religious Thought*, Bampton Lectures, 1858. *An Examination of the Rev. F. D. Maurice's strictures on the Bampton Lectures of 1858*, 1859.

MARSH, H. E.T. of J. D. Michaelis' *Introduction to the New Testament* with a Dissertation *On the Origin and Composition of our First Three Canonical Gospels*, 1801.

MARTIN, A. D. *Plain Man's Life of Christ*, 1941.

MARTINEAU, J. *The Seat of Authority in Religion*, 1890.

MASCALL, E. L. *Christian Theology and Natural Science*, 1956.

MASON, A. J. *The Conditions of Our Lord's Life on Earth*, 1896.

MATHESON, G. *Can the Old Faith live with the New?*, 1885.

MATTHEWS, C. H. S. Ed. *Faith and Freedom*, 1918.

MATTHEWS, W. R. *God in Christian Thought and Experience*, 1930. *Essays in Construction*, 1933.

MAURICE, J. F. D. *The Kingdom of Christ*, 1837. *Discourses on St. John's Gospel*, 1857. *What is Revelation?*, 1859.

MERZ, J. T. *History of European Thought in the XIXth century*, 1896.

MICHELL, R. *The Nature and Comparative Value of the Christian Evidences*, 1849.

MICKLEM, E. R. *Miracles and the New Psychology*, 1922.

MIDDLETON, C. *A Free Inquiry into the Miraculous Powers which are supposed to have subsisted in the Christian Church from the earliest ages through several successive centuries*, 1748.

MIDDLETON, P. *A Short View of the Evidences upon which the Christian Religion, and the Divine Authority of the Holy Scriptures, is Established*, 1734.

MILL, J. S. *System of Logic*, 1843. Three Essays on Religion: *Nature*, *The Utility of Religion*, and *Theism*, 1850–58.

MILLIGAN, W. *The Resurrection of Our Lord*, 1881. *The Ascension and Heavenly Priesthood of Our Lord*, 1892.

MILMAN, H. H. *The Character and Conduct of the Apostles considered as an Evidence of Christianity*, Bampton Lectures, 1827.

"Miracles": sermons and papers contributed to *The Guardian*, 1911.

Miracles, What they are, What they prove, and How to prove them, 1861.

MOBERLY, G. *The Sayings of the Great Forty Days*, 1844. *Some Remarks on "Essays and Reviews"* revised preface to second ed. of sermons on the Beatitudes, 1861.

MOBERLY, R. C. *Problems and Principles*, 1904: esp. *Reason in Relation to Christian Evidences*, 1891.

Modern Churchman, September 1921, papers of the Girton conference on "Christ and the Creeds".

Modernism, Programme of, E.T. A. L. Lilley, 1908, together with E.T. of *Pascendi Dominici Gregis* of Pius X.

MOFFATT, J. *Introduction to the Literature of the New Testament*, 1911.

MOORE, A. L. *Science and the Faith*, 1889. Inc. review of Drummond's *Natural Law*.

MORGAN, T. *The Moral Philosopher*, 1737.

MORISON, F. *Who Moved the Stone?*, 1930.

MOZLEY, J. B. *On Miracles*, Bampton Lectures, 1865.

MOZLEY, J. K. *Ritschlianism*, 1909. *Some Tendencies in British Theology*, 1951.

MURPHY, J. J. *The Scientific Bases of Faith*, 1873.

MURRY, J. MIDDLETON. *Life of Jesus*, 1926.

Mysterium Christi, ed. Bell, G. K. A. and Deissmann, A., 1930.

NEEDHAM, J., ed. *Science, Religion and Reality*, 1925.

NEWMAN, J. H. *The Ecclesiastical History of the Abbé Fleury from the Second Oecumenical Council to the end of the Fourth century translated with notes and an Essay on the Miracles of the Period*, 1842. *Two Essays on Scripture Miracles and on Ecclesiastical Miracles*, 2nd ed. 1870. *An Essay in Aid of a Grammar of Assent*, 1870.

NYE, S. *Historical Account and Defence of the Canon of the New Testament*, 1700.

OGILVIE, C. A. *Divine Glory manifested in the Conduct and Discourses of Our Lord*, Bampton Lectures, 1836.

OMAN, J. *The Problem of Faith and Freedom in the Last Two Centuries*, 1906. *The Natural and the Supernatural*, 1931.

ORR, J. *The Virgin Birth of Christ*, 1907. *The Resurrection of Jesus*, 1908.

PALEY, W. *Evidences of Christianity*, 1794. *Natural Theology*, 1802.

PASCAL, B. *Pensées*, 1670.

PATERSON, W. P. *The Rule of Faith*, 1912. *The Nature of Religion*, Gifford Lectures, 1924–25.

PEAKE, A. S. *Christianity, its Nature and its Truth*, 1908.

PEROWNE, E. H. *The Godhead of Jesus*, 1866.

PEROWNE, J. J. S. *Immortality*, 1869.

PRESTIGE, G. L. *The Life of Charles Gore*, 1935.

PRICE, R. *Four Discourses*, 1768.

PRIESTLEY, J. *Discourses on the Evidence of Revealed Religion*, 1794.

QUICK, O. C. *Liberalism, Modernism and Tradition*, 1922. *Modern Philosophy and the Incarnation*, 1924. *Doctrines of the Creed*, 1938. *The Gospel of the New World*, 1944.

RAGG, L. *Evidences of Christianity*, 1905.

RAINY, R., ORR, J. and DODS, M. *Supernatural in Christianity*, 1894.

RAMSAY, W. M. *Luke the Physician*, 1908. *Was Christ Born at Bethlehem?*, 1898.

RAMSEY, A. M. *The Resurrection of Christ*, 1945.

RANDOLF, B. W. *The Virgin Birth of Our Lord*, 1903.

RASHDALL, H. *Doctrine and Development*, 1898. *God and Man*—vol. 3 of his Collected Papers, ed. Major and Cross, 1930.

RAVEN, C. E. *What Think Ye of Christ?*, 1916.

RAWLINSON, A. E. J. *Dogma, Fact and Experience*, 1915. *Christ in the Gospels*, 1944.

REID, L. A. *Preface to Faith*, 1939.

RENNELL, T. *Remarks on Scepticism*, 1819. *Proofs of Inspiration*, 1822.

RICE, W. N. *Christian Faith in an Age of Science*, 1904.

RICHARDS, J. *The Canon of the New Testament Vindicated*, 1701.

RICHARDSON, A. *The Miracle Stories of the Gospels*, 1941. *Christian Apologetics*, 1947.

ROBBINS, W. L., ed. Robinson, A. W. *A Christian Apologetic*, 1902.

ROBINSON, C. H. *Studies in the Resurrection*, 1909.

ROBINSON, J. ARMITAGE. *Some Thoughts on the Incarnation*, 1903. *Some Thoughts on Inspiration*, 1905.

ROGERS, C. F. *The Case for Miracle*, 1936.

ROW, C. A. *The Supernatural in the New Testament*, 1875. *Christian Evidence Viewed in relation to Modern Thought*, Bampton Lectures, 1877.

ROMANES, G. J., ed. Gore, C. *Thoughts on Religion*, 1894.

RYLE, G. *The Concept of Mind*, 1949.

SALMON, G. Sermons: *The Reign of Law*, 1873. *Non-Miraculous Christianity*, 1881. *The Human Element in the Gospels*, 1907.

SANDAY, W. *The Life of Christ in Recent Research*, 1907. *Christology and Personality*, 1911. *Bishop Gore's Challenge to Criticism*, 1914. *The Position of Liberal Theology*, 1920.

SANDAY, W. and WILLIAMS, N. P. *Form and Content in the Christian Tradition*, 1916.

SCOTT, C. A. A. *Dominus Noster*, 1918.

SCOTT, E. F. *The New Testament Idea of Revelation*, 1935.

SCOTT, T. *The Dean of Ripon on the Physical Resurrection of Jesus*, 1872.

SEAVER, R. W. *To Christ Through Criticism*, 1906.

SEELEY, J. R. *Ecce Homo*, 1866.

SELWYN, E. G. *The Approach to Christianity*, 1925. *The Evidence of the Resurrection*, New Commentary, III.

SHAFTO, G. R. H. *Wonders of the Kingdom*, 1924.

SHARPE, G. *An Argument in Defence of Christianity*, 1755.

SHAW, J. M. *The Resurrection of Christ*, 1920.

SHERLOCK, T. *Tryal of the Witnesses of the Resurrection of Jesus*, 1729.

SHERLOCK, W. *A Discourse concerning the Happiness of Good men and the Punishment of the Wicked*, 1704.

SIMPSON, W. J. S. *Our Lord's Resurrection*, 1905. *The Resurrection and Modern Thought*, 1911.

SMALLBROOKE, R. *A Vindication of the Miracles of Our Blessed Saviour*, 1729, 1731.

SMETHURST, A. F. *Modern Science and Christian Beliefs*, 1955.

SMITH, D. *The Days of His Flesh*, 1905.

SPENS, W. *Belief and Practice*, 1915.

SPINOZA, B. DE. *Tractatus Theologico-Politicus*, 1670.

STALKER, J. *The Christology of Jesus*, 1899.

STANHOPE, G. *The Christian Interpretation of Prophecies Vindicated*, Boyle Lectures, 1701.

STANTON, V. H. *The Gospels as Historical Documents*, 1903.

STEBBING, H. *A Defence of Dr. Clarke's "Evidences of Natural and Revealed Religion"*, 1731.

STEPHEN, L. *English Thought in the XVIIIth Century*, 2 vols., 1876.

STILLINGFLEET, E. *Origines Sacrae, : or, a Rational Account of the Grounds of Natural and Reveal'd Religion*, Works, 1709 ed., vol. II. *A Rational Account of the Grounds of Protestant Religion*, Works, 1709 ed., vol. IV.

STORR, V. F. *The Development of English Theology in the XIXth Century*, 1913. *Christianity and Immortality*, 1918.

STREETER, B. H., ed. *Foundations*, 1912.

STREETER, B. H., ed. *Immortality*, 1917.

STROMBERG, R. N. *Religious Liberalism in Eighteenth-Century England*, 1954.

STRONG, E. L. *Lectures on the Incarnation of God*, 1917.

STRONG, T. B. *The Miraculous in Gospels and Creeds*, 1914. *Religion, Philosophy and History*, 1923.

SUMNER, J. B. *The Evidence of Christianity derived from its Nature and Reception*, 1824.

Supernatural Religion, Anonymous (W. Cassel), 1884.

SWEET, L. M. *The Birth and Infancy of Jesus Christ*, 1907.

SWETE, H. B. *The Apostles' Creed*, 1894. *The Appearances of Our Lord after the Passion*, 1907.

TAYLOR, A. E. *David Hume and the Miraculous*, 1927. *The Faith of a Moralist*, 1930. *Does God Exist?*, 1945.

TAYLOR, F. SHERWOOD. *The Fourfold Vision*, 1945.

TAYLOR, VINCENT. *The Historical Evidence for the Virgin Birth*, 1920.

TAYLOR, W. M. *The Miracles of Our Saviour*, 1891.

TEMPLE, F. *The Relations between Religion and Science*, 1884.

TEMPLE, W. *The Faith and Modern Thought*, 1910.

TENNANT, F. R. *Miracle and its Philosophical Presuppositions*, 1924. *The Philosophy of the Sciences*, 1932.

THIRLWALL, C. *Remains*, ed. J. J. S. Perowne.

THOMPSON, J. M. *Miracles in the New Testament*, 1911.

THOMSON, J. A. *Science and Religion*, 1925.

THURSTON, H. *The Physical Phenomena of Mysticism*, 1952.

TILLOTSON, J. *Works*, 1752 edition.

TINDAL, M. *Christianity as old as the Creation*, 1730.

TOLAND, J. *Christianity not Mysterious*, 1696.

TORRANCE, T. *Expository Studies in St. John's Miracles*, 1938.

TRENCH, R. C. *Notes on the Miracles of Our Lord*, 1846.

TULLOCH, J. *Movements of Religious Thought in Britain during the Nineteenth Century*, 1885. *Lectures on M. Renan's "Vie de Jésus"*, 1864.

TYRRELL, G. *Christianity at the Crossroads*, 1909, etc.

VAN MILDERT, W. *An Historical View of the Rise and Progress of Infidelity*, 1802, 1805.

VIDLER, A. R. *The Modernist Movement in the Roman Church*, 1934. *A Plain Man's Guide to Christianity*, 1936.

WACE, H. *On Inspiration and Old Testament Criticism*, 1894. *Christianity and Agnosticism*, 1895.

WARBURTON, W. *A Critical and Philosophical Enquiry into the causes of prodigies and miracles as related by historians*, 1727. *The Divine Legation of Moses Demonstrated*, 1738.

WARDLAW, R. *Systematic Theology*, 1856. *On Miracles*, 1852.

WATERLAND, D. *Scripture Vindicated*, 1730.

WATSON, H. A. *The Incarnation and Personality*, 1920.

WATSON, R. *An Apology for Christianity*, 1776. *An Apology for the Bible*, 1796.

WEBB, C. C. J. *Problems in the Relations of God and Man*, 1911. *Religious Thought in England since 1850*, 1933. *The Historical Element in Religion*, 1935.

WENDLAND, J. *Miracles of Christianity*, E.T. 1911.

WESLEY, J. *Letters*, standard ed. Telford, 1931.

WEST, G. *Observations on the History and Evidences of the Resurrection of Jesus Christ*, 1747.

WESTCOTT, B. F. *Characteristics of the Gospel Miracles*, 1859. *Gospel of the Resurrection*, 1866. *Revelation of the Risen Lord*, 1881. *The Gospel of Life*, 1892.

WESTON, F. *Ecclesia Anglicana*, 1913. *The Christ and His Critics*, 1919.

WHATELY, R. *The Christian Evidences. Historic Doubts relative to Napoleon Buonaparte*, 1819. *Essays on some of the Peculiarities of the Christian Religion*, 1825.

WHITE, A. D. *History of the Warfare of Science with Theology*, 1896.

WHITHAM, A. R. *Life of Our Blessed Lord*, 1910.

WHITEHEAD, A. N. *Science and the Modern World*, 1926. *Adventures of Ideas*, 1933.

WILBERFORCE, R. I. *The Doctrine of the Incarnation of Our Lord Jesus Christ in its relation to Mankind and to the Church*, 1848.

WILBERFORCE, W. *A Practical View of the Prevailing Religious System of Professed Christians in the Higher and Middle Classes in this Country contrasted with real Christianity*, 1797.

WILLEY, B. *The Eighteenth Century Background*, 1940.

WILSON, JAMES M. *Essays and Addresses*, 1887. *Science and Theology or an essay on the influence of scientific training on the reception of religious truth*, 1903.

WILSON, JOHN M. *Nature, Man and God*, 1885.

WINDLE, B. C. A. *The Catholic Church and its Reactions with Science*, 1927.

WOLLASTON, W. *The Religion of Nature Delineated*, 1725.

WOOD, H. G. *Belief and Unbelief since 1850*, 1955.

WOOLSTON, T. *Six Discourses on Miracles*, 1727–29.

WORTHINGTON, J. *The Doctrines of the Resurrection and the Reward to come considered as the grand motives to an holy life*, 1690.

WRIGHT, C. J. *Miracle in History and in Modern Thought*, 1930.

WRIGHT, T. H. Art. "Miracles", *Hastings' Dictionary of Christ and the Gospels*, 1908.

YOUNG, J. *The Christ of History*, 1855.

INDEX

INDEX OF NAMES

INDEX OF SUBJECTS